# How to Do Everything with Your

# Sony CLIÉ™

W9-DET-671

## Rick Broida
## Dave Johnson

**McGraw-Hill**/Osborne

New York  Chicago  San Francisco
Lisbon  London  Madrid  Mexico City
Milan  New Delhi  San Juan
Seoul  Singapore  Sydney  Toronto

**McGraw-Hill/Osborne**
2600 Tenth Street
Berkeley, California 94710
U.S.A.

To arrange bulk purchase discounts for sales promotions, premiums, or fund-raisers, please contact **McGraw-Hill/**Osborne at the above address. For information on translations or book distributors outside the U.S.A., please see the International Contact Information page immediately following the index of this book.

### How to Do Everything With Your Sony CLIÉ™

1234567890 FGR FGR 0198765432

ISBN 0-07222659-5

| | |
|---|---|
| **Publisher** | Brandon A. Nordin |
| **Vice President** | |
| **& Associate Publisher** | Scott Rogers |
| **Acquisitions Editor** | Marjorie McAneny |
| **Project Editor** | Jennifer Malnick |
| **Acquisitions Coordinator** | Tana Allen |
| **Technical Editor** | Denny Atkin |
| **Copy Editor** | Mike McGee |
| **Production** | |
| **and Editorial Services** | Anzai! Inc. |
| **Series Design** | Mickey Galicia |
| **Cover Series Design** | Dodie Shoemaker |
| **Cover Design** | Pattie Lee |

This book was composed with Corel VENTURA™ Publisher.

CLIÈ images courtesy of Sony Electronics, Inc.

## Dedication

For Caroline, who really is the best.
—Rick

For Kris, who really wants my NR70.
—Dave

# About the Authors

**Rick Broida** has written about computers and technology for more than a decade. A regular contributor to CNET and *Computer Shopper*, he specializes in mobile technology. In 1997, recognizing the unparalleled popularity of Palm handhelds and the need for a printed resource for users, he founded *Handheld Computing* (formerly *Tap Magazine*). He currently serves as editor of that magazine, which now includes all handheld platforms and devices. Rick also provides handheld-computing training seminars for corporate users and educators. He lives in Michigan with his wife and two children.

**Dave Johnson** is the editor of *Handheld Computing Mobility* magazine and writes about digital photography for *PC World* magazine. In addition, he's the author of two dozen books that include *Build Your Own Combat Robot*, *How to Do Everything with Your Digital Camera*, *How to Do Everything with MP3 and Digital Music* (written with Rick Broida), and *How to Use Digital Video*. His short story for early readers, "The Wild Cookie," has been transformed into an interactive storybook on CD-ROM. In his spare time, Dave is a scuba instructor and wildlife photographer.

# About the Technical Editor

**Denny Atkin** has been writing about technology since 1987, and about handheld computers since the Newton's release in 1993. After working with such pioneering technology magazines as *Compute!* and *Omni*, he's now editorial director of *Handheld Computing* and *Mobility Magazine*. Atkin lives with his wife, son, and giant Maine Coon cat in Vermont, a state where PDAs are nearly as popular as maple syrup.

# Contents at a Glance

# Contents

# Acknowledgments

This book was great fun to write, due in no small part to the great team at Osborne. Our thanks to Jane Brownlow, Tana Allen, Mike McGee, Margie McAneny, and the irrepressible Jennifer Malnick. We'd especially like to thank tech editor Denny Atkin, who corrected the wildly inaccurate things we wrote. Dave would also like to thank Rick for staying "on the wagon" long enough to finish this book. Good show, buddy! Rick: After writing another book with you, I *need* a drink!

More thanks to the people at Sony who helped us get what we needed when we needed it. In particular, we're grateful to David Yang and Rob Litt—consummate professionals who could teach other PR folk a thing or two.

Finally, thanks as always to our amazingly supportive families, who give us the time and space we need to get the work done without so much as a single complaint.

# Introduction

Clié handhelds are such great little devices that any book about them runs the risk of reading like a promotional brochure. We've written thousands of pages about the Windows platform, and half of them always seems to be apologetic. "Computer locked up again? You need to reboot and send $94 in cash to Microsoft. . . ." Books about computers are often more about getting them to work in the first place or explaining why they don't work right than about telling you what you can actually accomplish.

Not the Clié, though. It's one of the most forgiving, user-friendly, and non-crashable computers ever created. And because it suffers from so few technical glitches, we were able to devote most of this book to work and play—accomplishing stuff to make your life more fun and efficient.

This book starts at the beginning (unlike those that start around, say, the midway point). First we give you some of the history of handheld computers like the Clié (and the Clié itself), then discuss the various models and which one might best suit your needs (in case you haven't purchased one yet). From there you get a guided tour of your Clié and the accompanying desktop software. We teach you to navigate the core software, input data, and share information with your PC as well as other handheld devices.

In Part Two, "Everyday Stuff With Your CLIÉ," we show you the Clié's core applications and then tell you stuff you'd never think of—like how to get the most out of your Clié when you go on a business trip. Think your new handheld can't take the place of a laptop computer? Think again (and read Chapters 10 and 12).

Part Three thinks outside the box, and that's where things get really interesting. Read those chapters and you learn how to connect to the Internet, manage your finances, track your stocks, and balance your checkbook. We also delve into the arts, with chapters on painting pictures and playing music. You might not think there's a lot to say about playing games, but a whole world of entertainment awaits you—and we show you how to tap into it (pun intended). In fact, you might throw away your Game Boy after reading Chapter 20. And, yes, we said people rarely have trouble with their Cliés, but it does happen occasionally. We have that covered as well.

We wrote this book so you could sit down and read through it like a novel. But if you're looking for specific information, we made it easy to find. Plus, you can find special elements to help you get the most out of the book:

- ■ **How to...**   These special boxes explain, in a nutshell, how to accomplish key tasks. Read them to discover key points covered in each chapter.

- ■ **Notes**   These provide extra information that's often very important to gain an understanding of a particular topic.

- ■ **Tips**   These tell you how to do something smarter or faster.

- ■ **Sidebars**   Here we address related—and sometimes unrelated—topics. Sidebars can be pretty interesting, if only to see us bicker like an old married couple.

Can't get enough of Dave and Rick? See the back page of *Handheld Computing Magazine*, where we continue our lively "Head2Head" column. You can also send questions and comments to us at **dave@bydavejohnson.com** and **rick@broida.com**. Thanks, and enjoy reading the book!

# Part I

# Getting Started

# Chapter 1

# Welcome to CLIÉ

Stephen King novels. The entire *O Brother, Where Art Thou* soundtrack. A dozen different solitaire games. A collegiate dictionary. Your entire appointment calendar. A guide to more than 10,000 wines. An address book with pictures of every person. Episodes of *The Simpsons*.

All in your pocket.

It sounds like technology you might see on an episode of *Star Trek*, but you can have it right here in the 21st century. Thanks to remarkable strides in handheld computing, every item in the preceding list can be stored in a single device—a Sony Clié handheld PC. And that's just the tip of the iceberg. These amazing devices can send and receive e-mail, take digital photos, control your home stereo, open and edit Word and Excel files, and a lot more.

In the pages and chapters to come, you'll learn the history of handheld PCs like the Clié, the differences between models in the Clié line, and, of course, everything you need to know about using them.

# A Brief History of Handhelds

It all started with a block of wood. In 1994, Jeff Hawkins, founder of a little-known company called Palm Computing, envisioned a pocket-sized computer that would organize calendars and contacts, and maybe let travelers retrieve their e-mail from the road. This idea of a *personal digital assistant*, or PDA, was by no means new, but previous attempts—like Apple's highly publicized Newton MessagePad—had failed to catch on with consumers.

Hawkins knew he'd have a tough time selling the concept, so he decided to convince himself before trying to convince investors. His device would be roughly the size of a deck of cards—much smaller and lighter than the Newton—and fit in a shirt pocket. But would it be practical at that size? Would it be comfortable to carry around? Hawkins decided to find out. Before a single piece of plastic was molded, before a single circuit board was designed, the Palm Computing Pilot existed solely as a block of wood.

Hawkins cut a piece of balsa wood to the size he'd envisioned for his handheld device, put it in his shirt pocket, and left it there—for several months. He even took it out from time to time and pretended to take notes, just to see if the size and shape felt right. Though he quickly came to realize that such a form factor made perfect sense, doors slammed whenever he showed his "product" to potential investors. "The handheld market is dead" was the mantra at the time.

Fortunately, modem-maker U.S. Robotics didn't think so, and liked the idea of the Pilot so much that it bought Palm Computing outright. In March, 1996, the company unveiled the Pilot 1000, and the rest is history.

Flash forward six years. The Pilot—which would eventually be renamed PalmPilot and then just Palm—had become the fastest-growing computer platform in history, reaching the million-sold mark faster than the IBM PC or Apple Macintosh. In the interim, U.S. Robotics had been assimilated into networking giant 3Com, and Palm, Inc. along with it. The Palm line had grown to include a variety of models, and companies like Handspring, IBM, and Sony had adopted the Palm operating system for their own handheld devices.

Today, the *Palm platform* (an umbrella term used to describe not only the actual hardware, but the operating system that drives it) is dominant in the explosive handheld market. The Sony Clié series falls under that umbrella. It's a family of handheld PCs that run the Palm Operating System (OS)—the same OS used in handhelds made by Palm, Handspring, and other companies.

# What's an Operating System?

Windows is an operating system. Mac OS X is an operating system. The core software that drives any computer is an operating system. Hence, when we refer to the Clié's Palm OS, we're talking about the software built into the device—the brains behind the brawn. The Palm OS itself not only controls the Clié's fundamental operations, such as what happens when you press a button or tap the screen, but also supplies the built-in applications (the Address Book, Memo Pad, Date Book and so on—all of which we discuss in detail in later chapters).

The Palm OS is the key ingredient that links the various Palm devices, whether they're manufactured by Palm, Handspring, Sony or one of the other companies licensed to use the Palm OS.

**NOTE** *These "licensees" have been granted permission by Palm, Inc. to use the Palm OS in hardware of their own design. It's kind of like the way you can get PCs from a hundred different companies, yet they all run Windows.*

You can see that a Palm m100 looks quite a bit different from a Sony Clié N760C (see Figure 1-1), but on the inside they're fundamentally the same. They both use the Palm Operating System, and therefore operate in a similar fashion, each capable of running almost all the same software.

**FIGURE 1-1**    Palm OS devices don't all look the same, and, in fact, can look quite different, but they all use the same core operating system.

## What's the Difference Between a CLIÉ and a Palm?

It's easy to get confused between Palm, Clié, Palm OS, and other terms we use frequently in this book. Therefore, here's a lexicon to help you understand the basic terminology.

- **Handheld PC**  A portable, pocket-sized computer like the Palm m505, Handspring Treo, and Sony Clié.
- **Operating System**  The core software that makes a handheld PC function.
- **Palm, Inc.**  The company that makes handheld PCs which run the Palm Operating System (OS).
- **Palm OS**  The operating system used in Palm, Handspring, HandEra, Sony, and many other handheld PCs.
- **Palm Powered**  Denotes a handheld PC that runs the Palm OS. *Palm Powered* is a registered trademark of Palm, Inc.
- **PalmSource**  The division of Palm, Inc. responsible for developing the Palm OS.
- **PDA**  Short for Personal Digital Assistant, a generic term used to describe any handheld PC.
- **Pocket PC**  Microsoft's Windows-like operating system for handheld PCs. Found in devices from Casio, Compaq, Hewlett-Packard, and other vendors.
- **Sony**  Makers of the Clié series of handheld PCs.

# What Makes Handheld PCs so Great?

Why all the fuss? What makes Palm OS devices like the Clié so special? To answer these questions, we'll first need to look at what a handheld PC actually is. Put simply, it's a pocket-sized electronic organizer that enables you to manage addresses, appointments, expenses, tasks and memos. If you've ever used a Franklin Planner or any similar paper-bound organizer, you get the idea.

However, because a handheld PC is electronic, there's no paper or ink involved. Instead, you write directly on the device's screen, using a small plastic stylus in place of a pen. A key advantage here, of course, is that you're able to store all of your important personal and business information on a device that's much small and lighter than a paper planner.

What's more, you can easily share that information with your Macintosh or Windows-based computer. Handheld PCs are not self-contained: they can *synchronize* with a desktop computer and keep information current on both sides. This is an important advantage, as it effectively turns your handheld into an extension of the computer you use every day. Changes and additions made to your desktop data are reflected in the device, and vice versa (see Figure 1-2).

Saying that a Clié is an extension of your PC is only a half-truth. In reality, it has evolved into a computer in its own right. That's because it is capable of running software written by

**FIGURE 1-2**  A Clié connects to a PC via a HotSync cradle or cable, which allows data to be synchronized on both devices.

parties other than Palm, Inc., and those parties (known as software developers) now number in the tens of thousands. There are literally thousands of programs and databases that extend your Clié's capabilities, from spreadsheet managers and expense trackers to electronic-book readers and web browsers. Got five minutes to kill? You can play a quick game of *Bejeweled*. Need to check your e-mail while traveling? Snap on a modem and dial your Internet service provider.

**NOTE** *While the first several chapters of this book are devoted to the Clié's core capabilities—the things it can do right out of the box—the majority of it focuses on Clié's extended capabilities: the things that have elevated the device from a basic electronic organizer to a full-fledged handheld PC.*

Above all else, simplicity is a major key to the platform's success. The devices are amazingly easy to use, requiring no more than a few taps of the stylus to access your data and a little memorization to master the handwriting-recognition software. Most users, even those who have little or no computer experience (like Dave), find themselves tapping and writing productively within 20 minutes of opening the box.

# An Overview of the Different CLIÉ Models

Whether you're still shopping for a Clié or you've been fiddling with one for a month, it's good to have an understanding of the different models available. In Table 1-1, you can see that in a relatively short period of time, Sony released (and discontinued) quite a number of models. Fear not—even if you own or purchased secondhand a discontinued Clié, much of the material in this book is applicable (and darn useful, if we do say so ourselves). And even if Sony has introduced half a dozen new models by the time you're reading this, well, the same truth applies. A few features may change here and there, but the Palm OS remains.

NOTE    *If you live outside North America, you may encounter Clié models with slightly different numerical designations. In Japan, for instance, the T665C is known as the T650C.*

## What's Special about Sony's Handhelds

We're the first to admit it: Sony's first stab at a Palm OS handheld—the PEG-S300—was as dull as dirt. It looked kind of ugly and offered little to distinguish it from Palm's and Handspring's handhelds. But the company rebounded big time with a series of models packed with innovative and exciting features. Among the highlights: high-resolution color screens, a Memory Stick expansion slot, the ability to play MP3 music files, a "Jog Dial" for one-handed operation, and enhanced audio.

In the spring of 2002, Sony really pushed the outside of the handheld envelope with the introduction of the NR70V. It boasts the highest screen resolution of any PDA currently on the market (including Pocket PC devices championed by Microsoft) and offers a wealth of cool features. We talk more about them in later chapters.

| Model | Memory | Screen | Year Released | Status* |
|---|---|---|---|---|
| Clié PEG-S300 | 8MB | Grayscale | 2000 | Discontinued |
| Clié PEG-S320 | 8MB | Grayscale | 2001 | Discontinued |
| Clié PEG-S360 | 16MB | Grayscale | 2002 | Discontinued |
| Clié PEG-N610C | 8MB | Color | 2001 | Discontinued |
| Clié PEG-N710C | 8MB | Color | 2001 | Discontinued |
| Clié PEG-N760C | 8MB | Color | 2001 | Discontinued |
| Clié PEG-T415 | 8MB | Grayscale | 2001 | Discontinued |
| Clié PEG-T615C | 16MB | Color | 2002 | Discontinued |
| Clié PEG-T665C | 16MB | Color | 2002 | Available |
| Clié PEG-NR70/NR70V | 16MB | Color | 2002 | Discontinued |
| Clié PEG-NX60/NX70V | 16MB | Color | 2002 | Available |
| Clié PEG-SL10 | 8MB | Grayscale | 2002 | Available |
| Clié PEG-SJ20 | 16MB | Grayscale | 2002 | Available |
| Clié PEG-SJ30 | 16MB | Color | 2002 | Available |

*As of September 2002

TABLE 1-1    Sony Clié Models at a Glance

## Our Favorite Models

**Rick:** Well, obviously I'm partial to Charlize Theron, who's an actress now but did start out as a model, and....Oh! Sorry, wrong sidebar. I'm not afraid to say I'm head-over-heels for the NR70V, which has just about everything I want in a handheld PC: loads of memory, a gorgeous high-res screen, an MP3 player, and a built-in digital camera. The latter can't compare with today's multi-megapixel cameras, but it's great for capturing pictures of the kids being silly and other impromptu moments. I expect I'll be using the NR70V for quite some time to come.

**Dave:** This is a bad omen for the very first chapter—we never agree on anything—but I, too, love my NR70. More to the point, I love it with a passion that I usually reserve for Sandra Bullock and Halle Berry. I have loaded it almost exclusively with applications that can take advantage of the 320×480-pixel screen, and use it to watch movies, listen to music, and play games. Oh, yeah—and I use it for work occasionally, too.

## Where to Find the Best Prices

Still shopping for your Clié? Everyone likes to save a buck, and with a little research you can do exactly that.

- If you're comfortable shopping online, you can find some of the best deals on the Web. We recommend starting with a site called PriceGrabber (**www.pricegrabber.com**), which provides up-to-date price comparisons for most Palm devices and many accessories, drawn from a large number of web merchants. It even gives you shipping costs, so you know your out-the-door total before heading to the merchant's site. But buyer beware: the best deals tend to come from small, lesser-known merchants, and people have been known to get burned. Investigate a company thoroughly before buying anything from it.

- Another worthwhile online destination: web auctions. eBay is a treasure trove of new, used, and refurbished Sony devices. Just remember to use common sense: sometimes people get caught in a bidding frenzy and wind up paying as much for a used model as they would for a new one.

- Check Sony's web site for package deals. You may find bundles (like a handheld with a free case or memory module) that you won't find anywhere else, and at discounted prices.

- Another great source for inexpensive refurbished handhelds is ReturnBuy (**store.returnbuy.com**). We found a Clié T415 (a discontinued model, but still a nice one) selling for $149.99—half of what it cost originally. Just be sure to investigate the warranty policy for any refurbished item you buy. While ReturnBuy guarantees the reconditioned units to be in perfect working order, you may have to pay extra if you want a warranty—or you may not be able to get one at all.

**TIP**  *Auctions can also be a great way to sell your old Clié if you're moving up to a newer one. You can also try a service like SellYourPalm.net (**www.sellyourpalm.net**), which will buy your old handheld outright.*

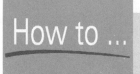

## How to ... Decide Which Model to Buy

Sorry, we can't help you with this one. So many great handhelds, so few hands. Virtually every Clié model available today has its merits. The key thing to remember is that right out of the box, every one offers the same great core capabilities: contact and calendar management, easy-to-learn handwriting recognition, seamless synchronization with your PC, and access to a wealth of third-party software. With that knowledge in mind, you can focus on other aspects you might find important: price, memory, screen quality (color or grayscale), multimedia features, and so on. In the end, you may just have to flip a coin. That's what we do.

## Where to Find It

| Web Site | Address |
|---|---|
| Sony | www.sonystyle.com/micros/clie |
| eBay | www.ebay.com |

# Chapter 2

# Getting to Know Your CLIÉ

## How to...

- Identify the buttons on a Clié
- Identify the infrared transmitter
- Work with the screen and Graffiti area
- Install (or charge) the batteries
- Turn on a Clié for the first time
- Use the Graffiti tutorial
- Reset a Clié
- Configure a Clié's preferences
- Reset the screen digitizer
- Work with the operating system
- Check how much memory is left
- Create and use shortcuts
- Work with Palm Desktop

Okay, enough history—it's time to dive in and start having fun. At the beginning of any lasting and meaningful relationship, you want to get to know the other person as well as possible—find out what makes them tick, what their boundaries are, where they keep their batteries. With that in mind, we tailored this chapter as a kind of meet-and-greet, to help you overcome that bit of initial awkwardness. Let's turn this blind date into a blissful marriage with two kids, a dog, and a white picket fence!

# A Guided Tour of the Hardware

By now, your Clié is no doubt out of the box and getting the once-over. You're seeing buttons, a screen, some little pictures, a little wheel sticking out of the side, and so on. What is all this stuff? What does it do?

 *Although fundamentally quite similar, there are some minor physical differences in the various Clié models. Many of the photographs in this chapter show the Clié N760C, which looks almost identical to the N610C, N710C, S320, and S360. If you have a T series or NR series model, things might look a bit different—but we'll jump in as necessary to alert you to important distinctions.*

## The Screen

Different Clié models have different kinds of screens. The now-discontinued S320, for instance, employs a grayscale screen with a resolution of 160×160 pixels. At the other end of the spectrum, the NR70 series boasts a 320×480-pixel screen that can display up to 65,000 colors. In between, the N, SL, SJ, and T series serve up color or grayscale screens with 320×320 resolution.

When you use a desktop computer, you use a mouse to navigate and a keyboard to enter data. With a Clié, you use a plastic-tipped stylus for both navigation and data entry. That's because the screen is, technically speaking, a *touchscreen,* meaning you interact with it by tapping it and writing on it. If you want to access, say, the To Do List program, you tap the To Do List icon that appears on the screen. If you want to remind yourself to buy milk, you write the words on the screen.

> NOTE
>
> *Many novice users think they have to double-tap the application icons, just like double-clicking with a mouse. Not true! A single tap is all you ever need when working with a Clié.*

## The Difference Between Tapping and Writing

Tapping the screen is the equivalent of clicking a mouse. You tap icons to launch programs, tap to access menus and select options in them, and tap to place your cursor in specific places. Writing on the screen is, of course, like putting a pen to paper. However, most writing you do on a Clié takes place in a specific area of the screen, which we discuss in the next section, "The Graffiti Area." But when you're working in, say, a sketchpad or paint program, you can scribble anywhere on the screen, just as though it were a blank sheet of paper.

> TIP
>
> *Don't press too hard with the stylus. The screen is fairly sensitive, and light pressure is all it takes to register a tap or stylus-stroke. If you press too hard, you could wind up with a scratched screen—the bane of every Clié user.*

## The Graffiti Area

As you have no doubt noticed, the bottom portion of the screen looks a bit different. That big rectangular box flanked by two pairs of icons is called the "Graffiti area," referring to the handwriting-recognition software that's part of every Clié.

> NOTE
>
> *The NR and NX series are a bit different from other Clié models in terms of the Graffiti area. That's because it's based in software rather than hardware. As a result, the Graffiti area is "collapsible," meaning it can disappear when not needed to give you more screen area for viewing your documents and applications. See Chapter 4 for additional information.*

Graffiti makes it possible to enter information using the stylus, but you can do so only within the confines of the Graffiti area (as seen in Figure 2-1).

> NOTE
>
> *We tell you more about Graffiti—how to use it and alternatives to it—in Chapters 4 and 15, respectively.*

What about those icons on either side of the Graffiti area? They serve some important functions. Here's an overview:

**The Home Button**    Represented by a picture of a house and located in the upper-left corner of the Graffiti area, the Home button is the one you'll tap more often than any other. From whatever program you're currently running, the Home button (see Figure 2-1) takes you back to the main screen—"home base," as it were (hence the house picture).

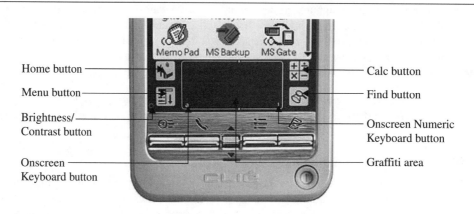

Home button — Calc button
Menu button — Find button
Brightness/ Contrast button — Onscreen Numeric Keyboard button
Onscreen Keyboard button — Graffiti area

**FIGURE 2-1**    The Graffiti area is where you write data into your handheld and access various options.

*TIP*    *When you're using any program, tapping the Home button returns you to the main screen. When you're viewing that screen, however, tapping the Home button cycles through the application categories, which we discuss later in this chapter in the "The Applications Screen" section.*

**The Menu Button**    Tapping the icon in the lower-left corner of the Graffiti area—a.k.a. the Menu button (see Figure 2-1)—gives you access to the drop-down menus that are part of the Palm Operating System. These menus vary somewhat from program to program, insofar as the options they provide, but they're fairly consistent within the core Palm OS applications.

*TIP*    *The Menu button works like a toggle switch. If you accidentally tap it or simply want to make the drop-down menus go away, simply tap it again.*

*TIP*    *Another way to access menus is by tapping the title bar in the top-left corner of whatever program is currently running—not unlike the way you use a mouse to access menus on a PC.*

**The Calculator Button**    Probably the most self-explanatory of all the buttons, Calc—located in the upper-right corner of the Graffiti area (see Figure 2-1)—launches the built-in calculator. This functions like any other calculator you've ever used—but you can learn a bit more about it in Chapter 9.

**The Find Button**    Finally, we get to the little magnifying glass in the lower-right corner. Because a Clié can store such vast amounts of information, and because sifting through all that information to find what you're looking for can be tedious, there's a handy little search feature called the Find button (see Figure 2-1). We talk more about it in Chapter 9.

**The a and 1 Buttons**    In the lower-left corner of the Graffiti area (see Figure 2-1) there's a little *a*. In the lower-right corner, a 1. As you'll learn in Chapter 4, these are used to bring up the onscreen keyboards (which serve as alternative input methods). Tapping the *a* launches the QWERTY keyboard, while the 1 brings up the numeric keyboard.

NOTE    *You can't access either keyboard unless there's a cursor in a data-entry field. If you're viewing the main screen—the one with all the icons—and tap either keyboard button, you'll just hear a beep. Try starting a new memo and then tapping one of the two buttons.*

**The Brightness/Contrast Button**    Below the Menu button (see Figure 2-1) resides a little icon that looks like either a starburst or a half moon. Tapping it brings up an onscreen slider that adjusts either the brightness or contrast of your Clié's screen (depending on whether it's color or grayscale). Tap and hold your stylus on the slider, then drag it left and right until you've found a comfortable setting.

TIP    *The brightness setting has a direct impact on battery life. If you travel a lot (meaning you're away from the charging cradle for long periods), try setting the brightness to, say, 50 percent. Your battery will last a lot longer, and you probably won't mind the slightly reduced brightness after you get accustomed to it. Of course, if your Clié spends most of its time in or near the cradle, crank the brightness to maximum. You might as well enjoy what the screen has to offer.*

**The NR/NX Status Bar**    If you own an NR- or NX-series Clié, you'll notice a row of icons beneath the Graffiti area (see Figure 2-2). This "status bar" duplicates three of the Graffiti-area buttons—Home, Menu, and Find—and supplies a clock, battery gauge, and Memory Stick indicator (a little icon appears when there's a Memory Stick inserted). There's also a little blue arrow icon used to collapse the virtual Graffiti area in applications that support this feature. Tap it once to collapse Graffiti, again to restore it. (If the icon appears *ghosted*, that means you're in an application or area that doesn't permit the Graffiti area to collapse.) As you may have figured out by now, the reason for the extra Home, Menu, and Find buttons in the status bar is for when the Graffiti area is minimized—you can access these features without having to restore it.

## The Buttons

Below the Graffiti area you can see a selection of buttons (see Figure 2-3). These serve some fairly obvious purposes: to turn the device on and off, to instantly launch the core applications (Date Book, Memo Pad, and so forth), and to scroll up and down in screens of data.

### The Power Button

The Power button is fairly self-explanatory. But it serves another function: to activate (or deactivate) your screen's backlight. If your Clié has a grayscale screen, you'd activate the backlight to make it more visible in low-light situations. With a color screen, you'd deactivate the backlight when venturing outdoors, in order to maximize battery life. Just hold down the button for two seconds to activate or deactivate the backlight.

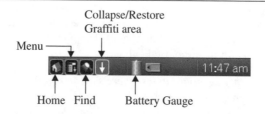

Menu

Collapse/Restore
Graffiti area

Home    Find    Battery Gauge

11:47 am

FIGURE 2-2    The NR and NX models have this status bar below the Graffiti area.

 TIP

*If you push the Power button and your Clié doesn't turn on, it probably means one of two things. Either the battery is dead, or you've accidentally engaged the Hold switch (see the upcoming section, "The Headphone Jack"), which can make it seem like the battery is dead. Try sliding it to the Off position and see if that resurrects your Clié.*

## The Four Program Buttons

So you want to look up a number in your address book. You could turn on your Clié, tap the Applications button to get to the main screen, then find and tap the Address button. There's a much faster way: simply press the Address button, which is represented by a picture of a phone handset. That serves the dual function of turning on the Clié *and* loading the Address Book program.

The same holds true for the three other buttons (see Figure 2-3), which launch Date Book, To Do List, and Memo Pad. You can use them at any time, whether the Clié is on or off, to quickly switch between the four core programs.

 SHORTCUT

*By holding down the Address Book button for two seconds, you can automatically beam your "business card" to another handheld user. In Chapter 6, you will learn how to designate an Address Book record as your card.*

 How to ... **Reprogram Your Handheld's Buttons**

Want the Memo Pad button to load your e-book viewer? Or the Calc button to load a sophisticated third-party number-cruncher instead of the built-in calculator? You can reprogram the Clié's four hardware buttons and Calc button to run any installed program. Just tap the Prefs icon, then select Buttons from the drop-down list in the top-right corner of the Preferences screen. Now, assign your desired applications to the various buttons. That's all there is to it!

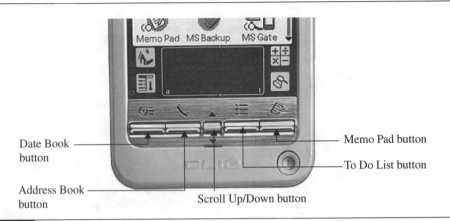

Date Book button

Address Book button

Scroll Up/Down button

Memo Pad button

To Do List button

**FIGURE 2-3**    Typical screen buttons

## The Scroll Buttons

Sandwiched between the two pairs of Program buttons, the Scroll buttons are used to cycle through multiple screens of data. If you're looking at, say, a memo that's too long to fit on the screen in its entirety, you'd use the Scroll Down button to move down to the next section—not unlike turning pages in a book. The Scroll Up button simply moves you back a page.

NOTE    *In many programs, onscreen arrows serve the same function. Instead of having to press the Scroll buttons, you can simply tap the arrows with your stylus. This is largely a matter of personal preference. Try both and decide which method you like better!*

## The Jog Dial Navigator

A little wheel protrudes from the left-hand side of every Clié. It's called the Jog Dial (see Figure 2-4), and gives the Clié an advantage found in few other handhelds: one-handed operation. Specifically, you can launch programs, navigate menus, and access data just by turning and pushing the Jog Dial. This can come in very handy if you have the Clié in one hand and, say, the phone or a live eel in the other.

As with so many aspects of your Clié, the best way to learn the Jog Dial is by experimenting. Turn it a few clicks in either direction or press it directly inward (the wheel doubles as a button) and see what happens. This combination of actions—turning the wheel and/or pressing the wheel—is all it takes to navigate your Clié with one hand. However, you'll also want to take advantage of the Back button, which is discussed in the next section. Later in this chapter, in the section called "Prefs," you'll learn how to modify a few Jog Dial and Back button settings.

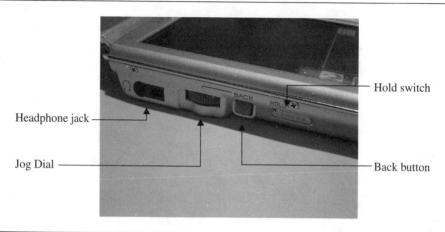

Headphone jack

Jog Dial

Hold switch

Back button

**FIGURE 2-4**    On the side of your Clié, you'll find items like the headphone jack, Jog Dial, Back button, and Hold switch.

## The Back Button

The Back button (see Figure 2-4) resides next to the Jog Dial and works in conjunction with it. When pressed, the Back button returns you to the previous screen you were viewing. When pressed for two seconds, it enables you to cycle through buttons, menus, and/or options (using the Jog Dial to make your selection). You can also set the Back button to double as a Power button, though we don't recommend this (it's too easy to hit by accident).

 *A few early-model Cliés don't have a Back button, which somewhat limits the functionality and value of the Jog Dial.*

## The Headphone Jack

If your Clié came with a pair of headphones, it's capable of playing music. Indeed, many Clié models double as damn fine MP3 players. That explains the headphone jack you see on the left-hand side of the unit (see Figure 2-4). We teach you everything you need to know about Clié music in Chapter 18.

### What Is the Hold Switch?

Not far from the headphone jack, you may notice a little switch labeled Hold (see Figure 2-4). This is a staple feature in MP3 players—it effectively locks out all the buttons on your handheld so you don't accidentally press one while you're jamming. At the same time, it turns off the screen to conserve battery life. Try sliding it to see what happens (you don't need to be listening to music). Your Clié more or less shuts itself off and doesn't respond to any button presses until you disengage the Hold switch.

TIP *When the Hold switch is engaged, your Clié appears to be dead. If you find that your unit won't turn on or respond to any button presses, check to make sure the Hold switch wasn't accidentally activated. More often than not, it's the culprit.*

## The Memory Stick Slot

Every Clié is expandable. If you run out of storage space, you can easily add more. If you want to outfit your Clié with a digital camera, you can do that, too. It's all thanks to the Memory Stick slot, which you can find at the top of your Clié.

Memory Stick refers to a kind of removable storage media created by Sony. True to its name, a Memory Stick (MS for short) is about the size of a stick of gum and provides extra storage space for your Clié—anywhere from 8MB to 256MB. You'll find out just how valuable extra memory can be when you get to the chapters on music and movies.

But surprise, surprise, the MS slot can be used for more than just memory expansion. Sony offers a digital camera module with an MS interface (see Chapter 16 for details), and, at press time, was rumored to be working on other expansion devices. There's already a Bluetooth MS module available in Europe and Japan, and we may yet see an MS GPS module.

Read more about Memory Sticks—where to buy them, how to use them, and so on—in Chapter 22.

## The Back of the CLIÉ

Flip your Clié over. Yes, it's pretty boring back there, but you should know about one important area: the Reset button. Every Clié has a little hole on the back that's used to reset the device. Hey, every computer crashes occasionally, and the Palm OS isn't entirely glitch-free. (We talk more about resetting in Chapter 24.)

## The Infrared Port

At the top of every Clié, there's a small black-plastic window. This is the *infrared port,* also known as the *infrared transceiver* or *IR port.* It's used to wirelessly beam data from one Clié to another and, if you have a model with the remote features, to control devices like your TV or stereo (which we discuss in Chapter 19). You learn more about beaming in Chapter 4.

## The Stylus

Last, but definitely not least, we come to the *stylus.* Every Clié has a small plastic or metal pen tucked away inside, usually accessible from the side or rear. What they all have in common is a plastic tip. Under no circumstances should you ever use any kind of ink pen or metal tip on a Clié's screen. That's a sure way to create a scratch, and a scratched screen is a damaged screen.

TIP *There's one exception: In a pinch, or if you just don't feel like extracting the stylus, you can use your fingernail for light taps on the screen.*

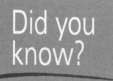

## On the Road Again

If you travel with a notebook PC, one that has an IR port of its own, you can HotSync your Clié to it without the need for a cradle. However, you'll still need a way to charge your handheld, so bringing along a HotSync cradle or cable might still make sense.

# Using Your CLIÉ for the First Time

Now that you're a bit more familiar with the hardware, you're ready to start using it. This means charging the battery, working your way through the startup screens, and checking out the Graffiti tutorial.

## Charging the Battery

Most Clié models use a rechargeable battery (the sole exception being the SL10, which uses everyday AAA alkalines). It gets charged and recharged via the very same HotSync cradle that links the handheld to your computer.

TIP *On several models, it's possible to charge the battery using just the AC adapter that plugs into the cradle. This makes a handy mobile-charging solution, as it eliminates the need to unplug and bring the cradle with you on road trips. Consult your Clié's documentation to see if your model has this capability.*

When you first unpack your Clié, it's vital that you fully charge the battery before using the handheld. You can do this by plugging the AC adapter into the cradle, then placing your Clié in it. (The cradle need not be connected to your PC.) Let the unit charge for a good four hours. It's a long time to wait, we know, but you can spend those hours reading ahead to some of the more entertaining chapters (namely, the ones Rick wrote).

NOTE *Never again should you have to wait four hours to fully charge your battery. Most of the time, you'll "top it off" by leaving it in the cradle for a few minutes. Even if the battery dies completely, it should take no more than an hour or so to recharge it.*

## Favorite Uses for Our CLIÉS

**Rick**: One of the reasons I'm so nuts about the Clié NR70V is its built-in digital camera. Sure, the resolution leaves something to be desired (namely, more pixels), but it's great for grabbing impromptu shots of my little girl, Sarah. It's great for entertaining her, too—when we're on an airplane or waiting for our food at a restaurant, I'll pull out the Clié and let her take pictures of herself. She loves making faces and seeing herself on the screen. I've also discovered some great "edutainment" software that teaches kids to count and identify the alphabet. Yep, my PDA has become my Parental Diversion Assistant.

**Dave**: I'm embarrassed to say this, but my favorite use for my Clié is Solitaire. Yep, you read it right. See, here's the deal: I play Acid Solitaire from Red Mercury, and it's a colorful, full-screen program for the NR70's 320×480-pixel mode. Whenever I have a spare minute, I invariably open Acid Solitaire. I'd love to tell you I read a book with Palm Reader or compose solutions for world hunger in Quickword, but the truth is I'm a Solitaire addict.

## The Welcome Screens

Once the batteries are in and you turn your Clié back over, you see a "welcome" screen that asks you to remove the stylus and tap anywhere to continue. You're about to undertake a one-time setup procedure that takes all of about 60 seconds. The two key tasks accomplished here are the calibration of the screen digitizer and the setting of the date and time.

### What Is Digitizer Calibration?

Put simply, *digitizer calibration* is the process of teaching a Clié to accurately recognize taps on the screen. As you know, the screen responds to input from the stylus, and this calibration process simply insures the precision of those responses. In a way, it's like fine-tuning a TV set.

NOTE
*Over time, you might discover your screen taps seem a little "off." For example, you have to tap a bit to the left of an arrow for the screen to register the tap. At this point, it's time to recalibrate the digitizer, which you can do in the Prefs menu. We tell you how later in this chapter in the "Setting Clié Preferences" section.*

### Setting the Date and Time

The last stage of the welcome process is choosing your country and time zone, then setting the date and time. To set the time, you simply tap the box next to the words Set Time, then tap the up/down arrow keys to select the current time (don't forget to specify A.M. or P.M.). Tapping the box next to Set Date reveals a calendar. Again, a few strategic taps is all it takes to select today's date. (Be sure to choose the year first, then the month, then the day.) When you've done so, tap the Today button.

Setup  3 of 4

1. Tap arrows and boxes to
change settings.

Country: ▼ United States

Time Zone: [USA (Eastern)]

Daylight Saving: ▼ On

Set Date: [7/19/02]

Set Time: [3:41 pm]

2. Tap Next to continue.

( Previous )  ( Next )

**NOTE** *If you find yourself in a different time zone and need to change your Clié's clock, you needn't repeat the whole "welcome" process to do so. The date and time settings can be found in the Prefs menu, which we discuss later in this chapter in the "Setting Clié Preferences" section.*

If you want your Clié to automatically adjust for Daylight Savings, tap the little arrow next to that field and select On.

## The Graffiti Tutorial

On the last screen of the welcome wagon, you're given this option: "To learn about entering text on your handheld now, tap Next." Doing so takes you to a brief but helpful tutorial on using *Graffiti*, the Clié's handwriting-recognition software. If you'd rather jump right into using your handheld and learn Graffiti later, tap Done instead of Next. You can revisit the Graffiti tutorial at any time, just by finding and tapping the Graffiti icon on the Home screen.

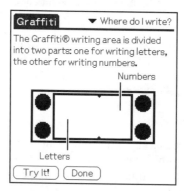

Graffiti          ▼ Where do I write?

The Graffiti® writing area is divided
into two parts: one for writing letters,
the other for writing numbers.

Numbers

Letters

( Try It! )  ( Done )

### Why Use the Tutorial?

Mastering Graffiti is arguably the most difficult aspect of using a Clié, because it requires you to learn and use a special character set. Thus, you should definitely spend some time with the tutorial. That said, most users can gain a working knowledge of Graffiti in about 20 minutes. And, after a few days' practice, you should be writing quickly, accurately, and effortlessly. We show you the ins and outs of Graffiti in Chapter 4.

> **TIP** *You may have discovered a Graffiti cheat-sheet sticker among the materials that came with your handheld. However, the Palm OS has a built-in cheat sheet of its own. Just draw a line from anywhere in the Graffiti area all the way to the top of the screen. Presto—a diagram of all the Graffiti characters!*

### What to Do If You'd Rather Not Use Graffiti

Psst! Don't tell anyone we told you this, but you don't have to use Graffiti at all. The Palm OS gives you an out, a way to enter data without drawing a single character. It's the built-in keyboard, which appears when you tap the little *a* in the lower-left corner of the Graffiti area. As you work your way to Chapter 4, which discusses Graffiti in much greater detail (the keyboard, too), you may find it's easier to enter data with the keyboard.

> **NOTE** *The keyboard appears only when you have a cursor—that is, only when there's a place to enter data. If you tap the little a when you're at the Home screen, nothing will happen (except perhaps a beep). The exception to this rule is the Clié NR series, which lets you switch between the Graffiti area and the keyboard at any time.*

# Getting to Know the Operating System

We aren't exaggerating when we say working with Cliés is roughly eight gazillion times easier than working with traditional computers. Though plenty powerful, Cliés are just a lot less complicated. There's no confusing menu system to wade through, no accidentally forgetting to save your document. Here we've highlighted some of the fundamental—but still important—differences between a Clié and a PC:

■ When you turn on a PC, you have to wait a few minutes for it to boot up. When you turn on a Clié, it's ready to roll instantaneously. Same goes for shutting it off: just press the Power button and the screen goes dark. There's no lengthy shutdown procedure.

■ On a PC, when you're done working with a program (say, your word processor), you must save your data before exiting that program. On a Clié, this isn't necessary. Data is retained at all times, even if you, say, switch to your to-do list while in the middle of writing a memo. When you return to Memo Pad, you find your document exactly as you left it. This holds true even if you turn the Clié off!

■ In that same vein, you don't "exit" a Clié program so much as switch to another one. This is a hard concept for seasoned computer users to grasp, as we've all been taught to shut down our software when we're done with it. There's no exit procedure on a Clié, and you'll rarely find that word in a drop-down menu. When you finish working in one program, you just tap the Home button to return to home base, or press one of the program buttons.

**NOTE** *We strongly encourage experimentation. Whereas wandering too far off the beaten track in Windows can lead to disaster, it's virtually impossible to get "lost" using a Clié. So tap here, explore there, and just have fun checking things out. Because there's no risk of losing data or running too many programs at once (impossible in the Palm OS), you should have no fear of fouling anything up. Play!*

## The Icons

*Icons* are, of course, little pictures used to represent things. In the case of the Palm OS, they're used largely to represent the installed programs. Thus, on the Home screen, you see icons labeled Address, Calc, Date Book, and so on—and all you do is tap one to access that particular program.

**NOTE** *Say, didn't you just learn that tapping a button in the Graffiti area is the way to load the calculator? And that you're supposed to press a button below the screen to load Date Book? In the Palm OS, there are often multiple ways to accomplish the same task. In this case, you can load certain programs either by tapping their onscreen icons or using their hardware-button equivalents.*

## The Menus

As in most computers, *drop-down menus* are used to access program-specific options and settings. In most Clié programs, tapping the Menu button (or the title bar at the top of any running program) makes a small "menu bar" appear at the top of the screen. You navigate this bar using the stylus as you would a mouse, tapping each menu item to make its list of options drop down, then tapping the option you want to access.

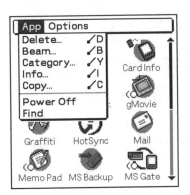

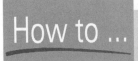 **Find Out How Much Memory Your Handheld Has Left**

As you start to add records and install new software on your Clié, you may wonder how to check the amount of memory that's available. From the Applications screen, tap Menu | App | Info. The screen that appears shows the total amount of memory on your device and how much of it is free. Notice, too, the other options that appear when you tap Menu | App. There's Delete (used to delete third-party programs), Beam (used to beam third-party programs), and Copy (used to copy programs to a Memory Stick—but we recommend using one of the methods discussed in Chapter 22).

## The Applications Screen

On a Clié, the *applications screen* (the screen you see when you tap the Home button) displays the icons for all the installed programs. (It also shows you the time and a battery gauge, as the following illustrates.)

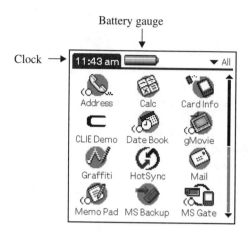

Battery gauge

Clock →

In the upper-right corner of the screen, you'll also notice a small arrow next to the word *All*. What this means is the applications screen is currently showing you all of the installed programs. If you tap the arrow, you see a list of categories (see Figure 2-5) into which you can group your programs.

## Why Use Categories?

The use of categories is entirely optional. They're intended solely to help you keep your applications organized. See, as you install more software, you wind up with more icons. Right out of the box, a Clié has only about a dozen of them—a manageable number. But, suppose you install all the bonus software that came with the Clié, plus a few third-party games, an e-book reader, and some spreadsheet software. Now things are getting a little cluttered, icon-wise.

Categories offer you a way to minimize the clutter. As you saw in the drop-down list, the Clié comes with a number of categories already created. You can use them if you want, or create your own.

**How to Create and Modify Categories**   Look again at the drop-down list in the upper-right corner of the applications screen (see Figure 2-5). Notice the last option: Edit Categories... Tapping this takes you to a screen where you can add, rename, and delete categories. To rename or delete one, first select it by tapping it with the stylus (you'll notice it's now highlighted). Then tap the appropriate button.

NOTE   *If you have a Memory Stick inserted, Edit Categories won't be the last item in the list. It will be Card.*

To create a new category, tap the New button, then write in the desired name. That's all there is to it!

**How to Assign Programs to Categories**   Once you tailor the categories to your liking, you must next assign your programs to them. This isn't difficult, but it may take you a few tedious minutes to complete. Here's how:

1. In the applications screen, tap the Menu button, then select Category...

2. Identify any one program you want to assign (you may have to scroll down the list, which you can do by using the onscreen arrows or scroll bar, or the Scroll buttons), then tap the little arrow next to it.

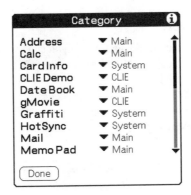

3. The list of categories appears. Pick one by tapping it.

4. Repeat the procedure for the other programs you want to assign.

5. Tap Done to return to the applications screen.

Now, when you tap the category arrow in the corner and select one, you see all your reassigned icons have been placed in their respective screens.

**FIGURE 2-5**    In the applications screen, categories can be used to organize your programs.

 *One way to change the displayed category is to tap the aforementioned arrow. However, there's a quicker way: if you tap the Home button repeatedly, the Clié cycles through the categories that have programs assigned to them. Again, the Clié offers us two ways to accomplish the same goal.*

# Setting CLIÉ Preferences

What would a computer be without a control panel where you can tweak the settings and customize the machine? The Palm OS has one, called *Prefs*. Find the Prefs icon in the applications screen, tap it, and meet us at the next paragraph.

Divided into several different sections (all of them accessible by tapping the arrow in the upper-right corner of the screen), Prefs is the place to reset your Clié's digitizer, change the date and time, input any necessary modem settings, and more. In listed order, here's the scoop on each individual Pref.

NOTE    *Depending on which Clié model you have, the Prefs options may be a bit different than what we have listed here. Most of the options are pretty self-explanatory, though, so don't worry.*

## Buttons

As we explained earlier, the four physical buttons below the screen are used to quick-launch the four main Palm OS programs (Date Book, To Do List, and so forth). However, it is possible to reassign these buttons to launch other programs instead. If you find you rarely use, say, To Do List, but you use Audio Player all the time, it may make sense to reassign the To Do List button accordingly.

After selecting Buttons from the drop-down menu in the Prefs screen, you see an icon that corresponds to each button. (You can also customize the Calc button.) All you do to change the function of any given button is tap the little arrow next to it, then select the desired application. The buttons can launch any installed application—you're not limited to just the core Clié apps.

Notice, too, the three options at the bottom of the Buttons screen:

- ■ **Default**   Restores the button assignments to their original settings.
- ■ **Pen**   Lets you choose what happens when you drag the tip of your stylus from the Graffiti area to the top of the screen. (This action can be made to load the built-in Graffiti help screens, invoke the onscreen keyboard, turn on backlighting, or one of several other options.)
- ■ **HotSync**   Enables you to reprogram the HotSync button on your docking cradle or optional modem—something we don't recommend doing.

## Connection

The *Connection* screen lets you set up whatever modem you might be using with your Clié, or choose to HotSync via the unit's IR port (instead of using the cradle). You probably won't need to fiddle with the modem settings.

## Date & Time

Flying into another time zone? Hit the Date & Time screen to change your handheld's internal clock (an important thing to remember so you don't miss your alarms!). You can also change the date if necessary, and set the Clié to automatically adjust for Daylight Savings Time.

## Digitizer

Noticing a little "drift" in your stylus taps? You tap someplace, but it doesn't quite register, or it registers in the *wrong* place? It may be time to reset your screen's digitizer. You should do so the moment you notice a problem; the worse the drift gets, the harder it may be to get to this screen. All you do is select Digitizer from the menu and follow the instructions.

*Digitizer drift does occur over time, but if it becomes a frequent occurrence, it could point to a hardware problem. If your Clié is still under warranty, contact customer service to see if a replacement is warranted. In the meantime, there are software utilities designed to compensate for digitizer drift. See Chapter 13 for more information.*

## Formats

Few users need to spend much time in the Formats screen, where you can change the way dates, times, and numbers are displayed. You can also specify whether you want the calendar week to start on Sunday (the default) or Monday.

## General

Probably the most frequently visited of the Prefs screens, *General* contains the following settings:

- ■ **Auto-off After**   To help preserve battery life, your handheld will turn itself off after a designated period of inactivity. Here you can set the interval, from 30 seconds to 3 minutes. The lower you set it, the better your battery life will be.

- ■ **Stay on in Cradle**   When this box is checked, your handheld will remain on while it's in the HotSync cradle. This can be handy if you spend a lot of time at your desk and frequently need to consult your handheld for addresses, schedules, and so on, or want to use the PhotoStand application (see Chapter 16) to turn your Clié into a digital picture frame.

- ■ **System Sound**   Adjust the volume for various system sounds (like beeps, HotSync tones, and so on). If you want your handheld to be silent, set this to Off.

- ■ **Alarm Sound**   Adjust the volume for alarms.

- ■ **Alarm LED**   On some models, the Power button doubles as an LED, which can be set to flash when an alarm goes off.

- ■ **Game Sound**   Adjust the volume for games.

- ■ **Beam Receive**   If this is off, you won't be able to receive programs and data beamed from other handhelds. However, keeping it off until you need it can help conserve power. Just *remember* that it's off so you don't pull your hair out trying to figure out why you can't receive a beam.

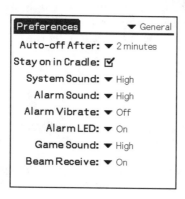

## HiRes

This option appears on those Clié models that have high-resolution screens. Although the vast majority of Palm OS programs were designed to run on lower-resolution screens, the Clié gives them a coat of "high-resolution paint" (meaning it enables them to take advantage of the extra screen pixels so they look sharper). This is accomplished via High Resolution Assist, which, by default, is enabled in this screen.

However, some applications—most notably games—may have difficulty working properly when "assisted" by High Resolution Assist. If you start a program and see a lot of garbage on the screen, or your Clié crashes, find the program in the HiRes list, then tap the check box next to it. That will make it run in its normal low-resolution mode, which should work.

NOTE    *You can't enable or disable High Resolution Assist for applications stored on a Memory Stick. But there's a freeware utility called SwitchDash that can.*

## Jog

The Jog screen enables you to tweak a few settings for the Jog Dial and Back button. We think the default settings are ideal for most users, so you probably won't need to fiddle with them too much. However, here's a rundown of what does what:

■ **Power On with BACK button** When checked, the Back button will turn on your Clié.

■ **Use JogAssist** JogAssist enables the Jog Dial to function in applications that don't innately support it. If you come across a third-party program that exhibits problems when the Jog Dial is used, you can disable JogAssist for that program. Just tap the Select Applications button, then check the program in the list that appears.

■ **Additional Menu** As noted earlier in this chapter, most applications have drop-down menus, just like on a computer. To make one-handed Clié operation even more practical, you can add extra functions (up to three of them) to the menus found in every program. Tap the Select Additional Menu button to see what options are available.

■ **Extended push of BACK button** You have two choices for what can happen when you hold the Back button for two seconds. Either it can turn off your Clié (that's the Power Off option), or it can give you a Jog Dial-accessible cursor for accessing buttons and menus. We highly recommend using the latter option, which is selected by default.

## Network

The slightly misnamed *Network* screen is where you enter the relevant information about your Internet service provider (ISP), if you're using a modem to dial into it. A handful of major ISPs are already listed in the Service menu, but you still need to provide your account username and password, plus the phone number for the ISP. The *Details...* button takes you to a screen with some advanced Internet settings, while *Connect* tells the modem to go ahead and dial in.

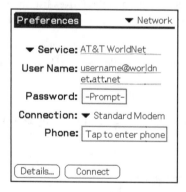

## Owner

In the tragic event that you lose your Clié, you'd probably be very grateful to have it returned. The Owner screen is where you can put your name and contact information (address, phone number, e-mail address—whatever you're comfortable with). Then, if you use the Palm Operating System's security features (which we detail in Chapter 9) to "lock" the device every time you turn it off, the information on the Owner screen is displayed when the unit is turned on again.

Thus, if someone happens to find your handheld, they know how to return it to you, but won't have access to all your data. Smart!

*Here's an even better way to retrieve a lost Clié: slap on a StuffBak sticker. Whoever finds your handheld simply needs to call a toll-free number or visit a web site to arrange its return. Get more information on this great service at **www.stuffbak.com**.*

## ShortCuts

Next, we come to *ShortCuts,* a tool designed to expedite the entry of often-used words and phrases. Let's say you're a Starfleet engineer, and you use your Clié to keep track of your repair duties. The phrase "holodeck emitters" comes up quite a bit—but do you really have to write it out every time? What if you could just write "h-e" instead, and have the words magically appear? That's the beauty of shortcuts.

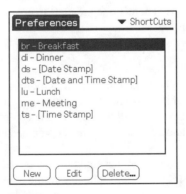

As you see when you reach the ShortCuts screen, a handful of the little time-savers have already been created. There's one each for your daily meals, one for "meeting," and even a couple of date and time stamps (used to quickly insert the date and time, natch). Let's walk through the process of creating and using a new shortcut:

1. Tap the New button.

2. In the ShortCut Name field, write the abbreviation you want to use for this particular shortcut. As an example, let's use "bm," for "Buy milk."

3. Tap the first line in the ShortCut Text field to move your cursor there. Now, enter the text you want to appear when you invoke the shortcut (in this case, **Buy milk**).

4. Tap OK. Now, let's invoke the new shortcut. Press the To Do button to launch the To Do List, then tap New to create a new task.

5. To invoke this or any other shortcut (in any application, be it Date Book, Memo Pad, or whatever), you must first write the shortcut stroke in the Graffiti area. This lets Graffiti know you're about to enter the abbreviation for a shortcut. The stroke looks like a cursive, lowercase letter *l* (see our Graffiti guide in Chapter 4). After you make the stroke, you see it appear next to your cursor. Now enter the letter *b*, then the letter *m*, and presto! The words "Buy milk" magically appear.

## Web Clipping

Very few users will need to bother with this screen. Consult your handheld's documentation if you need further information.

# An Introduction to Palm Desktop

So far, we've talked mostly about the Clié itself: the hardware, the operating system, the basic setup procedures and considerations. There's one area left to cover before you venture into real-world Clié use: Palm Desktop.

## What Is Palm Desktop?

Wondrous as a Clié is in its own right, what makes it even more special is its capability to synchronize with your computer. This means all the data entered into your Clié is copied to your PC, and vice versa. The software that fields all this data on the computer side is *Palm Desktop*. (If you use Microsoft Outlook or another contact manager, you needn't use Palm Desktop at all. More on that in the next section.)

Viewed in a vacuum, Palm Desktop resembles traditional personal information manager (PIM) or contact-management software. It effectively replicates all the core functionality of the Palm OS, providing you with a phone list, appointment calendar, to-do list, and memo pad. If you've never used such software before, you'll no doubt find Palm Desktop an invaluable addition, as it helps keep you organized at home or in the office (whereas a Clié keeps you organized while traveling).

## A Word about Synchronization

What happens when you synchronize your Clié with your PC? In a nutshell, three things:

- Any new entries made on your Clié are added to Palm Desktop.
- Any new entries made in Palm Desktop are added to your Clié.
- Any existing records modified in one place (the Clié, for example) are modified in the other (the desktop, same example), the newest changes taking precedence.

Therefore, synchronizing regularly assures your information is kept current, both in your Clié and in Palm Desktop.

> **NOTE** *Already entrenched in Microsoft Outlook? All Cliés come with software—a special version of Puma Technologies' Intellisync—that allows direct synchronization with Outlook (bypassing Palm Desktop). If you have a different contact manager (such as Lotus Organizer), you may need to upgrade to the full version of Puma's Intellisync.*

## Synchronizing with a Macintosh

Sorry, Mac owners. Unlike Palm and Handspring handhelds, Sony's models don't come with the software you need to synchronize. Fortunately, there's a third-party solution: The Missing Sync from Mark/Space. This $29.95 package provides everything you need to sync a Clié with a Macintosh.

# Where to Find It

| Web Site | Address | What's There |
|----------|---------|--------------|
| Puma Technologies | www.pumatech.com | Contact manager synchronization utility Intellisync |
| Mark/Space | www.markspace.com | The Missing Sync |

# Chapter 3

# Introducing Your CLIÉ to the PC

## How to...

- Charge your Clié
- Install the Palm Desktop software
- Configure the HotSync cradle
- Troubleshoot USB connection problems
- Set up the HotSync Manager
- Perform your first HotSync
- Interpret the HotSync log
- Keep your data synchronized just the way you like

A famous poet—it might have been Paul Simon, or perhaps John Donne—once said that no man is an island. Likewise, your Clié is not an island, either—it's designed to interact with your desktop computer to synchronize important data.

That's pretty neat, because it means you don't have to waste your time duplicating information on your PDA that already exists on your home computer. And if you should ever lose your data because the Clié crashes or does something catastrophic—like falls off the roof of a building or into a lake—you can restore every last bit and byte of data as easily as pressing the HotSync button on your desktop's cradle.

> NOTE *Not every Clié model comes with a cradle—some use HotSync cables instead. So, when we talk about placing your Clié into its cradle, you can also take that to mean "plug in the cable."*

Now that you've had a chance to explore your Clié in Chapter 2, it's time to learn about how the device works with your home computer. The Clié comes with a slew of tools designed for the desktop, including a synchronization application for making sure it has the same data as the desktop. Let's get started.

# Charging Your Clié

Most Cliés come with integrated rechargeable batteries. If yours does, be sure to fully charge your Clié (the first time usually takes about four hours) before you turn it on or start experimenting with it. To charge your PDA, place it in the HotSync cradle and plug the cradle into the AC adapter, as in the following illustration. Don't plug the cradle into your computer's USB port, though—that's a step you'll perform after the Palm Desktop software is installed.

Yes, we know you're anxious to play with your Clié. But if you don't let it fully charge before the first time you use it, you could limit its capability to charge and thereby cut down on its total battery life for as long as you own it.

NOTE    *Don't plug the cradle into your PC until you're told to. Connecting it too soon can complicate the setup procedure.*

After you're up and running, remember that your Clié will charge whenever it's sitting idly in its cradle. Just make sure the cradle is indeed plugged into the wall outlet via its AC adapter. If the cradle isn't plugged into the wall, it can't charge your PDA. You can tell your Clié is being recharged because a light on the cradle or the PDA itself will light up. If you don't see the light, check to see if the AC adapter has come loose from the wall or the HotSync cradle.

# Installing the Desktop Software

Before you can synchronize your Clié and desktop PC, you first need to install the Palm Desktop software suite on your computer. Palm Desktop is sort of like a personal information manager (PIM). It duplicates all the core applications from your Clié and serves as the headquarters from which you can use synchronized information from your Clié. While you definitely need to install Palm Desktop, you don't necessarily need to use it. If you already rely on Microsoft Outlook or another PIM, you can synchronize your Clié to that program instead and avoid the Palm Desktop entirely.

The CD-ROM that accompanies your Clié includes everything you need to connect the handheld to your desktop, including your choice of synchronization to Palm Desktop or Outlook. Installation is very straightforward. Follow the installation instructions that appear after you insert the CD-ROM.

## Installing Palm Desktop

The Palm Desktop CD-ROM includes a step-by-step installer that gets you up and running within minutes of taking your Clié out of the box. Most of the main installation is completely automated, but you have to make a few decisions:

- **Outlook or Palm Desktop?**  If you have a copy of Microsoft Outlook installed on your PC, the installer detects it and gives you the option of synchronizing your data to it if you so desire. What data are we talking about? Stuff like contacts from the address book and appointments from the calendar, as well as notes and tasks. If you're a regular Outlook user, you should certainly choose to synchronize your Clié with Outlook. Palm Desktop, on the other hand, is a serviceable PIM, though it's not as comprehensive as Outlook. If you use a PIM like Outlook, the software will install a copy of Intellisync Lite to manage the flow of data between your Clié and Outlook. If you sync with Palm Desktop, you don't need—and won't install—Intellisync.

# Palm Desktop is for the CLIÉ, too!

The Palm Desktop is so named because it was designed for the first Palm OS PDAs. It continues to work with all Palm OS devices like the Clié, though. So don't be thrown off by the name—the Palm Desktop is designed for Cliés just as well as Palms, Visors, and all the other Palm-powered devices out there. In fact, they really should have called it "Clié Desktop" just to minimize confusion, but Palm makes the operating system, so they make the rules.

> TIP
>
> *If you ever switch from a third-party PIM to Palm Desktop or vice-versa, just reinstall the Palm Desktop software and change your answer to this question to properly configure your computer's software.*

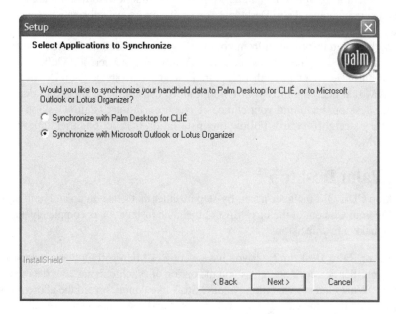

- **Configure Mail** Want to read and write e-mail on your Clié? The installer offers you a list of mail programs with which you can synchronize. Remember, you probably don't even have most of the programs in the list. Just choose the one you want to use (if you want to synchronize e-mail at all, that is—if you don't want mail on your Clié, just skip this step).

- **Assign a Unique HotSync Name** The HotSync Name is actually the name of your Clié. You can use your own name or give your handheld a unique descriptor—anything from **Dave's Clié** to **Clié-33A** to just plain **Mike** is acceptable. Is the name important? Yup. If you have more than one Clié, each one absolutely must have a different name. If you give two or more Cliés the same name, you can end up seriously messing up your data. If you forget your HotSync name and need to find it again, just tap the HotSync app on your Clié. The name will appear in the top-right corner:

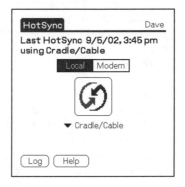

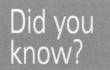
*Your Clié probably comes with a whole bunch of bonus programs—stuff like the Documents To Go office suite, sound editing software, and games like Bejeweled. You can install any or all of them from other options within the installation CD's setup program.*

## Did you know?

# HotSync Doesn't Have Anything to Do with Dating

HotSync, a term coined by Palm, Inc., refers to the act of synchronizing the data stored on your handheld and desktop computers. These days, all PDA companies use a special term that means more or less the same thing—for instance, Microsoft's Pocket PCs use the term *ActiveSync* instead.

## Installing the HotSync Cradle or Cable

Once the software is installed, it's time to connect the HotSync cradle or cable to your computer. Your HotSync cradle may look a little different depending on which Clié you're using, but its appearance doesn't matter—it performs the same function: transferring information between the PC and PDA. Plug the cradle or cable into an empty USB port on the computer or a USB hub. You don't even have to turn the computer off first.

 *As we mentioned earlier, make sure you've installed Palm Desktop before you connect the cradle or cable. If you don't, you could wind up with some serious setup headaches.*

### Troubleshooting the USB Port

USB is usually pretty reliable and any potential problems that crop up generally boil down to just a few things. For starters, you might not have anywhere to plug in your cradle, especially if you already have a few other USB devices. If that's the case, you need to run over to a local computer store and buy a USB hub. This device plugs into a USB port on your PC and gives you several extra USB connectors for additional devices.

However, if you plugged in your HotSync cradle and it doesn't seem to work, two likely causes exist:

- ■ Your USB port doesn't have enough power to run the cradle. If your USB port has several devices connected to it, such as through a hub, it may not be able to handle the power requirements of the connected devices. Make sure you're using a "powered" hub (it will come with its own AC adapter) and that it's plugged into the wall. If that checks out, you might need to swap some devices around between your PC's USB ports. This might take a little experimentation.

- ■ A related problem: your USB port might have run out of bandwidth—in other words, the capacity to transfer data. This can happen if you have some high-performance USB devices connected to the same port. Again, the solution is to move some things around between the ports. Dave found he simply couldn't run all the USB devices he wants to on his PC because they demand more total bandwidth than his PC's USB ports could deliver.

 *Many new PCs have USB 2.0 ports, which are much more robust and have far greater bandwidth than older USB 1.1 ports. Nonetheless, USB 2.0 ports work like older USB 1.1 ports unless USB 2.0-compatible devices are plugged in. Right now, all Cliés are plain old USB 1.1 devices.*

*You needn't plug the AC adapter into the HotSync cradle to transfer data between the PC and Clié. If you don't use the AC adapter, though, the batteries in the Clié won't recharge and, eventually, its batteries die and cost you your data.*

## Configuring Intellisync

If you opted to synchronize your Clié with some third-party PIM program like Outlook or Lotus Notes, you'll need to configure Intellisync before your first HotSync. If you are going to sync with Palm Desktop, skip to the next section, "Your First HotSync." No peeking... go already. Can't you see we have work to do?

After the installation program puts Intellisync on your desktop, you'll need to configure the program to your specific software. You'll see a dialog box that looks like this:

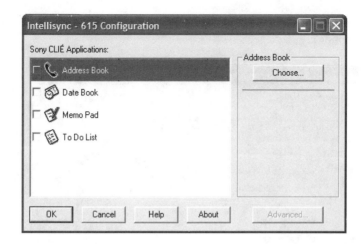

You can sync or ignore each of the four main Clié applications, but by default nothing syncs at all. Odds are that you'll want to synchronize all your Clié data with the desktop, so click each of the four check boxes. For instance, when you check the box for Address Book, you'll see a list of programs you can sync with. Select the program you actually use, then click OK. Repeat this process for each of the four programs on your Clié.

Also note that there's a button for advanced settings. For each of the four programs, you can click Advanced at the bottom of the dialog box and tell Intellisync how to handle conflicting data.

If you change the same entry on both the desktop PIM and the Clié, for instance, you can choose from among these options:

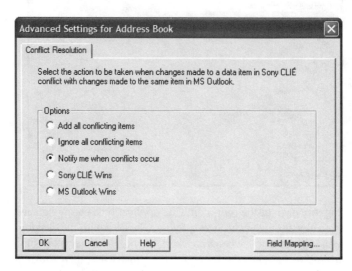

You can change these options at any time by running the Intellisync Configure application in your Start menu.

# Your First HotSync

After you load the software onto your computer, install your cradle, and have a nice, relaxing break watching television (Dave recommends *Andromeda*, though Rick prefers *Britney Spears in Concert*), it's time to perform your first HotSync.

HotSyncing—especially if you already use a PIM like Outlook—is pretty cool because it transfers all your desktop-based data (like appointments, contacts, and to-dos) to your Clié, so you don't have to enter any new data to get started with your new PDA. If you're starting from scratch with Palm Desktop, though, you'll have to enter your contacts and appointments because they aren't already on the computer. Here's what you need to do to make sure you're ready:

- Make sure your HotSync cradle is connected to the PC.
- Place the Clié in the cradle.
- If you have a rechargeable PDA, the AC adapter should also be connected. You see a charging light when the Clié is in the cradle.
- Make sure the HotSync Manager software is running. You should see the HotSync icon in the System Tray. If you don't see it, start it now. Choose Start | Programs | Sony Handheld | HotSync Manager.

**3**

## The Best Films of All Time

Taking that TV break before the HotSync got us just a tad distracted. Truth be told, we took the opportunity to go watch some movies. And that led to the inevitable arguments . . . what are the best movies of all time?

**Dave:** There's no way a rational person could disagree . . . *Aliens* is the best movie of all time. Space Marines fighting xenomorphs with twenty-third century machine guns! Woo hoo! What could possibly be cooler than that? And it has some of the best movie lines ever. This, mind you, is the film in which Bill Paxton made the words, "Game over, man," a part of my daily lexicon. After *Aliens,* my list gets a bit more introspective. *The Matrix, Memento, The Sixth Sense, Almost Famous,* and *O Brother, Where Art Thou* have to be several of the most amazing films ever made. Now let's see what lame movies Rick thinks are cool. My prediction: His favorite films include *Tron, Dirty Dancing,* and *Weekend at Bernie's 2.*

**Rick:** I've had just about enough of your *Weekend at Bernie's 2* bashing, mister. Don't make me tell everyone about your strange fondness for Will Smith. Anyway, in no particular order, my Top Five Movies are as follows: *Life is Beautiful, City Lights, The Shawshank Redemption, Toy Story 2,* and *Star Trek II: The Wrath of Khan.* Yes, I know only one of those movies has things blowing up, which means you won't care for the other four. The age of *Ah*-nold has passed, leatherneck. Grow up already.

**TIP**    *The System Tray is the region at the bottom of the Windows Desktop that's found to the right of the Taskbar. It contains the clock and icons for special programs like the HotSync Manager. If you use Windows XP, the icon may be "hidden"—click the little arrow to reveal all hidden icons and you should see the one for HotSync Manager.*

## Pressing the HotSync Button

Press the button on the HotSync cradle. Of course, a few Clié models don't have a cradle or HotSync button—if that sounds like yours, you'll need to find the HotSync application on the Clié (it's usually in the System category) and tap the big HotSync button that appears in the middle of the screen.

After you press the HotSync button, here's what should happen:

1.  Your Clié turns itself on (if it wasn't on already).

2.  You hear three tones indicating the HotSync has begun.

3.  A message box appears on the Windows desktop, which informs you of the HotSync status.

4.  You hear another set of tones when the HotSync is complete.

5.  The Clié displays a message indicating the HotSync is complete.

## Exploring the HotSync Manager

The HotSync Manager software does exactly what it sounds like—it manages the connection between your Clié and your computer, enabling you to HotSync. It contains all the options and configurations needed to keep the two devices talking to each other. To HotSync, you needn't mess with anything on the Clié at all. You only need to tweak the HotSync Manager.

To get to the HotSync Manager's options in Windows, you need to visit the HotSync menu. Click the HotSync Manager icon in the System Tray and a context menu appears.

**TIP** *You can click the HotSync Manager icon with either the right or left mouse button; the result is the same.*

These are the first options you encounter in the HotSync menu:

■ Local USB

■ Local Serial

■ Modem

■ Network

**NOTE** *If you're on a laptop or PC with an IR port add-on, you'll also see a fifth choice: Infrared.*

For now, the only one that must be checked is Local USB. This means you can perform a HotSync using the USB-powered cradle you've already installed.

### Configuring HotSync Setup

Click the Setup option on the HotSync menu. You should now see the Setup dialog box. This is the place where you get to configure how the HotSync manager behaves. Four tabs are on the Setup dialog box.

**The General Tab**    The General tab lets you specify how often the HotSync Manager "listens" to the USB or serial port for a HotSync request. It has three options, as you can see in Figure 3-1.

- ■ **Always available**    This is the default setting. As soon as you press the HotSync button on the cradle, you synchronize your data. It's fast and convenient, and is probably the way most people use their PDAs.

- ■ **Available only when the Palm Desktop is running**    This solution dates back to when PDAs connected via the serial port; these days, it's not that useful.

- ■ **Manual**    Just like it sounds, the HotSync Manager doesn't run at all unless you choose it from the Start menu (Start | Programs | Sony Handheld | HotSync Manager). This is the least convenient of all the options, but you might want to choose it if you HotSync only on rare occasions. Even so, we suggest sticking with the default, which is to always leave the HotSync manager running and available.

**The Local Tab**    The Local tab is for those poor suckers still using the computer's serial port instead of USB—don't worry about it.

**The Modem and Network Tabs**    Both of these tabs are used to specify settings for more advanced HotSync techniques. After you've seen all the tabs in the Setup dialog box, click OK to save changes or click Cancel to leave the dialog box without changing anything.

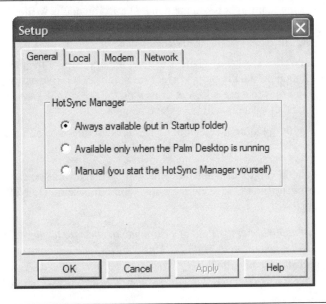

**FIGURE 3-1**    The General tab determines when the HotSync Manager runs and how easy it is to perform a HotSync.

## What's a Conduit?

Conduit is the term your Clié uses to describe the software that connects data on your PDA with similar data on your computer. The Calendar conduit, for instance, makes sure the Clié's Date Book and the computer's calendar stay completely in sync. Every application on your Clié that has a corresponding program on the PC is connected with its own conduit, and the Custom menu option is where you turn to adjust these conduits.

## Customizing the HotSync Operation

To customize the HotSync Operation, from the HotSync Manager menu choose Custom.

This is arguably the most important dialog box in the HotSync software because it enables you to specify with great detail exactly what data will get transferred. Before we look at this dialog box, however, we should describe a few conduit states the Clié uses to perform data synchronizations. Because if you make the wrong choice, you could delete data you need.

- **Synchronize the Files**    Suppose you added new files to both the PC and the Clié since the last HotSync. The new data from the Clié is copied to the PC, and the new data from the PC is copied to the Clié. Both devices will have a copy of everything. *This is the best setting to use most of the time. In fact, it's the default for most conduits.*

- **Desktop Overwrites Handheld**    This option supposes the desktop data is correct at the expense of anything that might be on the handheld. If you add new files to both the PC and the handheld, for instance, and then perform this kind of synch, the new files on the Clié will be lost. The desktop data overwrites whatever was on the PDA.

- **Handheld Overwrites Desktop**    This is exactly the opposite of the previous case. Assuming the handheld data is more correct for some reason (we assume you have your reasons), any files that are different or new on the desktop PC are lost after the synchronization. Both systems will have the Clié data.

- **Do Nothing**    With this option selected, no changes are made to either device during the HotSync.

Remember: each conduit can be adjusted independently. This means you can, say, set the Clié's Date Book to overwrite the PC's, while the e-mail conduit is set to Do Nothing and the Notes conduit synchronizes.

TIP    *If you're ever in doubt about the state of your conduits, be sure to check the action before you press the HotSync button by right-clicking the HotSync icon and choosing Custom. If you ever accidentally configure the HotSync Manager to Handheld Overwrites Desktop, for instance, you'll lose changes you made to the Palm Desktop or Outlook when you HotSync.*

With those options in mind, let's look at the Custom dialog box. As you can see in Figure 3-2, the top of the box displays the name of the Clié. Managing more than one Palm-powered device from each PC is possible, so you select the proper unit from the list menu before continuing. If you have only a single Clié, don't worry about this option.

This dialog box displays a list of conduits and their actions. As you can see from the list, there's a unique conduit for each kind of application on your Clié. Your Clié should include these conduits right out of the box:

- **Mail**   E-mail messages are synchronized between your desktop mail application and the Clié.

- **Date Book**   Shares data between the Clié and desktop calendar.

- **Address Book**   Shares data between the Clié and desktop address book.

- **To Do List**   Shares data between the Clié and desktop to-do list.

- **Memo Pad**   Shares data between the Clié and desktop memo pad.

- **Install**   Transfers Palm OS applications or data from your PC's hard disk to the Clié's system memory.

- **Install to Card**   Transfers data or applications to the Clié's memory card

- **System**   Transfers other files created by your Clié to the PC.

**NOTE**   *If you install new software, you may end up with more conduits. Many programs, like Documents To Go, come with their own conduits to control the flow of information between your Palm and desktop applications.*

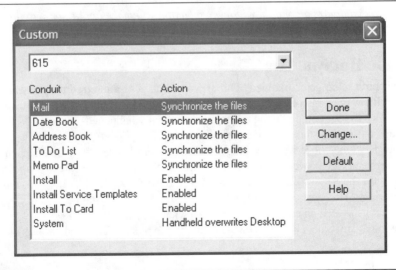

**FIGURE 3-2**   The Custom dialog box enables you to specify how each conduit behaves when you HotSync.

To configure a conduit, either double-click an entry or click it once and then click the Change button. Depending on which conduit you open, you'll find you have all four synchronization options, or perhaps fewer.

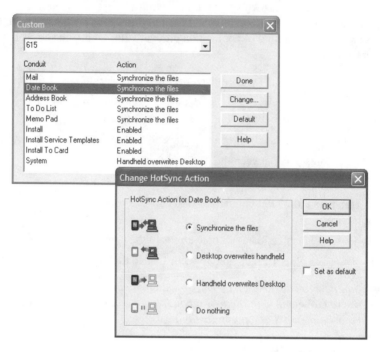

*When you configure a conduit, whatever selection you make applies only to the very next time you HotSync unless you check the box marked Set As Default.*

## Reading the HotSync Log

Did your HotSync session go as planned? Did all your data get transferred properly and did files get copied the way you expected? Usually, it's pretty obvious if everything went well, but sometimes it's nice if your computer can tell you what actually happened—especially if the HotSync dialog box reports some sort of error.

During each HotSync, the HotSync Manager makes a record of everything that happened. This log is easy to read and can answer that nagging question, "Why didn't the calendar update after I added an entry for the Sandra Bullock Fan Club?" If the HotSync Manager noticed something went wrong during a HotSync, it'll even tell you. Figure 3-3, for instance, shows the result of a HotSync that generated an error. The log reveals what happened.

To see the log at any time, click the HotSync icon in the System Tray and choose View Log.

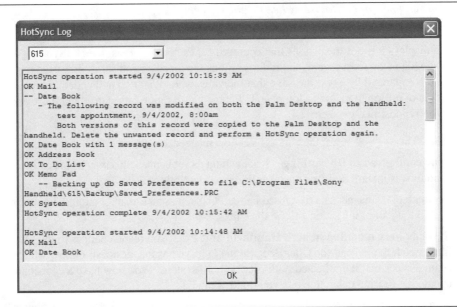

**FIGURE 3-3**   The HotSync log records the details of the last ten HotSyncs, as well as any errors that occurred along the way.

## How to ... HotSync

To HotSync, do the following:

**1.** Plug the cradle into your PC.

**2.** Set the Clié in the cradle or connect its HotSync cable.

**3.** Make sure the HotSync Manager software is running (by default, it should be already).

**4.** Verify the conduits are set properly to transfer and synchronize data just the way you want (by default, they should be already).

**5.** Press the HotSync button on the cradle.

**6.** Wait until you hear the "HotSync complete" tones before removing the Clié from the cradle.

*You can't perform a HotSync when the log is open.*

The log displays a list of the actions that occurred for each of your last ten HotSync sessions. The top of the log is the most recent, and older sessions are listed as you scroll down the page. Each session is separated by a text message that indicates when it started and ended.

What kind of information does a log reveal? Each conduit reports its status, and these are the messages you're most likely to see:

- **OK** This is good news; the conduit's action succeeded with no errors.
- **Sync configured to Do Nothing** If something didn't happen, this may be the cause—the conduit was intentionally, or mistakenly, set to Do Nothing.
- **Truncated** This means a file stored on the PC (such as an e-mail or address book entry) was so long all of it wouldn't fit on the Clié.
- **Records were modified in both Handheld and PC** You made changes to the same file on both the PC and the Clié. Because the HotSync Manager doesn't know which change is correct, it duplicated both files on both systems. You now have a chance to update the file and delete the one you don't want.
- **Synchronization failed** There can be any number of reasons for this—see Chapter 24 for troubleshooting information.

*The HotSync log is also available on the Clié itself, albeit only for the most recent HotSync session. To reach it, tap the HotSync application, then tap the Log button.*

# HotSync as a Way of Life

After your first HotSync, you may begin to see how convenient it is to have a duplicate of your desktop data on your Clié. But how often should you HotSync? The short answer is: as frequently as you like. Most people HotSync daily, while others—whose data changes much less frequently—update their Clié only once a week or even less. Use the following guide as a rule of thumb:

- HotSync any time you leave the office with your PDA.
- HotSync when you return from a trip to update your PC with new info stored on the Clié.
- Many AvantGo web channels (see Chapter 11) are updated daily. A HotSync each day keeps you current with the newest content.
- HotSync to install new applications on your Clié (discussed in Chapter 4).

## What HotSync Does to Files

After your first HotSync, you have a set of data on both your Clié and desktop. The goal of the HotSync process is to make sure the data stays the same on both systems. So what happens when you change data on one or both of the computers? This table, which assumes the conduits are set to synchronize the files, should help you understand the subtleties of the HotSync:

| Before the HotSync | After the HotSync |
|---|---|
| You add a file to the Clié (or the PC). | That file is added to the PC (or the Clié). |
| You delete a file from the Clié (or PC). | The file is also deleted from the PC (or Clié). |
| You change a file on the Clié. | The file is changed on the PC. |
| You changed the same file on both the Clié and PC—they're now different. | Both versions of the file are added to the Clié and PC. You need to modify the file and delete the one you don't want to keep. |

## Changing Conduits On-the-Fly

Often, you may find yourself changing all the conduits in your HotSync Manager save one or two. For instance, you might want to disable everything except the Install conduit to quickly get a new program onto your Clié, or set everything except AvantGo to Do Nothing so you can get your news onto the PDA as you're running out the door to lunch.

Whatever the reason, you'll soon find there's no easy way to disable several conduits at once. Successively changing five conduits to Do Nothing is almost as time consuming as performing the whole darned HotSync to begin with.

There's an easier way. Download the tremendously useful program called Ultrasoft NotSync from PalmGear.com. This program lets you quickly and easily change your conduits in just seconds. The change applies only to the very next HotSync, so it never affects your default settings.

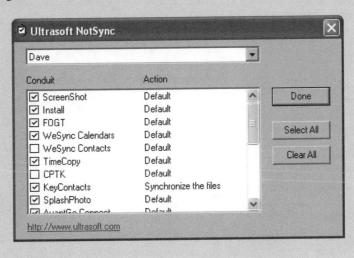

With this in mind, you might not always want to use the Synchronize The Files option for all your conduits. Why not? Any number of reasons. Here are a few situations:

- You might rely on your Clié to take notes you have no interest in copying to your PC. In other words, you want to keep one set of notes on the PC, which is relevant to what you do at your desk, and another set of notes for when you're on the road. In such a case, Do Nothing is probably the best option for your needs.

- You might take notes you don't need to keep after a trip is over. In such an instance, you can use Desktop Overwrites Handheld for that conduit. After your trip, the handheld notes will be erased during the HotSync and replaced by the desktop notes.

- Your computer has fallen victim to some kind of disaster, and now your Clié holds all your precious contact data. After you reinstall Windows, Palm Desktop, and so on, you should set everything to Handheld Overwrites Desktop to make sure the data is restored to the PC. After that, you can return to synchronizing the files.

 *Don't forget, you can configure each conduit individually, so the Address Book might be set to Synchronize the files, while the Date Book is set to Desktop Overwrites Handheld.*

## Where to Find It

| Web Site | Address | What's There |
|---|---|---|
| Sony | www.sonystyle.com | Software updates, news, and accessories |
| AvantGo | www.avantgo.com | Web page-like news and information channels you can carry on your Clié |
| PalmGear | www.palmgear.com | A great resource for Clié software |

# Part II

# Everyday Stuff With Your CLIÉ

# Chapter 4

# Getting Information In and Out of Your CLIÉ

## How to...

- Use Graffiti to enter data into your Clié
- Type using the onscreen keyboard
- Enter data using the Palm Desktop
- Use alternative gestures to write in Graffiti more effectively
- Eliminate the Graffiti area on certain Clié models
- Turn abbreviations into long text using shortcuts
- Display Graffiti help
- Receive data from another PDA via the IR port
- Beam items to another PDA
- Install new software on your Clié
- Delete old applications from your Clié

A handheld computer is only as good as the information you store inside it. Or, perhaps more to the point, it's only as good as the methods you have for getting information into it. After all, if you make storing your appointments on the computer too difficult, you won't bother doing it—and then you own an expensive paperweight with the word "calendar" written on it.

Here's an example: a tiny, credit card-sized PDA called the Rex that debuted and disappeared several years ago. This little guy was so small it slipped easily into your wallet, yet carried contacts and appointments like a champ. The problem? You couldn't update it away from your PC, so a schedule change or a new contact couldn't be entered on-the-fly. For some people, this wasn't a big deal, but public reaction was underwhelming. The Clié sells like hotcakes (the good ones, with the pecans in them) because of the very fact that it can be updated on the go, and quite easily as well.

You already know about some of the tools at your disposal for getting data in and out of your Clié. We talked about how to HotSync in Chapter 3, and you know you can enter data directly into the device using Graffiti, an almost-ordinary style of handwriting. In this chapter, you learn everything you might ever need to know about Graffiti. We also cover other data entry methods, including the onscreen keyboard and beaming data directly between handhelds using the built-in IR port.

# The Five Ways to Enter Data

Without a doubt, one of the first things you want to do with your new Clié is enter data—names, phone numbers, addresses, appointments, and so on—into your various applications. Hey, don't look so surprised. The core applications, like Date Book, Address List, Memo Pad, and To Do List, rely on you to fill them with interesting things you can later reference.

Certainly you can HotSync data into your Clié from your PC, but that's only part of the story. You can use any one of five completely different methods for entering information directly into your Clié, such as the following:

- Write by hand using Graffiti

- Tap-type using the onscreen keyboard

- Type with a built-in keyboard (if your Clié has one)

- Beam data wirelessly to your Clié from another Palm-powered device

- Enter data into the Palm Desktop, and then HotSync the data to your Clié

**TIP**   *You can also connect an add-on keyboard to your Clié and type the ordinary way. For information on keyboards, see Chapter 23.*

**4**

## Using Graffiti

$\wedge$ = A
$\urcorner$ = T

Graffiti is a specialized handwriting recognition system that enables you to enter text into the Clié almost error-free. Unlike other handwriting recognition systems, Graffiti neither interprets your handwriting nor learns or adapts to the way you write. Instead, you need to slightly modify the way you write and make specific kinds of keystrokes that represent letters, numbers, and punctuation. Don't worry, though, this isn't hard to do. You can learn the basics of Graffiti inside of a day—heck, you can probably master most of the characters in an hour or less.

When entering text into your PDA, you can't write directly on the part of the screen that displays data. Instead, you write inside the small rectangle at the bottom of the display—the one that sits between the four icons. We call this the "Graffiti area." For some Cliés, this is a special silk-screen region permanently positioned on the device. Some Cliés, though, feature a "virtual" Graffiti area that's actually a part of the main touchscreen. Software displays the Graffiti area and hence you can "collapse" it to get more screen space when you don't need to enter text. More on that later.

The rectangle is divided roughly in half: the left side is used to enter letters, while the right side is used to enter numbers.

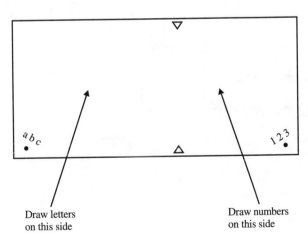

Draw letters
on this side

Draw numbers
on this side

TIP *If you aren't getting the results you expect from Graffiti, make sure you're writing on the correct side of the rectangle. The right side is for numbers, the left side is for letters, and either side works for punctuation.*

Your Clié came with a Graffiti "cheat sheet," either as a laminated card or a sticker. Take a look at this guide and you will see that most characters are single-stroke shapes (called *gestures* in Graffiti-ese). The characters must be drawn in the direction indicated on the Graffiti guide: the heavy dot indicates the starting position. To write a character, mimic the Graffiti guide by drawing the shape starting with the dot and—in most cases—finish the character in a single stroke without lifting the stylus.

For more details on writing in Graffiti, see the section "Getting to Know Graffiti," later in this chapter.

## Using the Virtual Graffiti Area

If you're lucky enough to own a Clié with a virtual Graffiti area, you have what may be the coolest PDA ever made. The screen resolution is either 320×320 pixels—four times the original Palm OS screen resolution—or a whopping 320×480 pixels if the Graffiti area is collapsed. That's the highest resolution of any PDA on the market, and an impressive screen to use for word processing, image viewing, or just about anything else. A small toolbar at the bottom of the screen lets you collapse the Graffiti area and use the entire screen for your main application. When the arrow points down, you can collapse the Graffiti area; when it points up, you can restore it to enter text.

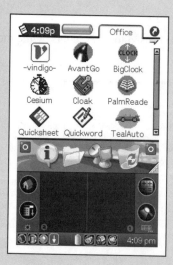

Fresh out of the box, though, you'll notice that the arrow is ghosted. Tapping it doesn't do anything. That's because Sony didn't enhance any of the core applications to work in the full-screen mode, which is called HiRes+. Since these programs don't know that the 320x480-pixel mode exists, the Graffiti area can't be collapsed. To use the HiRes+ mode, you need to install programs that support this resolution.

That's the bad news; the good news is that there are dozens of games, utilities, and applications that work with the Clié's HiRes+ mode. One of the best places to look for such programs is this site: **www.clieuk.co.uk/cphires.shtml**.

It keeps track of the programs that support HiRes+ and is one of the first places we go each week to see what's new in the world of Clié software. Right now, Dave has a Clié that's almost entirely HiRes+, with SilverScreen, DateBk5, QuickOffice, AcidSolitaire, PalmReader, Kinoma, and a handful of other programs making full use of the Clié's huge display. You can see the SilverScreen launcher, QuickOffice, and PalmReader next.

## Using the Keyboards

Even after you get comfortable writing with Graffiti, at times you'll need or want to input specific characters without using pen strokes. After all, remembering how to make some rarely used characters in the middle of taking real-time notes can be hard, and having access to a keyboard can be a real lifesaver.

**TIP** *When you have to enter a password, tapping it out on the keyboard is easier than writing it with Graffiti. Using the keyboard, you can be sure you're entering the right characters, error-free.*

All it takes to use the onscreen keyboard is a tap. At the bottom of the Graffiti area, you see the letter *a* on the left and the number 1 on the right. Tap either spot to call up the appropriate keyboard (alpha or numeric).

**NOTE** *The keyboard appears only in situations where it's appropriate—specifically, when a cursor is in a data field. If no application is open into which you can insert text, you simply hear a beep when you tap the keyboard dots.*

Once the keyboard is open, note that you can switch between letters and numbers by tapping the selector at the bottom of the screen. A set of international characters is available as well.

In addition to the onscreen keyboard, some Cliés come with a real, honest-to-goodness keyboard built in. If your Clié has such a keyboard, you'll find that it's a bit small and not conducive to touch typing. Nonetheless, once you get used to it, you'll be able to type at a reasonable speed. It's a good substitute for Graffiti when you need to create long documents—especially if you don't own an external keyboard.

Note that the built-in keyboard doubles-up on many keys. On the NR70 series, for instance, you need to hold down the Fn key to access numbers and punctuation. The ALT key enables you to make special characters, and the CTRL key controls shortcuts (CTRL-F, for instance, opens the Find dialog box).

# Using Palm Desktop

Those other methods are great when you're on the go, but what about getting data into your Clié when you're sitting comfortably at your desk? There's nothing wrong with entering notes into your Clié with Graffiti, even in the office, but long notes can get tiresome. Instead, you can use the keyboard on your desktop PC to type into Palm Desktop much more quickly and efficiently. When you're done entering the information into your PC, HotSync to transfer it immediately to the Clié.

**NOTE** *If you configured your Clié to synchronize with Microsoft Outlook or another PIM, use that program to copy data to your PDA instead.*

Let's add a note to the Clié's Memo Pad using the Palm Desktop. To do this:

1. Start Palm Desktop in Windows by choosing Start | All Programs | Sony Handheld | Palm Desktop for Clié.

2. Switch to the Memo Pad view by clicking the Memo button on the left side of the screen.

3. Click the New Memo button at the bottom of the screen and type a note.

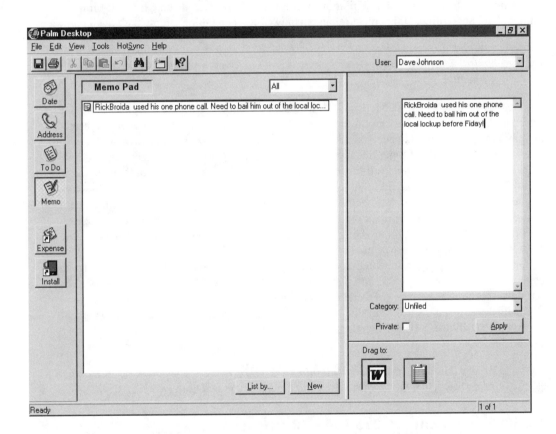

4. When you finish typing your note, close the New Memo dialog box by clicking OK. The note is automatically saved and the memo's subject line shows as much of the note as would fit on the line in the list.

5. When you finish entering data, place the Clié in its HotSync cradle and press the HotSync button. For details on how to HotSync, see Chapter 3.

# Getting to Know Graffiti

Earlier in the chapter, we took a quick look at using Graffiti. We're willing to bet that more than 90 percent of the time you need to add a note, contact, or to-do, you end up whipping out the stylus and entering your info with good old Graffiti. Thus, knowing Graffiti like the back of your hand is essential to using your Clié effectively.

As we pointed out earlier, Graffiti doesn't rely on interpreting whatever chicken-like scrawl you happen to draw into the Graffiti area. While it would be nice if the Clié could interpret unmodified handwriting, 100 percent reliable handwriting recognition simply isn't available yet.

**TIP** *Actually, there are third-party programs available that replace Graffiti with a more natural character set—nice for folks who just can't get the hang of it. See Chapter 15 for details.*

Consider Apple's Newton MessagePad. It was a great little PDA—the first, really—and it understood free-form handwriting. And while it did a darned good job, first-time users faced an uphill battle getting it to understand them. Not until you had a chance to use the Newton for a few hours did it start behaving like it comprehended English. To make matters worse, Apple insisted on putting MessagePads in stores with big signs inviting people to saunter over and try them. The result? People would scratch out a sentence in sloppy handwriting and the Newton would convert the result into total gibberish, kind of like what you think Lou Reed might be muttering in a Velvet Underground song. The public never got any confidence that Apple had a workable handwriting recognition engine; and, though the Newton actually was a great little PDA, it failed largely because of public perception.

Palm—the company from which Sony licenses the Clié operating system—didn't make the same mistake when it created the interface for its handhelds. Graffiti is designed to recognize particular gestures as specific characters, thus reducing the possibility of error. In fact, if you routinely draw the characters according to the template, you should get just about 100 percent accuracy. Graffiti doesn't have to understand 50 different ways of making the letter *T*, so it's both fast and accurate.

**TIP** *There's a Graffiti cheat sheet built into the Clié. By default, you can see it by making an upstroke from the Graffiti area up to the top of the LCD screen.*

## General Tips and Tricks for Graffiti

Before we get started with the nuts and bolts of writing with Graffiti, it might help to remember a few things. Despite Graffiti's simplicity, a few tips and tricks can make writing a lot easier.

- Draw your characters as large as possible, especially if you're having trouble with Graffiti misinterpreting what you're writing. Use all the Graffiti area, if necessary.

- Don't cross the line between the letter and number portion of the Graffiti area. Make sure to construct your gestures on the correct side of the fence to get the characters you want.

- Don't write at a slant. Some handwriting recognition engines can account for characters being drawn at an angle to the baseline, but Graffiti can't. Vertical lines should be perpendicular to the Graffiti area baseline.

- Don't write too fast. Graffiti doesn't care about your speed, but if you write too fast, you won't have sufficient control over the shape of your gestures and you can make mistakes.

- If you have a hard time making certain gestures consistently, try the character a different way. Specifically, refer to Table 4-1 for a list of primary and secondary gestures for each character. Use the ones that work best for you.

## Writing Letters and Numbers

The genius behind Graffiti—if that's not too strong a word—is that almost every letter and number at your disposal has two important characteristics:

- Every letter and number can be drawn in a single stroke of the stylus.

- Every letter and number bears a strong resemblance to its normal, plain English counterpart.

The easiest way to learn Graffiti is simply to practice writing the alphabet a few times. Use Table 4-1 for a guide on how to draw each character. We think you'll like the table better than the Graffiti card that comes with your Clié because we show you a few alternate gestures that might make certain characters easier to draw consistently. Give them a shot.

There's just one exception to the single stroke rule: the letter *X.* When you make an *X,* you can pick the stylus up off the screen to cross the letter in the traditional way. Of course, there's also a single-stroke alternative you can use as well (see Table 4-1 for the scoop on that).

You might notice some letters and numbers have identical gestures. The letter *L* and the number 4, for instance, are both made in the same way (see Figure 4-1). How does Graffiti tell the difference? That's an easy one—don't forget, the Graffiti area is divided into a number side and a letter side.

| Gesture | Character | |
| --- | --- | --- |
| L | L | 4 |
| I | I | 1 |
| 3 | B | 3 |

**FIGURE 4-1**    The letter L and the number 4 are made exactly the same. So are the letter I and the number 1.

| Letter | Gestures | Letter | Gestures |
|--------|----------|--------|----------|
| A | ∧ | S | S 5 |
| B | B B 3 | T | 7 ⟩ |
| C | C < | U | U ∨ |
| D | D D △ | V | V V |
| E | ε ξ | W | W W |
| F | Γ Γ | X | X ✗ |
| G | G G | Y | y γ |
| H | h ɥ | Z | Z 2 |
| I | ╎ | 0 | Ő Ŏ U |
| J | J J | 1 | ╎ ∧ |
| K | ∝ | 2 | 2 Z |
| L | L ∠ | 3 | 3 |
| M | m m | 4 | L < |
| N | N ∝ | 5 | 5 5 |
| O | O O | 6 | 6 ∞ |
| P | P P | 7 | 7 ⟩ |
| Q | ʊ ʊ | 8 | 8 8 8 |
| R | R R | 9 | 9 ε |

**TABLE 4-1**    The Graffiti Numbers and Letters

**TIP**    *If you're really having trouble mastering Graffiti, there's a great tutorial program called PenJammer (www.penjammer.com). It's not for Windows or Macintosh—it works right on your handheld, teaching you every Graffiti character via animated helpers. Very cool, very helpful, and very inexpensive (it's just $12.95).*

## The Hardest Characters

Everyone seems to have trouble with some Graffiti character. Even if you can never get your Clié to recognize your letter *B*, that doesn't make you a freak—it just means you should learn an alternative stroke for that letter or put extra care into drawing it carefully and slowly. Even we have trouble with some letters. . .

**Dave:** It's unfortunate my last name is "Johnson," because for the longest time I couldn't get Graffiti to accept my letter *J* to save my life. Usually, it was my own fault. As many times as I've made the *J*, I would forget to start at the top and curve down. I would always try to start at the bottom and hook up—which gives me a letter *U*. Even so, I sometimes end up with a *V* or a new paragraph, even when I think I've drawn it properly. Of course, now that I'm drawing it for this chapter, I can't seem to do it wrong—ten perfect *J*'s out of ten. I think the letter just hates me. And I know I'm not crazy, despite what my dog keeps telling me.

**Rick:** If you'd ever seen Dave's chicken-scratch excuse for handwriting, you'd understand why he sometimes has trouble with Graffiti. To be fair, though, a few characters seem tougher to make than others. It's the *V* that drives me up the wall—I always forget to put the little tail on the end of the upstroke. But I know a secret: if you write the letter backward, it comes out perfectly every time—and you don't need to draw the tail!

## Capitalizing Letters

You've probably noticed that there's no distinction in the Graffiti gestures for lowercase and uppercase characters. That's a good thing, actually—you don't have to learn over 50 gestures because uppercase and lowercase letters are drawn the same way. Here's how to tell Graffiti you want to make an uppercase letter:

- **One capital letter**   Before entering the letter, draw an uppercase gesture—a vertical line from the bottom of the Graffiti area to the top. This works only on the left side of the screen; it won't work in the number area. A symbol like the following indicates you're in Uppercase mode:

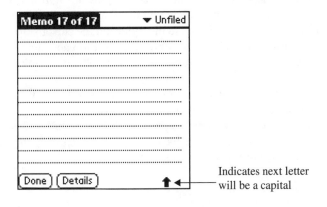

Indicates next letter
will be a capital

■ **All capital letters** To switch to All Caps mode and write in all capital letters, draw the vertical gesture twice. The following symbol indicates All Caps mode:

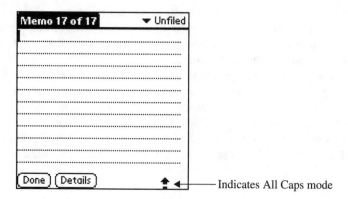

Indicates All Caps mode

■ **Lowercase letters** If you're already in All Caps mode, you can exit and write in lowercase again by making one more vertical gesture. The All Caps symbol should disappear to show you changed modes.

*Uppercase mode doesn't affect numbers, so it doesn't matter which mode you're in when writing numbers. This means you needn't drop out of Uppercase mode just to write numbers amid a bunch of capital letters.*

*One of our all-time favorite Hacks (see Chapter 15) is called TapPad. It changes the Graffiti area so you can tap out numbers keypad-style and get a capital letter by drawing it on the line between letters and numbers. There's a version with a thin plastic overlay for traditional Cliés and a software-based version for virtual Graffiti machines. Download it at **www.tappad.com**.*

## Spaces, Backspaces, and Deleting Text

Words are arguably more useful when you can put a space between them, thus enabling the casual reader to discern where each ends and the next begins. In Graffiti, it's easy to insert spaces. So easy, in fact, you might be able to figure it out on your own (but we'll tell you anyway). Draw a line that starts on the left and goes to the right, and the cursor skips ahead a space. You can use this gesture to insert spaces between words or to perform any other space-making task you might need. And, yes, you can insert multiple spaces simply by performing this gesture as many times as needed.

The backspace, not surprisingly, is exactly the opposite. Draw a gesture from right to left and the cursor backs up, deleting any text it encounters along the way.

Want to move the cursor forward or backwards by a character? Just do a variation on the space or backspace. For instance, to move the cursor back one space without deleting text, move the cursor back and then forward in a single stroke:

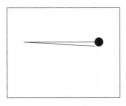

**TIP** *Space and backspace gestures work fine in both the letter and number sides of the Graffiti area.*

Using the backspace gesture is great if you want to delete one or two characters, but what if you want to delete a whole sentence? That backspace swipe can get tiring if you have a lot of text to kill or replace all at once. Luckily, an easy solution exists: select the text you want to delete. The next thing you write replaces the selected text. Here's how to do it:

1. On the Clié, find a region of text you want to replace.

2. Tap and hold the stylus down at the start of the text you want to select, then drag the stylus across the text and pick it up when you've selected all the text in question.

3. In the Graffiti area, write some new text. The old text is immediately erased and replaced with the new text. If you simply want to delete the text, use the backspace gesture instead.

## Adding Punctuation

To add punctuation to your prose, you need to (surprise, surprise) enter Graffiti's special Punctuation mode. All it takes is a tap in the Graffiti area. A dot then appears, indicating you can now enter punctuation. Table 4-2 displays the punctuation gestures you commonly need.

The most common punctuation mark is a period; and because it's simply a dot, you can add a period to the end of a sentence by performing a quick double-tap. Some other symbols are trickier, though, and may take some practice. The comma, parenthesis bracket, and apostrophe are so similar, for instance, getting one when you're trying to gesture another isn't unusual.

| Punctuation | Gestures |
| --- | --- |
| Period | • |
| Comma | /    (draw low) |
| Question mark | ? ⌐ |
| Exclamation point | ! |
| Colon | V |
| Semicolon | ν |
| Open parenthesis | C |
| Close parenthesis | ) |
| Tab | ⌐ |
| Apostrophe | !    (draw high) |
| Quotes | N |
| Slash | / |
| Backslash | \ |
| At Symbol | O |
| Asterisk | ⋉ |
| Number sign | ν h |
| Greater than | < |
| Less than | > |
| Percent | ∪∪ ⋈ |
| Equal sign | Z |
| Plus sign | α |
| Dollar sign | S |

**TABLE 4-2**    The Most Common Graffiti Punctuation Gestures

TIP

*If you have a lot of trouble with specific symbols, you can always use the onscreen keyboard along with Graffiti to write your text.*

*TIP*   *If you enter the Punctuation mode by tapping on one side of the Graffiti area, you need to complete the punctuation gesture on the same side. Tapping once on the number side and again on the letter side has no effect, for instance.*

## Using Shortcuts

If you're a big fan of using CTRL-S in Microsoft Word to save your work, then you should love this. The Clié has its own menu shortcuts you can access with Graffiti. To do this though, you must know two important items:

- How to draw the Graffiti command stroke
- What the shortcut character is for the menu command you want to invoke

*TIP*   *If your Clié has a virtual Graffiti area, you can use "skins" in conjunction with a very handy utility called PageDown Hack to activate the Command mode by tapping Location in the status bar under the Graffiti area. See Chapter 13 for details.*

The command stroke is easy. To put your Clié in Command mode, draw the gesture on the left. After you draw the gesture, your Clié displays the Command bar. You simply need to write the proper character to invoke the menu item.

To learn what the shortcuts are for each menu item, display the menu (tap the Menu soft button on your Clié and something similar to Figure 4-2 appears). You'll notice that many menu items have associated shortcuts.

*NOTE*   *The Command mode only lasts about two seconds. If you don't write the shortcut character quickly, Command mode is deactivated and you need to perform the command stroke again.*

### The Command Bar

So, you tried entering a command, but you're curious about the Command bar. What are all those little symbols and what do they do?

Actually, the Command bar is a clever tool you can use to access common features of your Clié rapidly. It's context sensitive, which means the bar will look different—it'll have different icons—depending on when you make the command stroke.

Try this: make the command stroke when you're on the Applications screen. The three icons on the right side of the Command bar represent Info, Beam, and Delete (just as if you tapped the menu button and selected Info, Beam, or Delete from the Applications menu).

FIGURE 4-2    Many menu items have Graffiti shortcuts associated with them.

Now open the Date Book and select an appointment by dragging the stylus across some text. Make the command stroke again and… voilà! You now have all new choices, like Cut, Copy, and Paste. You can experiment with the Command bar in various locales around your Clié to see what kinds of shortcuts you can create.

# Beaming Data Between PDAs

On *Star Trek,* transporters are used to beam people and equipment from one location to another. While we're a long way from being able to beam physical things around, the Clié makes it possible to beam almost any kind of data between handheld users.

All Cliés—in fact, all Palm-powered PDAs—have an infrared port. On most models, you can find it on the top edge of the case. If you haven't located your Clié's IR port yet, find it now. It's a small, black, translucent strip of plastic. Using this IR port, you can beam information in a surprising number of ways. You can:

- Use your Clié as a TV and stereo remote control
- Send data between your Clié and a cell phone or pager

- Print data on an IR-equipped printer
- Beam data to other PDA users
- Give another PDA user your "business card"
- Play two-player games "head-to-head"
- Perform a wireless HotSync with a laptop

While you can do a lot of things with your Clié's IR port, usually you'll want to exchange mundane business data with other PDA owners. All the core applications support beaming, so you can beam Address List entries, your own "business card" from the Address Book, appointments and meetings, memos, and to-dos. In addition, you can beam entire applications to other Palm-powered PDA users. If you download a freeware program from the Internet and want to share it with friends or co-workers, go ahead: it's a snap to transmit the item wirelessly.

## How to Beam

No matter what you're planning to beam—or receive—the process is essentially the same. Actually seeing the process demonstrated is faster than reading about it, but because neither Dave nor Rick is handy to stop by your office today, here's the process in a nutshell:

1. Orient the two devices so their IR ports face each other, being anywhere between four inches and three feet apart. If you're any closer than four inches, the PDAs may have a hard time locking onto each other; too far away and the signal won't be strong enough to reach.

2. As the sender, you should choose the item you want to beam. You can beam items from the menu in all of the Clié's main applications. Or, to beam a program, choose App | Beam from the PDA's application screen.

**TIP**   *If you beam often, you might want to use the beam shortcut—a command slash gesture followed by the letter B. Or you can configure your Clié so a stroke from the bottom of the Graffiti area to the top of the screen can start a beam. To do that, tap the Prefs icon, then select the Buttons item in the list at the top-right corner of the screen. Tap the Pen button and choose Beam Data.*

3. A dialog box appears to indicate the beam is in progress. First, you see a message that your Clié is searching for the other PDA. That message then goes away and the data is transmitted.

4. After the beam, your Clié goes back to business as usual—you won't get a message indicating the beam was successful. The receiver's handheld, on the other hand, gets a dialog box that asks permission to accept the beamed data. As the receiver, you need to decide what category to file the information into and tap either Yes or No, depending on whether or not you want to keep the item. If you tap Yes, the data is integrated into your Clié in the category you specified.

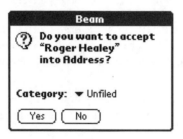

TIP *There's a way to receive a beam from someone even if you have disabled beaming in Preferences. When someone starts to beam something to you, draw the shortcut gesture and double-tap to make a period. Then draw the letter I. You receive the beam just that one time. You must receive a beam signal within about five seconds or you revert to No-beaming mode.*

Remember that not all applications are free, so don't use your Clié's beaming capability for piracy. Actually, many commercial programs are "locked" to prevent beaming, and shareware applications often require an unlock code to access all the features in the registered version. You can beam trial versions around, but don't share registration codes—that's piracy.

Indeed, not all programs can be beamed. The core applications that come with your Clié are "locked," making them non-beamable. Many commercial programs are also locked, and some programs have a resistance to beaming—like Hacks (discussed in Chapter 13). In addition, if you have a program that requires supporting database files, the files won't be beamable. This means you must go home and install the program the old-fashioned way, using your PC.

 **Install New Applications**

1. Start Palm Desktop by choosing Start | Programs | Palm Desktop | Palm Desktop.

2. Click the Install button on the left side of the Palm Desktop screen. The Install tool appears.

3. Click the Add button. You see the Open dialog box for selecting applications.

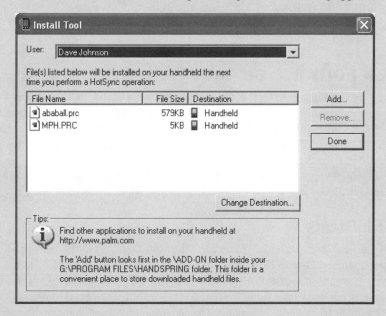

4. Locate the program you want to install and select it. Click the Open button.

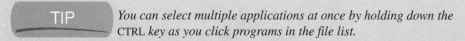 *You can select multiple applications at once by holding down the CTRL key as you click programs in the file list.*

5. With your application displayed in the Install Tool dialog box, click Done.

6. The next time you HotSync your Clié, the selected application is installed.

## Installing to a Memory Card

If you've added a Memory Stick to your Clié, you can install applications directly to the external memory. That's handy, especially if you want to install a huge application or data file that simply wouldn't fit if copied to the more limited internal memory.

When you open the Install Tool dialog box, click the Change Destination button. You'll see the Change Destination dialog box. Then just click the program you want to copy directly to the memory card, and click the arrow to move it to the right side of the screen, which represents the PDA's memory card.

When you've configured all the to-be-installed applications to your liking, click OK, close the Install Tool, and HotSync.

# Installing New Software on Your CLIÉ

Did you know that you can install tons of additional programs on your Clié? Thousands of free and commercial applications are out there, just waiting to be installed. They include enhancements to the core applications, utilities, games, and more. In fact, one of the best reasons for choosing a Palm OS device (instead of a competing Pocket PC device or some other kind of organizer) is that such a wealth of software exists.

But you might wonder: how the heck do I get all this cool stuff onto my Clié? The answer is that Palm Desktop includes a handy Install tool for loading applications.

## Installing Shortcuts

Not everyone likes to use Palm Desktop. If you use Microsoft Outlook, for instance, and you don't need to open Palm Desktop to HotSync or enter data, then don't feel compelled to open Palm Desktop simply to install applications on your Clié. Instead, you can start the Install tool directly. Choose Start | All Programs | Sony Handheld | Install Tool. The Install tool starts without Palm Desktop running at all. You don't even need to use the Add button; you can drag and drop files from the Windows desktop into the Install dialog box, or just double-click them to add them to the install queue.

NOTE    *You may have discovered a folder on your hard drive called Install. If you don't know where it is, look in C:\Program Files\Sony Handheld\your username\Install. This folder holds applications waiting for the next HotSync to be installed on the PDA. Don't mess with this folder! You can't just drag files to this folder because the Install tool needs to tell Windows that files are waiting to be installed.*

## After the HotSync

Any programs you want to install are stored in the Install tool's queue until you HotSync. After the HotSync, the programs are copied to your Clié, as long as the Install conduit is set to Install Handheld Applications (see Chapter 3 for details on configuring conduits).

After the HotSync, remember two things about your applications:

- New applications end up in the Unfiled category on your Clié.

- On your PC, the files are moved to a folder called Backup. The Backup folder can be found at C:\Program Files\Sony Handheld\\*your username*\Backup. This folder is used by Palm Desktop to reinstall all your applications, just in case your Clié suffers a total memory failure and you need to reinstall programs from scratch. In a bizarre twist on logic, though, you can't always count on Palm Desktop to restore 100 percent of these applications when you have a total failure. If you want more backup security, try a dedicated backup program like the one discussed in Chapter 13.

## Removing Applications from the CLIÉ

You won't want to keep every application you install on your Clié forever. Some programs you won't like, others will outlive their usefulness. And, quite often, you need to eliminate some applications to make room for more, because the Clié has limited storage space.

Deleting programs is easy. Tap the Home button on your Clié, then tap Menu | Delete. You see a list of all the applications currently stored on the handheld. At the top of the screen, you also see a bar showing how much memory remains on your PDA.

To delete an application, select it and tap the Delete button. This is similar to the Beam interface, and, in fact, it's so similar you should be careful you don't accidentally delete an application you're trying to beam to a friend.

# Chapter 5 The Date Book

## How to...

- Use the Day, Week, Month, and Agenda Views
- Customize the Date Book's appearance
- Add appointments to the Date Book
- Beam an appointment to someone else
- Create an appointment using the Address Book
- Create repeating events
- Add a note to an appointment
- Make an appointment private
- Edit appointments in the Date Book
- Delete events in the Date Book
- Set an alarm for an appointment
- Use the Clié with Outlook or Palm Desktop

Are you busy on Tuesday at 3 p.m.? If you have your Clié handy, you'd probably already know the answer to that question. In an informal survey conducted in Dave's living room, we found that Date Book is the single most popular core application on the Clié. In the old days—before Sony packed Cliés full of multimedia tools—people would buy a PDA just for the scheduling software.

Indeed, the Date Book is a modern miracle. It can show you your schedule by day, week, or month. The Date Book handles recurring appointments and can notify you about upcoming events. It synchronizes precisely with your desktop calendar. And the Date Book fits in the palm of your hand. It's better, Rick might tell you, than *Star Trek*. Dave, on the other hand, would be inclined to say it's better than *Babylon 5*.

# Viewing Your Appointments

When you switch to the Date Book, by default, it starts by showing you any appointments you have for today. Start the Date Book by pressing the Date Book button on your Clié or tapping the Date Book icon in the Application screen.

## Operating System Oddities

Although most Cliés work more or less the same way, they don't all use exactly the same operating system. Likewise, the Palm Desktop software on your PC may vary a bit depending on which model you own. We wrote this book with version 4.1 of the Palm OS in mind, though your Clié may differ slightly—especially if you have a new Clié with OS 5 under the hood. Nevertheless, the basic functionality of applications like Date Book remains the same, so don't worry if you have a different OS.

## Navigating the Day View

When you start the Date Book, the first thing you see is the Day View. You can see that it shows the currently selected date in the tab at the top of the screen. Next to that are seven icons, one for each day of the week.

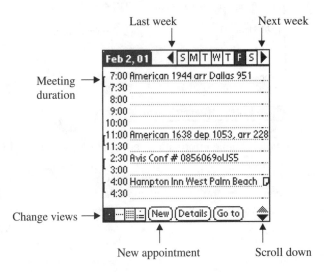

In the middle of the screen, you see the current day's calendar. You can enter new events on the blank lines. If you have any appointments already entered, note that long appointments (those lasting for more than 30 minutes) have duration brackets. *Duration brackets* appear to the immediate left of the appointment time and show you what time an appointment is scheduled to end.

Other icons also appear near appointments. In fact, you should get used to seeing these three icons:

■ **Alarms** This icon indicates you'll get notified by the alarm sound that the appointment is due to start.

■ **Notes** If you attach a note to your appointment (perhaps with directions to the location or agenda details, for instance) you see this icon.

■ **Repeating meetings** If the meeting is configured to happen more than once, this icon appears.

If you tap any of these icons, shown in Figure 5-1, you see the Event Details dialog box, which we discuss in detail later in this chapter.

> **TIP** *Tap and hold the date tab to see the current time. If you let go too quickly, the Record menu will drop instead.*

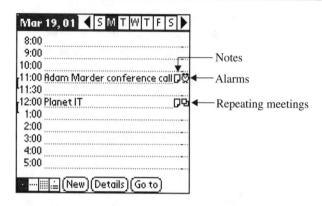

**FIGURE 5-1** These icons tell you valuable information about your appointment. Tap on them to edit the details.

Finally, the bottom of the screen has several important controls. Icons exist to change the current view, as well as to create a new appointment, to view the Event Details dialog box, and to go to a specific day.

## Changing View Options

By default, the Day View compresses your calendar by not showing blank times of the day. This way, you can have appointments that span from 6 A.M. to 11 P.M. and have them all appear onscreen without needing to scroll at all. Whenever it can, it includes blank events between existing events for better readability.

What happens if you have such a busy day that all your appointments won't fit onscreen at once? You need to tap the Scroll button at the bottom of the screen. It only appears when needed.

5

**NOTE** *Lots of users try pressing the Scroll button or rolling the scroll wheel to see more appointments in the same day. Of course, that simply changes the view to the next day.*

Not everyone likes the Day View compression. If you frequently add events to your schedule during the day, for instance, you might want to have blank lines available for all the hours of the day. If this sounds like you, here's how to turn off compression:

**1.** Choose Options | Display Options from the menu.

**2.** Uncheck the Compress Day View option.

**3.** Tap the OK button.

Now when you use the Day View, you see all the blank lines for your day. On the other hand, using this setting virtually guarantees you need to use the Scroll button to surf around your daily schedule.

When you configure your Day View, you also have to decide what kind of person you are. Are you:

■ Neat and orderly—and opt for less clutter whenever possible?

■ Impatient—and want everything at your fingertips all the time?

■ Apathetic—and don't want to bother changing the default settings?

You can change the display of the Date Book to accommodate the way you want your Clié to look. If you're the neat and orderly sort, for instance, you might want the Date Book to be a blank screen, unless it actually has appointments already scheduled for that day. If this is the case, choose Options | Preferences and set the Start Time and End Time to be the same thing—like 7:00 A.M. After configuring your Clié in this way, you should find days without appointments are essentially a blank screen with a single blank line—the time you set in Preferences.

More of an impatient sort? Then choose Options | Preferences and configure your Start Time and End Time to span the full range of hours you plan to use. If you ever add events to the evening, for instance, set the End Time for 10 p.m. or later. This way, you have a blank line available immediately for writing a new entry.

If all this sounds extremely pointless to you, leave the Preferences alone. The default settings cover most of the hours you routinely need.

### Getting Around the Days of the Week

As you might expect, several ways exist to change the view to a different day. You can figure out most of them on your own, but we bet you can't find 'em all. Here's how you can do it—use the method that's easiest for you:

- Switch to a specific day by tapping the appropriate day icon at the top of the screen (see Figure 5-2).

- To move ahead one week at a time, use the forward button to the right of the week icons, as shown in Figure 5-2. If you're currently on Tuesday, for instance, tapping the arrow takes you one week ahead to the following Tuesday. Obviously, you can go back a week at a time by tapping the Back arrow instead.

- To move forward or backward one day at a time, press the hard Scroll button. If you hold it down, you scroll quickly, like holding down a repeating key on a computer keyboard.

- If you want to find a specific day quickly, tap the Go To button and enter the date directly in the Go to Date dialog box. When you use Go To, remember to choose the year and month first, because you go to the selected date as soon as you tap a date.

- To get back to "today" from somewhere else in the calendar, tap Go To, and then tap Today on the Go to Date calendar dialog box.

## Navigating the Week View

Now that you're used to the Day View, we'll let you in on a little secret: there's more where that came from. That's where the icons at the bottom of the screen come in. Tap the second one to change to the Week View.

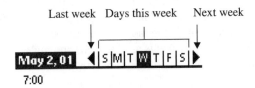

Last week   Days this week   Next week

FIGURE 5-2   Navigate the Day View with these controls.

5

TIP

*The Date Book button also serves as a view changer. Every time you press the button, the view cycles from Day View to Week View to Month View to Agenda View and back to Day View again. It's convenient to jab with your thumb as you view your various schedule screens.*

This screen uses a grid to display your appointments. The top of the grid is labeled by day and date, while the left side contains time blocks throughout the day. The gray blocks represent scheduled events. Obviously, this view isn't ideal for determining your daily schedule in detail, but it's handy for getting your week's availability at a glance. Use it to pick a free day or to clear an afternoon, for instance, when you're in a meeting and trying to choose a good time to get together with an equally busy person.

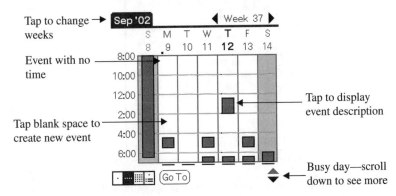

TIP

*If you have an appointment you need to move to another time anywhere in the week, tap the event, hold the stylus down, and then drag it to another place on the schedule. As you move the block around, you can see the exact time to which the event is being moved. To abort this process without changing anything, move it back to its original location without lifting the stylus.*

## Navigating the Month View

If you press the Date Book button again or tap the third icon at the bottom of the screen, you're transported to the Month View. It displays an entire month at a time.

Blocks of busy time are now replaced by little hash marks. You can't tap on these marks to see the appointment details because they don't actually represent individual events. Instead, the three possible marks represent events in the morning, afternoon, and evening, as seen in Figure 5-3. In addition, this view shows untimed events as plus signs and multiday events as a series of dots that span several days. If you tap any day in this view, you're automatically taken to the Day View for that day.

*By default, both of these special display features are disabled on your Clié. To turn them on, choose* Options | Display Options *from the Day View screen. Then, in the Month View section of the Display Options dialog box, enable Show Untimed Events and Show Daily Repeating Events.*

# Managing Your Day from the Agenda View

The last of the Date Book views—the Agenda View—is a favorite for many people. Why is the Agenda View so cool? Because, like some desktop day planners, it combines your appointments and to-do tasks into a single screen. You can see at a single glance all your responsibilities for the day without switching screens or pressing buttons.

Take a look at the Agenda View:

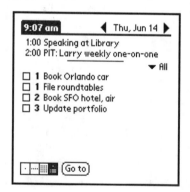

You can see that the top of the screen shows you any appointments and untimed events that may be scheduled for the day. After a horizontal line, your Clié lists your To Dos.

You can change the current day by tapping the arrows at the top of the screen to change a day at a time. If you want to hop directly to another day, tap the date between the arrows. This displays the Go To Date dialog box, just as if you had tapped the Go To button at the bottom of the screen.

*To jump to the current date, tap the Go To button and then tap the Today button at the bottom of the Go to Date dialog box.*

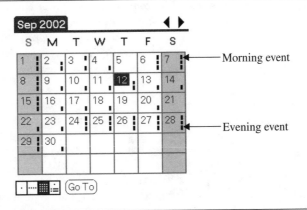

— Morning event

— Evening event

**5**

If you enable the right features in preferences, you can see untimed and multiday events in the monthly calendar.

# Filtering Your To Dos

You might not always want to see all the to-do tasks stored in your Clié. If you're at work, for instance, you might not want to see any to-dos filed in a personal category.

To fine-tune the To Do List, tap the down arrow for the category list and choose the category you want to see displayed. You can choose any category you like, including All, as shown next.

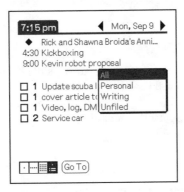

# The Agenda Zoom

The Agenda View is great for viewing your day's schedule, but it's also a cool way to make changes to your daily itinerary. Just tap on a calendar item to switch to the Day View so you can make schedule changes. Or tap a To Do item to go to the To Do List for editing.

NOTE    *It would be great if you could automatically start your Clié in Agenda View all the time. Alas, you can't quite do that. But, if you set your Clié to the Agenda View and then visit another application, the Agenda View automatically returns the next time you start the Date Book. If you're in a hurry, remember, you can always press the Date Book button several times to cycle through the Date Book's various screens to arrive at the Agenda View.*

### The Best Sci-Fi

**Dave:** The Clié is like science fiction come alive, which begs the question: which sci-fi? Rick obsesses over some of the lamest sci-fi shows ever, like *Star Trek: Voyager* and *The West Wing* (Martin Sheen as the president? Yeah, that's gotta be sci-fi). I am partial to shows with plausible technology, engaging plots, and a real sense of drama—that's why *Babylon 5* and *24* are perhaps the two most compelling television shows ever. Meanwhile, Rick is watching a repeat of another "very special" episode about The Doctor and his desire to become a Real Boy. Oh, and now The Doctor is into photography! Woo Hoo!

**Rick:** Speaking of sci-fi, aliens have taken over Dave's brain. I know because he thinks *24* is science fiction and *Star Trek: Voyager* is lame (when it is, in fact, the best-written, best-acted and most enjoyable Trek show since the original series). Even scarier, Dave thinks *Enterprise* is even better (when it is, in fact, the worst-written, worst-acted, and dullest Trek show ever). Alas, alien-Dave can't seem to compute that. And, obviously, anyone who doesn't like *The West Wing* must be controlled by some evil influence. Oh, that's right, Dave's a Republican.

# Creating New Appointments

Now that you've mastered the fine art of viewing your schedule from every conceivable angle, you probably want to know how to add new events to the schedule. There are two ways to add appointments to your Clié: via the PC—which we discuss later in this chapter in "Importing Alarm Settings"—and right from the Clié itself. The only place you can actually enter data about a meeting is from the Day View.

## Add Events

Most of the time, your schedule will be full of meetings that take place at a specific time of day, such as:

```
Meet with Susan from accounting
3-5 P.M. in Conference Room A.
```

This is what the Clié refers to as an *event*—but most people call it an appointment. No matter what *you* call it, here are three ways to add an event to your Clié:

■ **Use the New button**   Tap the New button on the Day View. Then, within the Set Time dialog box, select a Start Time and an End Time, and tap OK. Now, enter the meeting information on the blank line provided for you.

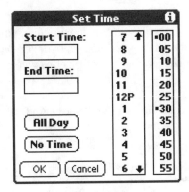

■ **Start writing**   Tap on a blank line that corresponds to the meeting start time and write the details of the meeting on the line.

■ **Pick a time from the Week View**   If you're looking for a free space to place a meeting, the Week View is a good place to look because it gives you the "big picture" of your schedule. When you find a spot you like, tap it and the Day View should open to the desired start time. Then write the meeting info.

*A fast way to create a new event at a specific time is to write the start time in the Graffiti area. A Set Time dialog box appears and you can proceed from there. For example, writing a '4' automatically launches the Set Time dialog box for 4* P.M.

## A Closer Look at the Set Time Dialog Box

To set a time in this dialog box, tap an hour (in the selector on the left) and a minute (on the right) for both the Start Time and End Time. You can change your mind as often as you like, but the time must be in increments no smaller than five minutes. You can't set a Start Time of 11:33, for instance.

You can also use Graffiti to set the time, a real convenience for folks who are faster at writing than tapping. 335 is interpreted as 3:35. To change between A.M. and P.M., write an *A* or a *P* in the letter side of the Graffiti area.

If you need to back up and start over, use the backspace gesture. When you want to move between the Start Time and the End Time box, use the Next Field gesture. Finally, when you've finished entering times, use the Return gesture to simulate tapping OK. Now you're back at the Day View, ready to write in your meeting name.

*You can also create activities that don't have a specific time associated with them; they appear at the top of the Day View and attach themselves to the entire day.*

 **Make a Date**

If you're setting up an appointment with someone in particular, you can have a lot of fun with your Clié. Okay, it's not better than listening to Pink Floyd with the lights out, but it's pretty cool, nonetheless. Suppose you need to meet with someone who's already in your Address Book. Switch to the Day View and tap on a blank line at the time you want to start your meeting. Then choose Options | Phone Lookup. You see the Phone Number Lookup dialog box, which displays all the names in your Address Book. Find the name of the person you're meeting with and tap it. Tap Add. What do you get? The person's name and phone number positioned at the start time of the meeting.

Now it gets even better. Does your associate have a Clié or some other Palm OS device? If so, make sure the appointment is still selected and choose Record | Beam Event. You've just given your associate a copy of your meeting in her PDA. She now has no excuse if she's late.

## Making Your Appointments Repeat

Some schedule events just don't go away. Weekly meetings, semiannual employee reviews, and the monthly dog grooming sessions are all examples of events you might want the Clié to automate. After all, you don't have the time or energy to write the same weekly event into your Clié 52 times to get it entered for a whole year. An easier way exists. To create a recurring event, do the following:

1.  Select the entry you want to turn into a recurring event and tap the Details button at the bottom of the Day View screen.

2.  In the Event Details dialog box, the Repeat box is currently set to None. Tap it. The Change Repeat dialog box should appear.

3. Now you need to tap a repeat interval. Will the event repeat daily, weekly, monthly, or annually? In other words, if the event takes place only once a year, or once every five years, tap Year. If you have a meeting that takes place once a month, or every other month, tap Month. For meetings that occur every week or every five weeks, use the Week button. Finally, if you need to schedule meetings daily, every other day, or every ten days, tap Day.

4. You now have more options, depending on which interval you choose. A common interval is Week, which would enable you to set up a weekly meeting. Tell the Change Repeat dialog box how often the meeting will occur, such as Every 1 Week or Every 3 Weeks.

5. If you selected a monthly interval, you can also choose whether the meeting will repeat by day (such as the first Monday of every month) or by date (as in the 11th of every month).

6. If the event will repeat more or less forever (or at least as long as you can imagine going to work every day), then leave the End On setting at the default, which is No End Date. If you are creating an event with a clear conclusion, tap End On to set the End Date for this repeating event.

7. Your selection is turned into a plain English description. If you agree the repeat settings are what you want, tap OK.

> TIP
>
> *If you're attending a multiday event, such as a trade show, you can display this in your Clié by creating an untimed event and setting it to repeat daily (Every 1 Day). Don't forget to set an End Date.*

## Making an Appointment Private

You may not want all your appointments to be available to the public. While we generally believe honesty is the best policy, you can flag certain appointments as private—and they'll be hidden from everyone except you. If you want to hide an appointment, do this:

1. On the Day View screen, select an appointment.

2. Tap the Details button.

**3.** On the Event Details dialog box, tap the Private box to add a check mark. Once you select this option, the current record is flagged for privacy. Tap the OK button, and you see this dialog box:

**4.** Tap OK to close the dialog box.

You might notice the event probably isn't hidden yet. To make it go away, you need to enable the Private Records feature in the Security application. For details on how to do this, see Chapter 9. Using this feature, you can hide and show private data whenever you want.

 *You can display more than one calendar on your Clié at once. If you collaborate with coworkers or a spouse and want to see their calendars side by side with yours, try* **www.wesync.com** *or DualDate at* **www.palm.com/support/dualdate.**

## Editing Recurring Meetings

With most appointments or events, you can alter them just by tapping and entering the needed change with a little Graffiti. Changes to repeating meetings require a little more care. In general, when you change some aspect of a meeting that repeats, the Clié asks you whether you want to change only this one meeting or every meeting in the series.

If you need to move a specific meeting—like the one in November—to a different time, but all the other meetings are held at the traditional time, select Current. The event is actually unlinked from the series and any changes you make to the rest of the repeating event don't affect the one you changed. On the other hand, if the meeting is moving to a new day permanently, choose All:

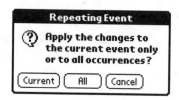

There's an exception to this rule: if you change any text in the name of the appointment, then the Clié makes the change to the entire series without asking. If you want to change the text of one instance of the event without changing the rest, you need to unlink it from the series. To do that, follow these steps:

1.  Change something else about the event, like its time.

2.  You're asked if you want to change the current event or all of the events. Choose Current. The event is now unlinked from the series.

3.  Change the name of the unlinked event.

4.  If you need to, fix whatever you changed in Step 1.

# Working with Alarms

If you need a reminder about upcoming events, then you should use the Clié's built-in alarm feature. Any event you enter can be set to beep shortly before the event, giving you enough time to jump in your car, pick up the phone, or start saving for the big day. You can assign an alarm setting to your events as you create them, or at any time afterward.

**NOTE**    *Timed events play an audible sound. Untimed events don't play a sound, but instead show a screen advising you the event is pending.*

## Setting Alarms for Specific Events

To enable the alarm for a particular appointment, do the following:

1.  In the Day View, select an appointment.

2.  Tap Details.

3.  In the Event Details dialog box, tap the Alarm check box. You should see a new control appear that enables you to set the advance warning for the event.

4.  Select how much advanced warning you want. You can choose no warning (enter a zero) or set a time of up to 99 days in the future. The default is five minutes.

5.  Tap OK.

## Picking Your Own Alarm Sound

If, like us, you're easily bored, you might be interested in changing your Clié's default alarm sound. It's easy to do—just visit PalmGear.com and search for alarm sounds. You'll find tons of downloads that give your Clié alternative sounds. Keep in mind that if your Clié has "enhanced sound," many of the ordinary alarm replacements won't work. You'll need a special program, like CLIÉ Sounds (which you can find at **www.palmgear.com**). Alarm replacement programs can give you special effects like science fiction or animal sounds, while others deliver complete songs, TV themes, and movie scores. If you've ever wanted your Clié to sound like a Star Trek communicator, here's your chance.

Of course, it's not all fun and games—a distinctive alarm sound can make your Clié easier to hear in noisy environments.

## Setting Alarms for Everything

By default, the Clié doesn't turn the alarm on for your appointments. Instead, you need to turn the alarm on for every event individually. If you find you like using the alarm, though, you can tell the Clié to turn the alarm on automatically for all your appointments. Then it's up to you to turn the alarm off on a case-by-case basis when you don't want to be notified of any events.

To enable the default alarm setting, do the following:

**1.** In the Day View, choose Options | Preferences.

**2.** Tap the check box for the Alarm Preset. Set your alarm preference; configure the alarm time, the kind of alarm sound, and how many times the alarm will sound before giving up.

**TIP** *You can try out each of the alarm sounds by selecting them from the list. After you choose a sound, it plays so you can hear what it sounds like.*

**3.** Tap OK.

## Importing Alarm Settings

Much of the time, you probably get appointments into your Clié via your PC—you HotSync them in from Palm Desktop or Outlook. In that case, the rules are different. The Clié keeps whatever alarm settings were assigned on the PC and doesn't use the Preference settings on the Clié. If you want a specific alarm setting, you need to change the alarm setting on the desktop application before HotSyncing, or change the alarm on the Clié after you HotSync.

> **TIP**  *Some folks would like to have two separate sets of alarms for their appointments: one for the Clié and another for their desktop calendar program. If you have a PC and Microsoft Outlook, try Desktop to Go. This alternative conduit enables you to configure the Clié to use a completely independent set of alarms from Outlook.*

**5**

## Controlling Your Alarm

If you use an alarm clock, you know the only thing better than having an alarm is being able to turn it off.

Keep in mind that the Clié really isn't all that loud. If you need to hear your Clié, don't bury it in a backpack or briefcase where the sound will be hopelessly muffled. However, what if you're in a quiet meeting room with a CEO who turns into Darth Vader every time a cell phone rings? In that case, temporarily silence it (before he silences you). To do so, open Prefs and choose the General view, where there's an option for Alarm Sound. Choose Off from the Alarm Sound list.

# Working with Palm Desktop

If you use Palm Desktop as the calendar on your desktop PC, you benefit because it looks similar to the version on your Clié. Granted, Palm Desktop is a lot bigger than your Clié screen and it's in color. But aside from that, you find the modules share a common appearance and the overall philosophy of the program is similar.

## Using the Day View

The Day View looks similar to the Clié display. Look at Figure 5-4 for an overview of the major elements in this display.

> **TIP**  *The easiest way to double-book a time slot is to click the Time box. A new blank appears to the right of the existing appointment.*

You might recall that on the Clié, you can create an appointment by using the Phone Lookup feature—this grabs a name and phone number from the Address Book, and places it in a time slot in the Date Book. You can do the same thing in Palm Desktop. Under the calendar, you can see the To Do List and Address Book minilists. Choose which you want to see by clicking Address or To Do. Then drag a name (or even a To Do) into a time slot.

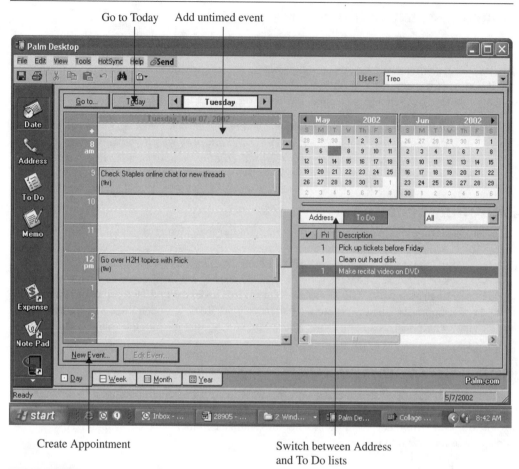

FIGURE 5-4    The Day View combines appointments with either To Dos or Addresses,
depending upon how you configure the screen.

## Editing Appointments

You can make lots of changes with the mouse. To change the duration of an event, drag the
arrow-shaped duration handle up or down; to move an appointment, drag it by its event handle
on the right edge; and to see the Edit Event dialog box, which lets you edit the text and includes
alarm and privacy controls, double-click anywhere in the event.

TIP    *You can move an appointment to another day by dragging it via the event handle to the
calendar and dropping it on the desired day.*

## Using the Week and Month Views

Both of these views are quite similar to their Clié counterparts. In the Week View (shown in Figure 5-5), though, the event blocks work a little differently than you might expect. The following is a general rundown:

- To move an event to a different time, drag it by the event handle.

- To display the Edit Event dialog box and change options like text, time, repeat settings, or the alarm, double-click the event.

- To change the duration of the event, drag its duration handle up or down.

The Month View is a bit more helpful than the one in your Clié. The Month View actually shows you what events are scheduled, not just that you have a mysterious "something" scheduled. You can't edit the events in this view, though. Instead, you can double-click the appropriate day to get to the Day View or add a new event to a specific day by right-clicking the day and choosing New Event from the menu.

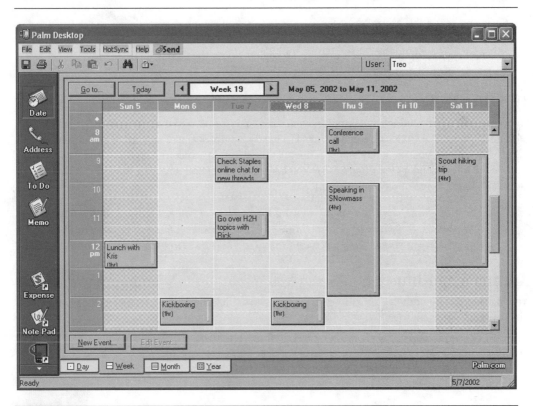

FIGURE 5-5   The Week View enables you to add and edit appointments.

## Using Alarms on the Desktop

Want to be notified about upcoming events while working at your desk? You need to use Palm Desktop's Alarm Manager—a new feature in Palm Desktop 4.1, which you can download from Sony's web site if you have an older Clié. While Alarm Manager is linked to Palm Desktop, it's technically not a part of it. What we mean is that it runs outside of the program and hangs out in the Windows System Tray, just like HotSync Manager.

To activate the Alarm Manager, choose Tools | Options and then click the Alarm tab. You'll see three choices in the Options dialog box:

- **Always Available**   When you choose this option, Alarm Manager loads when you start Windows, even if Palm Desktop itself isn't running. It ensures that you hear all of your alarms. Most folks, we think, want this option.

- **Available only when the Palm Desktop is running**   This is pretty self-explanatory—but we can't think of a lot of reasons why you'd use this option.

- **Disabled**   Alarms won't ring at all—which makes sense if you don't need to worry about event alarms or you actually use another PIM, like Outlook.

Once you set up the Alarm Manager to your liking, you can configure alarms in the Clié Desktop when you create new events. At the bottom of the New Event or Edit Event window, you'll find the alarm options (which work just like they do on the Clié itself).

# Using Outlook

Of course, Microsoft Outlook synchronizes with the Clié just fine, and many people use it instead of Palm Desktop. The Outlook Calendar View is a handy tool for seeing your current and upcoming events. By default, you see today's appointments. To switch to a specific day, click the date you want in the minicalendar (see Figure 5-6). You can also see several days at a time. To do this, click-and-drag a range of days in the minicalendar.

TIP   *The toolbar includes buttons for viewing the work week, an entire week, and a month at a glance. To switch back to a single view of today, you need to click both Day (to switch to a single day view), and then Go To Today (to view the current day).*

## Adding Appointments

You can add an appointment to Outlook in several ways. Pick the method that's easiest for the kind of event you want to add.

■ Create a simple 30-minute meeting: Simply click a time slot and start typing. Press the ENTER key when you finish.

■ Create a simple meeting that lasts for 60 minutes or more: Click a time slot and drag the mouse down to extend the length of the appointment for an hour or more. When a block of time is selected, type the subject of the meeting and press ENTER.

■ Create a meeting that repeats or has detailed notes: Find the start time of the meeting and double-click the block. An untitled Appointment window should appear. Fill in the meeting details as needed.

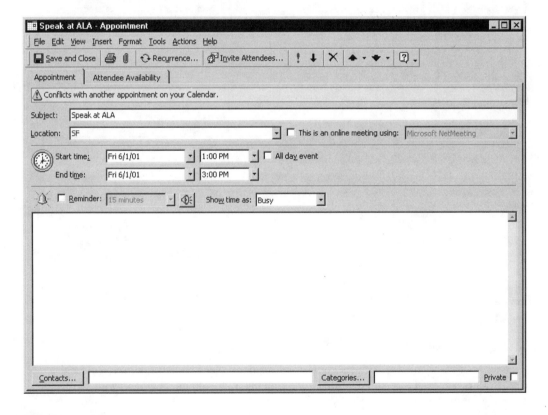

NOTE    *If you use the Location line of the Outlook appointment box, this information appears in parentheses after the subject text on your Clié.*

Toolbar                                        Minicalendar

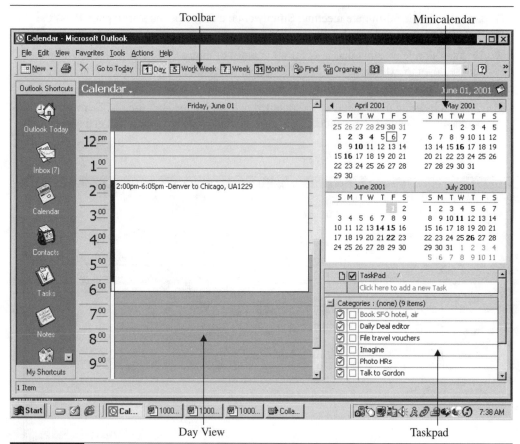

Day View                                      Taskpad

**FIGURE 5-6**    Many users synchronize with Outlook instead of Palm Desktop.

# Tweaking Alarms for the CLIÉ

By default, every Outlook appointment comes with an alarm that sounds 15 minutes before the
event. If you create most of your appointments within Outlook, you might end up with alarms
you don't want on the Clié after a HotSync. To change the length of the default alarm—or to
disable alarms entirely—choose Tools | Options from the Outlook menu and click the Preferences
tab. In the Calendar section, edit the Default Reminder option to suit your needs. If you remove
the check mark, the alarm is then disabled for new appointments.

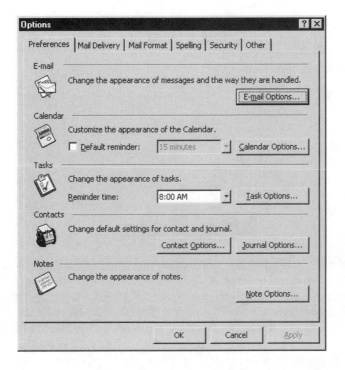

## A Better Date Book

Looking for an alternative to the Date Book that comes with your Clié? Then look no further than DateBk5 (downloadable from **www.pimlicosoftware.com**), probably the most popular replacement for the built-in Clié applications (it takes advantage of the full screen for Cliés with a collapsible Graffiti area).

Technically, DateBk5 is just a replacement for the Date Book, but the program has so many features, so much depth, and so much raw power that it redefines the way you use your Clié.

One of the program's most interesting features is its split screen—you can see your To Dos, Memo Pad, or Address Book atop the screen, with the calendar below. DateBk5 lets you "link" items from the various applications to each other, so an appointment can have a link to both an Address Book entry and a memo. This is an incredibly useful feature, since you can open information related to an appointment with just a single tap.

That's just the beginning. DateBk5 understands time zones, for instance, which allows you to schedule distant events to occur in their own time zone. Instead of making time zone conversions in your head, just enter a teleconference for 2 P.M. EST, and the appointment will appear in your calendar at the right local time. The repeat control for recurring appointments also has an "irregular" mode that lets you pick any sequence of dates from the calendar, which is great for oddball meeting schedules. And if you place a four-digit year in the description of an annually-recurring appointment, it'll automatically report how many years it's been since that date—just the thing to keep track of birthdays and anniversaries.

Another powerful feature is its capability to make countdowns to specific appointments "float" through the calendar, giving you advance warning that they're approaching. You can even create items with special formatting. For instance, select the color of the text and foreground, as well as bold or enlarged text—so certain appointments appear in red, or important tasks have a highlighted background. Likewise, you can tack icons onto the front of items. DateBk5 comes with a wide array of color and grayscale icons to dress up your calendar. It's well worth a few dollars—give it a try.

## Where to Find It

| Web Site | Address | What It Does |
|---|---|---|
| WeSync | www.wesync.com | Sync with other peoples' calendars |

# Chapter 6 The Address Book

## How to...

- View Address Book entries
- Customize the Address List display
- Search for an entry by name
- Search for an entry by keyword
- Create new Address Book entries
- Add pictures to your Address Book
- Display a specific phone number in the Address List
- Use the custom fields
- Assign a category to an entry
- Delete Address Book entries
- Use the Windows Address book
- Use your Clié with Outlook

What's the big deal? It's only an address book. Yes, but as one of the four big "core" applications—the main programs that ship with your Clié—you'll use the Address Book a lot. And the Address Book is an elegant program, designed to get the information you need quickly, perhaps more quickly than any other contact manager on the market.

We're sure you'll get a lot of mileage from the Address Book. You can store thousands of entries and not run out of memory. Despite how many names you add to the list, your Clié never slows down. In addition, the Address Book isn't really a stand-alone application (though it can be if you want). The Address Book synchronizes with desktop applications like Palm Desktop and Microsoft Outlook. This means you only need to create a contact list once and then it's maintained on both your PC and your Clié.

# Viewing Your Addresses

When you switch to the Address Book, the program displays all the entries in your list onscreen. As you might expect, you can start the Address Book by pressing the Address List button on your Clié or tapping the onscreen Address icon in the Clié's applications.

As you can see in Figure 6-1, the Clié lists your contacts alphabetically in a view called the Address List. There's room for 11 entries onscreen at one time; the rest appear above or below the screen, depending on where you are within the Address List. To get around in the Address List, just use the Scroll buttons. Each time you scroll, the Clié moves the list by one complete page of entries.

You can also get around with categories. If your contacts are divided into more than one category, every time you press the Address button, you switch categories. You can cycle through the first page of names in each category by repeatedly pressing the Address Book button.

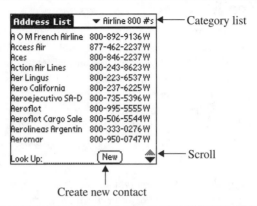

Category list

Scroll

Create new contact

**FIGURE 6-1**    The Address List is a database with all your contact information.

## Viewing by Company Name

For most folks, the default Address List is great. This list displays the entries by name (last, first) and a phone number. If you prefer to work with your contacts according to the company they work with, you can change the Address List.

To change the View mode of the Address List, do this:

1. Display the Address List View.

2. Choose Options | Preferences from the menu.

3. Choose Company, Last Name from the List By list.

4. Tap OK to save your changes.

Notice that after making the change, you can see the company name in the list. If no company is associated with a particular entry, then you only see the individual's name, as you did before. You can switch back to the default view at any time.

## Finding a Specific Name

If you're looking for a specific entry in the Address List, you can simply scroll down until you find it. If you only have a few dozen contacts, that's not so hard. But what if you're like us and your Address List is brimming with over a thousand contacts? Scrolling might take a while, especially if the guy you're looking for is named Nigel Walthers or Earnest Zanthers. That's when you use the Look Up function.

To search for a specific name, start writing the person's last name in the Look Up field at the bottom of the screen. The Address Book adjusts the display as you write; so if you enter the letter **J**, it displays all the names that begin with the letter *J*. If you write **JO**, it narrows the search and shows names that begin with those letters.

*If you're using the List By: Company, Last Name option in the Address List View, it's a little more complicated. If the entry has a company name, you need to search for that entry by company name. If the entry doesn't have a company name, though, you must find it by the last name.*

Once you start searching, you can keep writing letters until the Clié displays exactly the name you want, or you can write one or two letters, and then use the Scroll button to find the name you need. If you want to clear the Look Up field to write in a new name, just press one of the Scroll buttons.

## Conducting a Detailed Search

You may have noticed that the Look Up field only searches by last name. What happens if you want to find someone, but you can only remember that person's first name or the company where he works? The Look Up field won't do you any good.

In this case, use the Find tool. Tap the Find button, enter the word you want to search for, and then tap OK. You get a list of every entry in the Clié with that word—even items from the other applications—as shown in Figure 6-2. The current application is searched first, so make sure you're in the Address Book before you start using the Find tool.

```
                    Find
         Matches for "Airline"
         ──────── Addresses ────────
         A O M French Airlin   800-892-9136 W
         Air Inter-French Air  800-237-2747 W
         Air North Airlines    800-764-0407 W
         Airatlantic Airlines  800-223-5552 W
         Alaska Airlines       800-426-0333 W
         ALM Antillean Airlin  800-327-7197 W
         America West Airlin   800-235-9292 W
         American Airlines     800-433-7300 W
         ( Cancel ) ( Find More )
```

**FIGURE 6-2**    The Find Tool is a powerful way to locate an entry even if you don't remember the person's exact name.

## Viewing a Name

Once you locate the name you were looking for, tap on it. You'll see the Address View, which displays the contact's name, address, and phone numbers, as shown in Figure 6-3.

# Creating New Entries

To create a new Address List entry on the Clié, tap the New button at the bottom of the screen. From there, start filling in the blanks. Start by writing the last name of the person you're adding. When you're ready to move on to the first name, you need to change fields. You can do this two ways:

■ Tap the next field with the stylus, and then write in the Graffiti area

■ Use the Next Field gesture to move to the next field

6

**TIP** *The Next Field gesture takes a little practice because it's easy to get the letter U by mistake. Although the gesture template shows a curve in the first part of the stroke, you get the best results by going straight down, and then straight up again.*

Even though you only see a single line for text in each field, the Address List secretly supports multiple lines of text in each field. If you're entering the company name, for instance, you can use two or more lines to enter all the information you need about the company, department, and so on, for the individual. To write multiple lines of text in a field, use the Return gesture to create a new line. You won't see the multiple lines in the Address List, but you can see them when you select the entry and view the Address View.

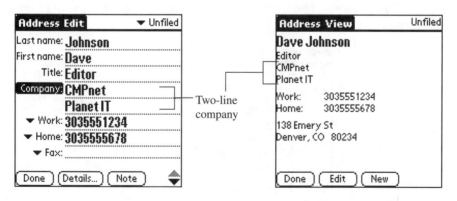

When you've finished adding information about this new person, tap the Done button.

**TIP** *What if you're Canadian, French, or living in some other non-American location? The Clié defaults to address details like city, state, and ZIP code—which may not be appropriate for your locale. The solution is to tap on the Prefs icon in Apps and select Formats from the menu. Then set the Preset To: menu to whatever country you desire.*

**FIGURE 6-3**   The Address Book shows you all the details about the selected individual.

## Using Multiple Phone Numbers

The Address List gives you a few options when you enter contact information. Specifically, you can set what kinds of phone numbers your Clié has for each contact. Conveniently, this needn't be the same for everyone. For one person, you might list a home phone and a pager, for instance, while another entry might have a work number and an e-mail address. The Clié keeps track of everything for you.

To control these numbers, tap on the phone number list and choose the desired label. Then, write the number or e-mail address in the field next to the label. You can specify up to five entries for each person in your Address List.

If you're on the ball, you might wonder which of those numbers shows up in the Address List View. Remember, the list shows the name and a phone number for each contact—this means you may not have to open an entry simply to dial a phone number because it's right there in the List view. The answer, though, is that the first phone number you enter into the Edit view is the one that appears in the List view—no matter where it appears in the list of phone numbers.

*If you later decide you want a different number to appear in the List view, tap the Details button and select the number label you want from the Show In List menu.*

## Using Extra Fields

The Address List has plenty of preconfigured fields (like name, company, and phone numbers) for most users, but it's also flexible enough to accommodate the special needs of everyone else. You might want to track birthdays, web pages, spouse names, or other personal information. If so, you're in luck—four custom fields are at the bottom of the Address Edit view, which you can rename as you like.

To label these four bonus fields into something more useful, do the following:

**1.** Choose the Address Book. Any view will do.

**2.** Choose Options | Rename Custom Fields from the menu.

**3.** Select the text on the first line (which should say Custom 1) and write a name for the field. Name the other fields—or as many as you need—in the same way.

**4.** Tap OK when finished.

Once you create labels for these fields, you can find them at the bottom of the list of contact info in the Address Edit view.

NOTE *The custom fields are global. This means you can't have different custom fields for each entry or even for each category. Once named, the custom fields apply to all entries in the Address List. You needn't fill them out for every entry, though.*

## Adding Pictures to the Address Book

Most Clié models come with a very cool feature in the Address Book—the capability to attach photos to your contacts. This is great, since it allows you to associate names and personal information with the individual's actual picture. If you have a lot of acquaintances you don't know very well in your Clié, this can be a wonderful feature for jogging your memory before a meeting.

Does *your* Clié support pictures? There's an easy way to find out:

**1.** Start the Address Book and tap on an entry.

**2.** Tap the Edit button at the bottom of the screen.

Do you see the words "No Image" in the upper-right corner of the screen? If so, you can add pictures to your Clié. The spot that says No Image is where the picture appears.

There are two ways to get pictures into the Address Book: the easy way and the not-so-easy way. That translates to using a Clié digital camera or an external digital camera. If you import digital images from some source other than the Clié camera, you'll have to transfer them to the Clié through your PC. Let's look at both methods.

*If you delete an image from your Clié—or even just move it to a Memory Stick that's still installed on the PDA—any Address Book entries that used the picture will lose it. An image needs to be stored on the Clié in order to appear in the Address Book.*

## Dialing Your Phone with a CLIÉ

Now that you've got hundreds of phone numbers stored on your Clié, it's better-equipped to place phone calls for you than the speed dial feature on your desktop phone. If you don't mind investing in a gadget called the Parlay Autodialer, you can point your Clié at your phone and automatically dial phone numbers.

The Autodialer is a small infrared receiver that plugs into your telephone (sort of like an answering machine) and intercepts beams from your Clié. Beam an Address Book entry toward your phone, and it dials the associated phone number. It's as simple as that.

If you change the Clié's preferences so a single upstroke across the display starts the beaming process (that's something you can configure in the Clié's Prefs program, explained in Chapter 4), dialing is effortless: just find an Address Book entry, point your PDA at the Autodialer, and beam. Pick up your handset or turn on the speakerphone to complete the call.

## Using Your CLIÉ Camera

To use your Clié camera, do the following:

**1.** Activate your Clié's camera. It doesn't matter whether you have a built-in camera, like the one in the NR70V, or you're using a Memory Stick camera you've attached to your PDA.

**2.** Make sure your camera is set to store images on the Clié itself—not the Memory Stick—and the images are in the Clié's own PGP format.

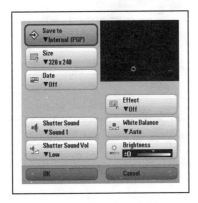

**3.** Take a picture of someone.

**4.** Start the Address Book and open the entry for the person you just photographed.

**5.** Tap the Edit button to get to the Address Edit page.

**6.** Tap the No Image text in the upper-right corner of the screen. You should see thumbnail images for all the pictures stored on your Clié.

**7.** Tap the picture you want to display for this entry.

That's all there is to it! Remember: you can always change pictures later. You can even remove a picture. To do that, enter the Address Edit page, tap the image, and choose No Images from the bottom of the screen.

TIP    *If you have a picture on your Clié's Memory Stick you'd like to use in the Address Book, simply import it back to the Clié. To do that, open the image in PictureGear Pocket and choose Image | Import/Export from the menu.*

## Our Favorite Books

**Dave**: Rick, it occurs to me that we often argue about movies, but rarely talk about our favorite books. I realize that's because you only recently got your equivalency diploma and mastered chapter books, but I was wondering if you were ready to weigh in with a few titles. Personally, I think that Orson Scott Card's *Ender's Game* is perhaps one of the very finest, but most under-appreciated novels in American literature—it's probably dismissed by academics because it's a genre title. After Ender, though, I'd count Joseph Heller's *Catch 22*, C. S. Lewis' *Perelandra*, and T. H. White's *The Once and Future King* among my very favorites. In a nutshell, I seem to have a thing for authors with three names.

**Rick**: I'm really surprised you didn't mention your collection of Little Lulu comic books or fondness for *Go, Dog. Go!* Well, I enjoyed Ender's Game, but certainly wouldn't call it great literature. For that I'd point to modern gems like *The Corrections* and *The Amazing Adventures of Kavalier & Clay*. I would also count *Angela's Ashes*, *The Good Earth*, and *Microserfs* among my favorite novels. Oh, by the way, there are only two names in "Joseph Heller." Didn't *Go, Dog. Go!* teach you anything?

### Using Images from Your PC or Digital Camera

If you have images on your digital camera or PC's hard disk, you have to execute an extra step or two. Here's what you should do:

1. Start by running PictureGear on your desktop PC. You should have received PictureGear with your Clié or your Clié digital camera. You may not have installed it, however. If you didn't, dig out the original CD-ROM and install it now.

2. Find the picture—or pictures—you want to use by browsing your computer's hard disk drives.

3. When you find the images, select them. You can hold down the CTRL key while clicking images to select more than one.

4. Choose File | Output Services | Install The Image During The Next HotSync.

5. When you see the Install dialog box appear, click the Still Settings button.

6. Change the size of the image to Small, since that's all you'll need for the Address Book. Click OK twice to close both dialog boxes.

7. Perform a HotSync. Afterward, the images will appear on your Clié and you can use them in your Address Book.

NOTE    *There's a big downside to attaching pictures to your Address Book entries: memory. Each image you leave on your Clié eats up at least 40KB, and large, higher-resolution images can consume much more—170KB, at least. Be selective about how many images you use and monitor the free space remaining on your Clié.*

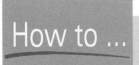

How to ...   **Create an Address Book Entry**

In summary, here's how you can create entries in the Address Book:

1. Press the Address Book button on your Clié to switch to that application.

2. Tap the New button on the bottom of the Address List view.

3. Enter all the information to create an entry for the person in question.

4. Tap the Details button and assign the entry to a category, and then tap OK.

# Assigning Categories

Your new contact can easily get lost within a sea of names and addresses if you aren't careful. With only a few names to manage, this isn't a big deal. But what if you have 500 or 1,000 contacts in your Address List? This is when categories could come in handy.

## Choosing a Category

As you might remember from Chapter 2, categories are simply a way of organizing your Clié data more logically into groups you frequently use. To assign a contact to a specific category, do the following:

1. From the Address Edit screen, tap Details. The Address Entry Details dialog box should appear.

2. Tap the Category List and choose the category name you want to assign to this contact.

3. Tap OK to close the dialog box.

Of course, you needn't assign a category if you don't want to do so. By default, new contacts are placed in the Unfiled category.

*The Clié's Address Book doesn't support as many categories as Microsoft Outlook. If you have dozens of categories assigned in Outlook, you might want to look at an alternative Clié Address Book, like KeyContacts.*

# Editing and Deleting Addresses

In this fast-paced world, a contact once entered in an address book isn't likely to stay that way for long. You may need to update an address, phone number, or e-mail address, or to delete the entry entirely.

To edit an entry, all you do is find the entry in the Address List and tap it. You're taken to the Address View where you can see the existing information. Then, tap the screen and the display changes to the Address Edit screen, which you can change to suit your needs.

If you have a contact you simply don't need anymore, you can delete it from the Clié to save memory and reduce data clutter. To delete a contact, do the following:

**1.** Choose the entry from the Address List. The Address View should appear.

**2.** Choose Record | Delete Address from the menu.

*If you check the box marked Save Archive Copy on PC, then a copy of this entry is preserved in Palm Desktop in archive form. In general, you probably needn't archive your data but it lets you restore deleted data in a crisis.*

# Creating and Beaming Your Business Card

One of the coolest things about taking your Clié to meetings and trade shows is the capability to beam your personal information into other peoples' PDAs. This is a lot easier and more convenient than exchanging a business card. Heck, a paper business card? That's so . . . '80s! Use your Clié instead.

Before you can beam your personal information around, though, you need to create a business card. That's not hard to do. Find your own personal information in the Address List (or, if you haven't done this yet, create an entry for yourself). After you select your card and can see your personal information on the Address View screen, choose Record | Select Business Card from the menu.

From here on, you can beam your card to others either by choosing Record | Beam Business Card from the Address List menu or, more simply, by holding the Address List button down for two seconds.

*Is your Address List entry selected as your business card? If so, on the Address View screen you should see an icon representing a Rolodex page at the top, just to the right of the title.*

# Working with Palm Desktop

Palm Desktop obviously has its own counterpart to the Address Book found in the Clié. Using Palm Desktop, you can not only create, edit, and refer to entries on your PC, but you can also put them to use in ways unavailable on the Clié itself. Next, we look at Palm Desktop.

Using the Address Book in Palm Desktop is a radically different experience than using the one in Clié. In most respects, it's better because the larger desktop screen, keyboard, and mouse enable you to enter and use the data in a more flexible way. After you start Palm Desktop, you can switch to the Address Book by clicking the Address icon on the right side of the screen or by choosing View | Address Book (see Figure 6-4).

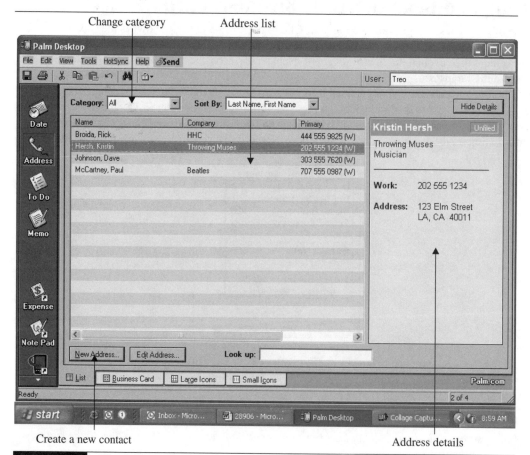

FIGURE 6-4    The Address Book looks sparse, but has more features than the Clié itself.

The Address Book interface enables you to see both the Address List and Address View simultaneously. To see a specific record's contents, click on it in the list and the information then appears in the column on the right.

*You can print a detailed address book based on your Clié contacts by choosing File | Print. The address book is nicely formatted.*

## Creating and Editing Entries

Some of the most dramatic differences in the Address Book appear when you create and use the Address Book. Remember these notes:

- To create a new entry, click the New button at the bottom of the screen or double-click a blank spot in the Address List.

- The Edit and New dialog boxes allow you to enter the same information as on the Clié. The dialog box also has a list box for specifying the category and a check box to make the entry private.

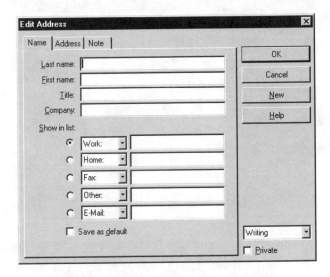

- To specify which phone number will appear in the Address List, click the radio button to the left of the appropriate phone number.

- To edit an existing entry, either double-click the entry in the Address List or its equivalent in the Address View on the right.

- You can also change the custom fields in Palm Desktop. To do so, choose Tools | Options and click the Address tab.

## Importing Contacts Into Palm Desktop

If you have a history with another contact manager, you could have dozens or even hundreds of names and addresses that should be copied over to Palm Desktop to be synchronized with the Clié. Thankfully, Palm Desktop makes importing all those contacts possible with a minimum of fuss. All you need is a contact manager capable of saving its data in either a comma-separated (CSV) or a tab-separated (TSV) format. To import your data from another program, do the following:

1. In your old contact manager, find the menu option to export your data in either CSV or TSV format. If the program gives you an option to remap your data as it's saved, don't worry. We'll map it properly as it's imported into Palm Desktop. Save the exported data to a file on your hard disk. (Make a note of where you save this file because you need to find it again in about two steps.)

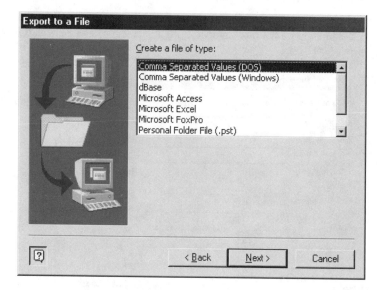

2. In Palm Desktop, choose File | Import. The Import dialog box should appear.

3. Select the file you just created with the old contact manager. You may have to choose the proper file extension (like CSV or TSV) from the Type of File list box to see the file you created. Choose Open.

4. Now you see a Specify Import Fields dialog box, as shown in Figure 6-5. This is the hardest part of the process and the one step that isn't terribly automated. Here's the deal: the data in a typical contact entry includes items like name, phone numbers, and address. But those fields won't be in the same order in any two contact management programs, so you need to help Palm Desktop put the old data in the right fields as it imports. To map the fields properly, drag each field on the left (which is Palm Desktop) until it's lined

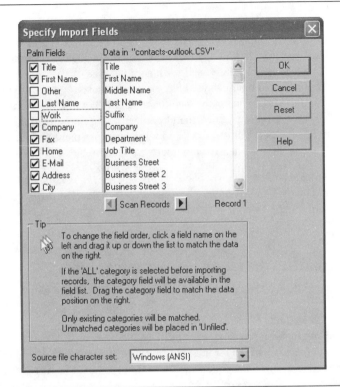

**FIGURE 6-5**   Carefully rearrange the fields in the Specify Import Fields dialog box so your old data is imported properly into Palm Desktop.

up with the proper field on the right (which represents the old program). Line up last name with last name, for instance, and match phone numbers, e-mail addresses, and any other important fields. If you don't want to import a certain field, deselect its check box.

**TIP**   *You can use the arrows to cycle forward through the database and make sure you've assigned the fields properly.*

**5.** When you finish lining up the fields, click the OK button.

If you did everything right, you should see your contacts in Palm Desktop. Any newly imported entries are highlighted. If you messed something up, all isn't lost. Simply delete all your records, and then try to import your contacts file again.

# Using Outlook

As we mentioned in Chapter 5, Outlook is a perfectly good alternative to Palm Desktop. To see your contacts in Outlook, start by clicking the Contacts icon in the Outlook Shortcut bar. Outlook should switch to the Contacts view where you'll see a complete list of your names and addresses.

You can view your contacts in many ways. That's good, because if you're anything like us, you have hundreds of entries—and sorting through them can be like finding a virtual needle in a digital haystack. To see your options, click the Organize button in the Outlook toolbar. The Organize pane should open. Click Using Views and you can experiment with arranging your contacts by category, by company, or nearly any other way imaginable.

 *To find a contact quickly from any view in Outlook, type the person's name in the Find A Contact field on the Outlook toolbar and press ENTER. Outlook displays a list of names that matches your criteria or, if only one name appears, displays its entry.*

## Address Book Alternatives and Enhancements

Don't think you have to stick with the Address Book just because it came with your trusty old Palm. Personally, we prefer the Clié's Address Book to most of the alternatives, but here are a few you might want to look into if you feel like expanding your contact management horizons:

This Address Book replacement combines the To Do List, Date Book, and Address Book to deliver a single, integrated interface for tracking, alarming, and viewing your daily itinerary. This program has lots of die-hard fans because of its many powerful features for managing contacts. You can try it out at **www.iambic.com**.

- **KeyContacts**   This replacement's claim to fame is the way it duplicates almost every aspect of Outlook on the Clié—it supports all of Outlook's categories, plus nearly all of the most obscure fields from Outlook are perfectly synchronized on the PDA. It's the best choice for avid Outlook users. Download a trial from **www.chapura.com**.

- **PopUp Names**   This "Hack" (see Chapter 13 for details on Hacks) pops the Address Book onto the screen with a simple stroke of the stylus, and puts it away when you're done. This lets you keep the application you were using open so you don't lose your place or have to hunt around to get back to what you were doing. You can find it at **www.benc.hr**.

## Where to Find It

| Web Site | Address | What's There |
| --- | --- | --- |
| Synchroscan | www.pda2phone.com | Parlay Autodialer |

# Chapter 7 The To Do List

## How to...

- View To Do List entries
- Create new To Dos
- Create a To Do based on an Address Book entry
- Prioritize your To Dos
- Add notes to your To Dos
- Edit To Dos from the List view
- Customize the To Do List view
- Beam To Dos to others
- Use Palm Desktop for Windows
- Export To Dos to Word and Excel
- Using Outlook with the Clié

The To Do List is admittedly one of the smallest of the core applications, but don't let that fool you. There's a lot of convenience under the hood. What good is this little program? Well, think of it this way: would you be more organized if you actually carried a list of things you needed to do—big and small—with you all the time? Finish a task and cross it off the list for a sense of immediate gratification. Or, think of something you need to do while you're away from the office and add it immediately to your Clié, knowing the entry will be added to your PC's master To Do List as soon as you HotSync. The To Do List is a way to take charge of all the little things that make up your daily agenda.

# Viewing the To Do List

As with most of the core applications in your Clié, you can start the To Do List by pressing its button (it's the one that looks like three "checklist" lines) or by tapping its icon on the Application screen.

As you can see in Figure 7-1, the Clié lists your To Dos in a fairly straightforward list that you can use to see what tasks you have coming up or, in some cases, that are past due (you might want to take care of those pretty soon, by the way). A standard Clié screen has room for 11 entries at one time; the rest appear "off the screen," and you can scroll to them. Getting around is easy. Simply scroll down to see more names, either with the onscreen scroll arrows or the Scroll buttons on the case.

Each time you scroll, the Clié moves the list by one complete page. This means that if you scroll down, the bottom entry on the page becomes the top entry after scrolling.

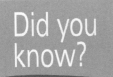

<br>

**FIGURE 7-1**   The To Do List displays all of your pending tasks.

7

Another way to get around is by using the categories. If your tasks are divided into more than one category, every time you press the To Do button, you switch categories. You can cycle through the first page of tasks in each category by repeatedly pressing this button.

## Did you know?

# The Agenda Shows To Do Items

You can view your To Do items in the Date Book. The Agenda view lets you see all of today's appointments and upcoming To Dos at a glance, all on the same screen. (See Chapter 5 for more.)

## Creating a To Do

To add a To Do to your Clié, just start writing in the Graffiti area. The text appears automatically in a brand new To Do entry.

*If you want to create a task with a specific priority, tap on a To Do entry that has the priority you want, and then tap New. The new To Do takes the priority of the previously selected task, saving you the trouble of choosing a priority later.*

While most tasks can be summarized in only one line of text, there's no reasonable limit to how long you can make a To Do entry. If you need more than one line of text to describe your task, you can use the Enter gesture to get the Clié to display a new blank line in the same To Do.

Remember, though, creating multiline To Dos might make it hard for you to read your tasks later, as you can see here:

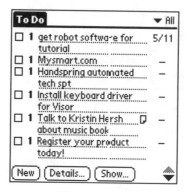

Instead of making long, multiline tasks, we recommend you add a note to your task instead (explained in the next section, "Adding Some Details").

## Friends Are a Chore

It's true! Having friends and coworkers can be actual work. Suppose you need to meet with Ed Grimpley from accounting sometime this week to talk about why you've gone through 18 mouse pads in the space of a month. You don't have an appointment in your calendar; you'd rather pop in sometime when it's convenient. The To Do List is your answer. Create a new To Do and choose Options | Phone Lookup from the menu. Find Ed in the Phone Number Lookup dialog box and tap Add. What you get is Ed's name and phone number in the To Do entry. It's a handy way to remind yourself to call someone without setting up a rigid appointment in the Date Book.

## Adding Some Details

Once you finish entering the name of the task, tap elsewhere on the screen to save the entry. If you prefer, you can add additional information, like a priority, category, and due date. You don't have to enter any of these special settings, but using them enables you to track your tasks with greater accuracy. Here's what you need to do:

1. Select the task you want to edit by tapping the name of the To Do.

2. Tap the Details button.

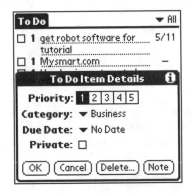

3. Tap a number to represent the priority of your task. You can select any number from one to five (the lower the number, the higher the priority).

4. Choose a category from the Category list.

5. Choose a due date from the Due Date list. You can choose to make a task due today, tomorrow, or in a week, or you can choose a date directly from the Calendar dialog box.

6. Tap OK to save your changes to the task.

## To Do or Appointment?

We know what you're thinking—if you can assign due dates to items in the To Do List, why bother with appointments? Or, from the other perspective, why use To Dos if you have the Date Book? That's a good question. We use the To Do List whenever we have tasks that need doing by a certain date—but not at a certain time of day. If it requires a time slot, we put it in the Date Book. So, stuff like "buy lemons" or "finish Chapter 20" (hint, hint, Rick . . .) are To Dos. "Meet with Laura for lunch at 11:30" is a Date Book entry. There's also the matter of alarms: your Clié has an alarm for appointments, but not for To Dos. If that bothers you, consider trying DateBk5, a program that lets you alarm To Dos as well as appointments.

TIP    *While you can make a task almost any length, most people find it's better to keep the To Do short, and add a note. To add a note to a To Do, select your To Do, tap the Details button, and then tap Note.*

# Working with the List View

When you switch to the To Do List, all of your existing tasks are arranged onscreen, usually in order of importance (as determined by the priority number assigned to each To Do). As you can see in Figure 7-2, six elements are associated with each task:

- **Check box**   If you complete a task, you can indicate it's done by tapping the check box. That places a check mark in the task. Depending on how you configured the To Do Preferences, the entry either disappears or remains onscreen, but nevertheless it's marked as done.

- **Priority**   Not everything is the most important thing on your task list. If you want to arrange your tasks by importance or urgency, use the priority numbers—one through five. Tap the number to get a list of all the priority choices.

> **TIP**   *We recommend you use priority numbers for your tasks—they help you sort through the clutter of your various To Dos and determine what's really important from one day to the next.*

- **To Do description**   You can edit the description of the task by tapping in this field and editing the existing text.

- **Note icon**   If you already created a note for the task, you can read the note or edit it by tapping the icon to the right of the To Do name field. If no note already exists, you can add one by selecting the task and choosing Record | Attach Note from the menu.

- **Due date**   You might have tasks that need to be accomplished by a specific date. If this is the case, use the final column. If a dash is in that slot, this means you haven't yet assigned a due date. Tap it and choose a date. You can also change the due date in the same way.

- **Category**   Change the category to which a task is assigned by tapping the category column and choosing the desired category from the list.

**FIGURE 7-2**    The To Do List lets you modify your tasks without tapping the Details button.

*Some of these columns aren't displayed by default—to enable them, tap the Show button and choose the columns you want to appear in the To Do Preferences dialog box.*

## Changing the View Options

If you're anything like us (and that could be a very, very bad thing, if you know what we mean), you may be perfectly happy with the default look of the To Do List. It's easy to modify, though. Tap the Show button and you see the To Do Preferences dialog box. Here are your options:

## Sorting Options

The first item you encounter in the Preferences dialog box is a Sort By list. This determines the way the To Do List shows the tasks onscreen. The four options are shown next:

- **Priority, Due Date**   This groups all the priority one tasks first, followed by priority two, and so on. Within each priority group, the earliest deadlines are listed first, while tasks with no deadlines are listed last. This option works best if you need to work on tasks with the highest priority and due dates aren't particularly important to you.

- **Due Date, Priority**   This selection arranges all the tasks by due date, with the soonest due dates listed first and those tasks with no due dates listed last. If several tasks have the same due date, they're listed by priority order. This is probably the best display option for most people. Tasks due soonest are listed at the top of the page, and within each group of due dates, top priorities are arranged first.

- **Category, Priority**   Arranges your tasks by category, with categories arranged in alphabetical order. If you have more than one task in a given category, they're arranged by priority order within the category. Use this category if seeing tasks visually arranged into different categories—like work and personal—is more important to you than arranging them by due date or category.

■ **Category, Due Date**   This selection also arranges your tasks by category, where the categories are arranged in alphabetical order. If you have more than one task in a given category, they're arranged by due date within the category. Tasks with the nearest deadlines appear first while those with no due date are listed last in each category.

## Using Filters to Customize the Display

The next section in the To Do Preferences dialog box controls what kind of tasks are displayed onscreen. Actually, that's not true, but we're trying to apply some logic to the way Clié chooses to group the items on this screen. Here's what each of these three items does:

■ **Show Completed Items**   As you check off tasks you complete, slowly but surely they clutter up your screen unless you do something about them. If you uncheck this option, completed items are hidden. If you need to see items you have completed, simply check Show Completed Items and they reappear.

**NOTE**   *If you hide completed tasks in this way, they're not deleted. They still take up memory on the Clié. To find out how to get rid of them for good, see "Deleting Old To Dos" later in this chapter.*

■ **Show Only Due Items**   If you're only concerned about tasks due today, check this item. Any tasks with a due date after today disappear from the screen and only reappear on the day they're due.

**CAUTION**   *Be careful with this option because it hides To Dos from the screen that aren't due today, regardless of priority. It's easy to get caught off guard by a major deadline this way.*

■ **Record Completion Date**   This interesting little feature changes the due date of a completed item to the date it was completed. If you didn't assign a due date to a task, the completion date becomes the due date. In this way, you can track what day you completed each of your tasks.

**CAUTION**   *This option overwrites the due date with the completion date. You can't get the original due date back even if you uncheck the task or turn off the Record Completion Date option.*

## Modifying the Task Columns

As you probably already saw, you can tweak the data the To Do List shows you for each task in the list. That tweaking occurs here, in the last three options of the To Do Preferences dialog box. Your To Do List can look sparse, highly decorated, or anything in between by changing the Show options, as shown here:

- ■ **Show Due Dates**   The due date format is day/month, which takes some getting used to. If you don't assign a due date to a task, you see a dash instead. On the To Do List, if you tap a due date, you see a list for changing the date.

- ■ **Show Priorities**   This displays the priority to the left of the To Do name. The priority can be adjusted by tapping the number on the To Do List view.

- ■ **Show Categories**   The category of the task appears on the right edge of the To Do List view if you use this option. You can assign a category to an unfiled To Do (or change the category of a previously filed entry) by tapping the category name on the To Do List view.

## What Sony Does Best

**Dave:** The optimist in me says that what Sony does best is release absolutely stunning hardware. They push the boundaries and create cool PDAs with clever features—like universal remote control software, digital cameras, music players, and super-hi-res screens. For me, looking at a new Clié is always like being in a hi-tech candy store. But the pessimist in me says that what Sony does best is tease us with half-baked technology. What's the point of having a proprietary Memory Stick format if it's only available in capacities far smaller than all of the other formats? I want 256MB and 512MB Memory Sticks—you know, like I can get in a Compact Flash or SD card right now—but Sony won't budge. To make matters worse, they have cool stuff like Bluetooth and GPS Memory Sticks, but won't sell them in the US. If I had a Palm, I could have Bluetooth and GPS right now. But not from Sony. Why do they torture me so? Are they crazy, or just insane?

**Rick**: Funny how you used the two words that describe you best! It is indeed ironic that Sony has been so slow with Memory Stick while they've been cranking out new Clié models at the rate of one per month (seriously!). But just be patient: MS capacities will increase, and the runaway success of the Clié line (which, as of this writing, must still be taking Sony by surprise) guarantees more MS goodies like Bluetooth and GPS. I do wish they'd let some other manufacturers get in on the action instead of being so proprietary with the technology. It's like making a fabulous sports car that everyone loves, but forcing you to use special gasoline only available at a handful of stations.

# Deleting Old To Dos

For most people, To Dos are not like diamonds—they don't last forever. After you check off a task that says "pick up a loaf of bread," how long do you need a record of having accomplished that goal? That's why your Clié provides a method of removing tasks you no longer want. There are two ways to eliminate tasks:

- **Delete them one at a time**    If you need to delete only one To Do, tap the To Do to select it. Now choose Record | Delete Item from the menu and the To Do is gone forever.

- **Delete a whole bunch at once**    If you use the To Do List a lot and develop a back list of hundreds of completed tasks, axing them one at a time could become a full-time job. Instead, purge them. A *purge* deletes all completed tasks, so be sure you want to do this. To purge your To Do List, choose Record | Purge from the menu. The Purge dialog box appears, asking if you really want to delete your completed To Dos. Tap OK.

TIP    *If you want to preserve a copy of your completed tasks, check Save Archive Copy on PC, and then load the archive into Palm Desktop when you need to refer to the entries.*

# Sharing Your To Dos

Delegation is the key to successful management. At least that's what we've been told. We don't actually supervise anyone, but it sounds like solid business advice, nonetheless. You can use your Clié as a solid delegation tool by beaming tasks to other people. Just like in other applications, you can beam a single item or all the items in a specific category. Here's the skinny:

- **Beam a single To Do**    To beam one To Do to someone, choose a task by tapping inside the To Do name. Then choose Record | Beam Item from the menu.

- **Beam a whole bunch of items**    You can beam an entire category's worth of To Dos at once. To do this, switch the current view to show the category you want to beam. You can choose a category from the list at the top right of the screen or press the hard To Do button several times until the category you want appears. Then choose Record | Beam Category from the menu.

# Working with Palm Desktop

Who says the only place you can enter To Dos is on your Palm? Not us! Palm Desktop has a module dedicated to tracking your tasks. Using Palm Desktop, you can enter To Dos and have them appear on your Clié when you're away from your desk.

# The Windows To Do List

The To Do List's interface is a bit more spacious than the one in your Clié. As a result, Palm Desktop pulls off a cool trick—it displays both the list itself and the contents of the Details dialog box onscreen simultaneously, as you can see in Figure 7-3. Click a To Do and the details on the right automatically update to show you more information about the particular task you selected.

## Turn To Dos into Appointments

Your Clié understands there's a tight relationship between your calendar and your tasks. Switch to the Date Book in Palm Desktop and you'll find the right side of the screen has a window for displaying either addresses or To Dos. Click the To Do box to show To Dos; click Address to return to the Phone Number Lookup mode. What good is it? Well, you can actually grab a To Do and drag-and-drop it into a calendar appointment. That lets you turn a task into a bona fide appointment. Unfortunately, you can't go the other way and turn an appointment into a task.

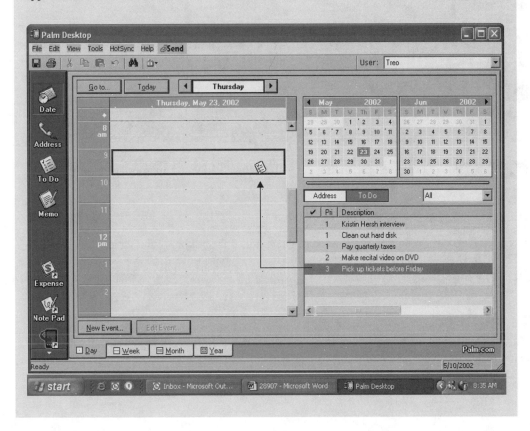

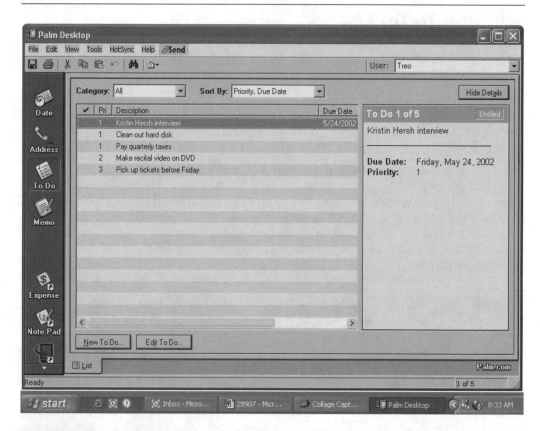

**FIGURE 7-3** You can see the details on any To Do by clicking the appropriate description on the left side of the screen.

## Creating and Editing To Dos

To create a new To Do, just click the New To Do button at the bottom of the screen. You'll see the New To Do dialog box, where you can enter text, assign priorities, and even set a due date for your task.

# Using Outlook

If you're an Outlook user, you probably already know that Palm's To Do items become Tasks in Outlook. In fact, that's pretty much all you need to know to use Outlook with your Clié. To see your To Dos in Outlook, click the Tasks icon in the Outlook Shortcuts bar. The tasks are also displayed in the Taskbar section of the Calendar. But remember that To Do categories and certain fields don't make the trip from Outlook to the Clié—stuff like % Complete, Status, and Owner aren't supported by the Palm OS.

**TIP** *When you mark a task as completed in Outlook, it isn't deleted. To reduce clutter and save disk space, you might want to delete tasks occasionally. To do this, right-click a completed task and choose Delete from the menu.*

## Understanding Task Priorities

The Clié and Outlook use two slightly different ways of assigning priority to tasks and To Dos. Thankfully, the two systems work together and are easy to figure out. Use this guide to correlate the Clié and Outlook systems:

| Clié | Outlook |
| --- | --- |
| 1 | High |
| 2 | Normal |
| 3 | Normal |
| 4 | Normal |
| 5 | Low |

7

# Chapter 8

## The Memo Pad

## How to...

- View the Memo List
- Create new memos
- Cut, copy, and paste text in a memo
- Assign categories to memos
- Customize the appearance of memos in the Memo List
- Beam memos
- Make memos private
- Delete old memos
- Import text files into Windows memos
- Use memos in other Windows applications
- Use Outlook with the Clié

As you've already seen, applications like the Date Book, Address Book, and To Do List let you attach long notes to your entries. A note in the Address Book, for instance, enables you to list directions to the person's house, the names of all their kids, or ten reasons not to visit them for Thanksgiving. But there's also an application designed to do nothing but create notes. These memos can be memory joggers, information you need to take on a trip, or anything not explicitly connected to an address, an appointment, or a to-do. The Memo Pad is your chance, in a sense, to color outside the lines and leave yourself any kind of message you want.

# Viewing the Memo Pad

The Memo Pad has two views—the *Memo List* (which, not surprisingly is, a list of all the memos you created) and the Memo View, which shows you the contents of whatever memo you select from the Memo List. When you start the Memo Pad, it always starts in the Memo List view. As you can see in Figure 8-1, the Clié displays each of your memos in a list, with the first line of the memo visible as a kind of title that lets you know what's inside. Getting around is easy—just scroll up or down to see more memos.

 *Another way to get around the Memo List is by using the categories. If your memos are divided into more than one category, every time you press the Memo Pad button, you switch categories. You can cycle through the first page of tasks in each category by repeatedly pressing this button.*

# Creating New Memos

You've probably noticed the New button at the bottom of the Memo List—but you don't need to use it to create new memos. Instead, start writing in the Graffiti area and the Clié automatically switches from the Memo List View to the Memo View.

**FIGURE 8-1**    The Memo List displays all of your memos.

The memo can be as long as you want—up to 4,096 characters, or about 700 words. That's pretty long and it should suit your needs most of the time. You can include blank lines and divide your memo into paragraphs—anything you need to make it logical and readable.

**TIP**    *You can't name your memos in the sense that you can save files on the PC with a specific filename, but the first line of the memo is what appears in the Memo List. To keep things neat and organized, you can write a brief description of the memo on the top line, and then start the memo itself on the next line.*

## Using Editing Tools

The familiar cut, copy, and paste tools are available in every Clié application, but nowhere are they more important than in the Memo Pad, where you're likely to be writing more than a sentence or two. Remember, you don't have to create text from scratch all the time. Using these edit tools, you can move text from other applications and rearrange it to suit your needs.

Suppose, for example, you previously had a Date Book appointment that read:

```
Meeting with Ted
```

Within that appointment, you might have created a note that looked like this:

```
Discuss performance review
Get feedback on budget for 2Q
Agree on approach for marketing plan
```

If you want to have a record of your meeting with Ted, take notes in a memo. Open the appointment note and select the three lines of text from the note. With the text selected, choose Edit | Copy from the menu (or use the Command gesture and write *C*). Then switch to the Memo Pad, create a new memo, and paste the text into the memo using Edit | Paste (or COMMAND-P using the Graffiti shortcut).

After pasting the text into the memo, you can use it as your agenda items—and insert notes as needed, giving you a complete record of the meeting. When you HotSync your Clié, you can then paste that data into Word or some other application and generate a formal report.

## Cool Things to Do with the Memo Pad

Do you know what surprises us? Lots of things, actually. Dave is surprised Rick has no appreciation for the fine arts—specifically, bands like *Pink Floyd*, *the Velvet Underground*, Kristin Hersh, and *Throwing Muses*.

More to the point, we're surprised at how many people can't seem to come up with good uses for the Memo Pad. They let it languish while they use the Address Book and Date Book all the time. To help you fully realize the potential of this cool little application, here are some helpful suggestions for how to use the Memo Pad:

- Create a **Million-Dollar Idea** memo. No matter when or where you come up with one of those incredibly amazing ideas to help you retire before you turn 50, pull out your Clié and jot it down.

- **Trade show category** Got a lot of booths to visit at next month's lawn care trade show? Create a category and put all the memos for that event in the category. As you walk the show floor, you can reference your notes about the show in one easy-to-find set of memos.

- **Store passwords** This one is dangerous, so make sure you keep it private. But, if you have a lot of passwords you routinely need—for your ISP, web sites, computer logons, and that kind of thing, you can store them all in one place in a memo for passwords. Note, we have to reiterate the danger in this—if your Clié is stolen, you could give all your passwords away if they're not protected properly. No IT department on Earth would sanction this particular tip, and we won't even admit to writing it down if questioned in court.

- **Meeting notes** Take notes during a meeting and beam the memo to others when the meeting is over.

- **A "Phone Messages" memo** Name a memo Phone Messages and when you check voice mail, jot down notes in your Clié using this memo. If you're diligent about it, you won't end up with a million yellow stickies all over your desk after each VM-checking session. Plus, names and phone numbers will be in your Clié where you need them, not splayed all over your desk.

- **Store your new words** Dave makes up new words in an effort to evolve the English language at a grass roots level. If you, too, make up new words frequently (and that's a beautiquious thing to do), store them in a **New Words** memo so you don't accidentally forget them. Chizzy! (Rick is working on a way to delete that particular memo from Dave's Clié, perhaps by using a large hammer.)

## Memo Pad Assistants

Many tools can enhance the experience of creating long notes in the Memo Pad. Here are a few examples you might want to try.

A pair of programs—*TextPlus* and *WordComplete*—can suggest common words as you write, even before a word is complete. By offering likely options for what you might be writing, either of these applications can significantly reduce the time you spend creating text in the Memo Pad.

*MultiClipHack* expands the Clié's clipboard. It keeps track of your last 16 cut and copy operations and allows you to pick them from a drop-down menu to insert in your memo as you write.

## Assigning Categories

After you accumulate a few memos, you might find the Memo List View getting a bit crowded. Clean it up with the Clié's ever-helpful category filing system. You can assign a category by doing the following:

**8**

1. Create a new memo.

2. Tap the Details button. The Memo Details dialog box appears.

3. Choose a category from the Category list.

4. Tap OK to close the Memo Details dialog box.

After your memos are arranged into categories, you can cycle through them easily by pressing the Memo Pad hard button on the Clié case.

## Arranging Memos in the Memo List

Computer users are, for the most part, fanatical organizers. We tend to spend hours straightening up the Desktop so icons appear in exactly the right place when the computer starts each morning. That said, we're sure you will want to organize your memos. This isn't pointless busy work: if you need to open the same memo over and over, having the memo appear at the top of the list whenever you open the Memo List can help. At the very least, we're sure you'll want to understand how to take control of the way memos appear onscreen.

## Peering Into Madness: Dave's and Rick's Memos

**Dave:** I have a Memo Pad category called Lists. In this category, I have a bunch of memos I refer to all the time. I have a list of movies—whenever I think of a film I want to rent, I add it to the list. Then, when I go to **Netflix.com**, I can add it to my queue. I also have a Songs memo where I can jot down the names of songs I hear on the radio that I might want to download from an MP3 service. I have a list called meals—things I'd like to eat—that I can refer to when I go grocery shopping and get the appropriate ingredients. Finally, I have a Top 10 list. When I think of a funny Top 10 topic—like "Restaurants you won't want to eat at" or "Reasons to own a Clié"—I jot it down, so I have something funny to start a speaking engagement.

**Rick:** If Dave ever starts reading one of his "funny" Top 10 lists in your presence, turn and run the other way as fast as you can, unless you're really good at polite laughter. Anyway, I compile similar lists of books I want to read, movies I want to rent, and wines my wife and I have tried and liked. I also use memos to jot down business ideas, and any other brainstorms I don't want to forget.

When you add memos to the Memo List, by default, the newest ones always appear at the end of the list. The default order of Memo List entries is essentially chronological, with the oldest entries at the top and the newest ones at the bottom.

It's a little more complicated than that, though. You can specify the sort order of memos by choosing Options | Preferences. You get two choices:

■ **Manual**    This is the default mode your Clié uses out of the box. New memos are added to the bottom of the list, but you can actually drag-and-drop memos to different positions in the list. Suppose you have a frequently used memo which you want to appear at the top of the screen. Tap and hold the stylus on the entry, then drag the stylus up to the position where you want it to appear. You should see a line move with the stylus, indicating where the memo will land if you release the stylus.

■ **Alphabetic**   This option sorts all entries into alphabetical order. If you select this option, the drag-and-drop method of moving memos won't work unless you revert to the manual method.

## Blank Lines for Emphasis

Here's a trick you can try if you think the Memo List is too cluttered. If you use the manual ordering method and arrange your memos in a specific order in a near-fanatical way, you might be bothered by the fact that memo number four is "touching" memo number five. Rick, for instance, is adamant about not eating his mashed potatoes if they come in contact with his peas. Maybe you suffer from the same kind of problem with your Clié.

Try this: Create a new memo with a blank first line. You have to enter at least one character on the second line, because the Clié doesn't let you create a completely blank memo. Close the memo and you will see you've made a new memo with a blank header. Drag this memo between two memos you want separated and voilà—you've found a way to separate memos.

## Working with Your Memos

You have the same 4,096-character limit on writing memos as you have with notes in other parts of the Clié suite of applications. That's plenty of space to write, as long as you're not trying to draft your autobiography (if you are trying to create an extremely long document, see Chapter 17 for details on applications that let you do that).

## Beaming Memos

You can send a memo or a group of memos to another Clié owner just as easily as beaming any other kind of information. Here's how:

- **Beam one memo**   To beam a memo, you need to tap on the memo you want to beam—this displays the memo in the Memo View. Then choose Record | Beam from the menu. That's all there is to it.

- **Beam a bunch of memos**   To beam more than one memo, they all must be in the same category. Make sure you're in the Memo List View and switch to the category you want to beam. You can do this by choosing the category from the list at the top right of the screen or by pressing the Memo List hard button on the Clié case until you see the category you want. Then choose Record | Beam Category from the menu.

## Making a Memo Private

If you have private information stored in a memo, you can easily hide specific memos from prying eyes. The procedure is essentially the same as with other Clié applications. To do this:

1. In the Memo List, select a memo by tapping it.

2. Tap the Details button. The To Memo Details dialog box appears.

3. Tap the Private box to add a check mark. Now the entry is marked as private. Tap OK and you see this dialog box:

4. Tap OK to close the dialog box.

If the memo isn't hidden yet, there's one more step you can take. To make it disappear entirely, you need to enable the Private Records feature in the Security application. For details on how to do this, see Chapter 10.

## How to ... Create New Memos

Working with the Memo Pad is a snap. In summary, here's what you need to do to create memos:

1. Press the Memo Pad button on your Clié.

2. Start writing in the Graffiti area to create a new memo.

3. Tap the Details button and assign your new memo to a specific category.

4. Tap the Done button to close your new memo.

5. Drag the memo to put it in a specific place in the Memo List.

8

### Deleting Memos

No matter how much you like your memos, eventually you may need to delete some. To delete a memo, tap the memo you want to delete. Then choose Record | Delete Memo from the menu. The memo is then deleted from your Clié. If you prefer, you can save a backup of this memo to Palm Desktop by choosing Save Archive Copy On PC.

## Working in Palm Desktop

You can create and review your notes and memos on Palm Desktop. That's good, because many kinds of memos might come in handy on the desktop. For instance, if you took our earlier advice about creating a Phone Messages memo, you'll appreciate having the capability to type directly into the PC when the phone rings.

## The Palm Desktop Memo Pad

Because the Clié has pretty limited real estate on the small screen, you have to switch between the Memo List and Memo View. But, on Palm Desktop, you can see both at once. To see a memo, click the header on the left, and the memo's contents appear in the window on the right. It should look like Figure 8-2. Double-clicking a memo header has no effect.

Most of the Memo Pad's operation is obvious. The controls aren't identical, though. Here are some things to remember:

- You can't rearrange memos, but you can sort them alphabetically or by how they appear on the Clié. Use the Sort By drop-down menu at the top of the screen.

- You can display memos in a list or through icons (like Outlook's Notes) using the tabs at the bottom of the screen.

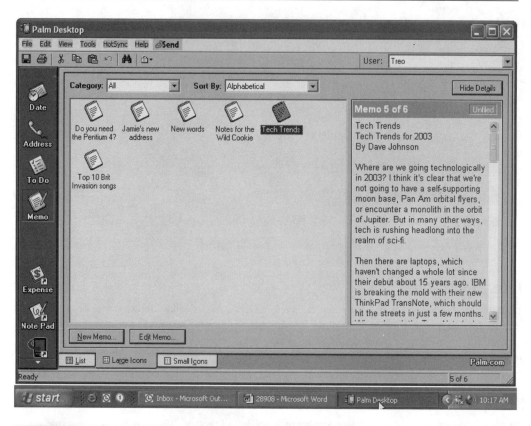

**FIGURE 8-2**    On the desktop, Palm Desktop memos look a lot like memos in Outlook—except that Palm Desktop adds a convenient text window on the right.

## Importing and Exporting Memos

You don't need to create memos from scratch. Heck, you don't even have to cut-and-paste to create a memo. Palm Desktop lets you import text files from elsewhere on the computer. To import a text file, do the following:

1. Choose File | Import. The Import dialog box appears.

2. Choose Text (*.txt) from the File Of Type list box.

3. Find the file you want to import. It has to be a plain text file in ASCII format—no Word or other specially formatted file types are allowed. Select the file and click the Open button. You then see the Specify Import Fields dialog box.

**4.** The text file should be ready to import, with the text lined up with the Memo field. If it isn't, drag the Memo field on the left until it lines up like the one shown in Figure 8-3.

**5.** Click OK.

**6.** If your text file is too large to fit in a single memo, the Palm Desktop automatically divides it into multiple memos.

**7.** Click OK.

What about the other case, where you have a memo that you'd like to get into Microsoft Word? Piece of cake! Just right-click a memo and choose Send To | MS Word from the menu. The text will automatically appear in a new blank document in Word.

8

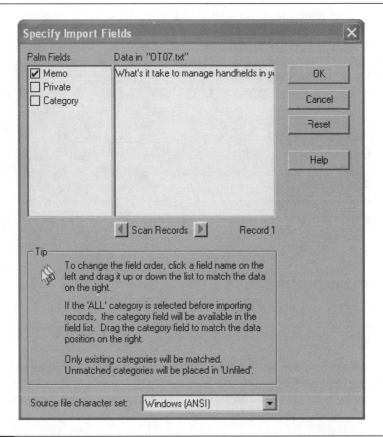

**FIGURE 8-3**    The text should be lined up with the Memo field as shown here.

# Using Outlook with the CLIÉ

Outlook's Notes View, like the Clié's Memo Pad is, a place to store free-form notes of any kind. You can use it to record phone messages, jot down reminders, leave long-term documents (like things to bring on a trip), or remind yourself about web sites you want to visit. It doesn't matter what you put in these notes. By default, Outlook's notes look like little Post-it notes. You can change their appearance in two ways:

1. To change the color of a single note, right-click it and choose Color from the menu. You can choose from five colors to make certain notes stand out visually.

2. To change the default color and size of all notes, choose Tools | Options from the Outlook menu and click the Preferences tab. Click the Note Options button and set your preferences. Click OK to close the dialog boxes. All new notes you create appear with these settings.

## Look Ma, No Scroll Bar!

Outlook's notes have an annoying glitch—lacking scroll bars, it's hard to read a long note that trails off the bottom of the sticky note window. Don't know what we're talking about? Copy a long Word document into a new note. Or create a really long Clié memo and HotSync. You'll find the text extends beyond the bottom of the note window in Outlook and there's no scroll bar to get at the rest of it.

The solution is deceptively simple: click in the note window to place the cursor in the note, then use the down arrow key on the keyboard to scroll through the document.

Why do we mention this? Rick didn't realize there was any way to scroll through the document at all—he thought anything that didn't fit in the sticky note window was totally inaccessible—until Dave showed him the keyboard arrow trick. So, if you were ever perplexed by the missing memo text, now you are at least as smart as Rick (fill in your own jokes here).

## Quirks Between Outlook and CLIÉ

While the Outlook Notes View and Clié Memo Pad are perhaps the simplest of all the features in these two programs, there are a few things you should know to ensure everything works smoothly when you HotSync:

- The Clié Memo Pad has a size limit—but Notes in Outlook don't. This means you can create a very long note in Outlook that doesn't transfer properly to the Clié. If you create a huge note in Outlook, only the first 4,096 characters appear in the Clié Memo Pad. You'll also see a warning saying this occurred in the HotSync log.

- The Clié's categories aren't used by Outlook. This means your Clié memos, when they appear in Outlook as notes, are unfiled. The same is true in the other direction.

## A Memo Pad Alternative

Is the Memo Pad not powerful enough for you? Then flip over to Chapter 12, where we introduce you to a few powerful word-processing alternatives to the Memo Pad, such as Documents To Go and WordSmith. Or, there's a program called Memo PLUS (a good substitute for Memo Pad), which enables you to attach drawings to your memos, use templates, and more. You can find Memo PLUS on the Web at **www.handshigh.com**.

## Where to Find It

| Web Site | Address | What's There |
|----------|---------|--------------|
| SmartCell Technology | www.smartcell.com | TextPlus |
| Hands High Software | www.handshigh.com | Memo PLUS |
| PalmGear | www.palmgear.com | Tons of additional software |

8

# Chapter 9

# The Rest of the Palm OS Team

## How to...

- Access security features
- Set records as private
- Hide or show private records
- Set a security password
- Password-protect your Clié
- Find third-party security measures for your Clié and data
- Use the Find feature
- Find third-party utilities that extend your search capabilities
- Use the calculator
- Find third-party calculators
- Work with Expense
- Identify the rest of the Clié's bundled software

Now that we've looked at the stars of the Palm OS—the Address Book, Date Book, Memo Pad and To Do List—let's turn our attention to the supporting cast. We're talking about the Security program, which enables you to hide private records and "lock" your Clié; the Find feature, a search tool that helps you quickly sift through all your data; the calculator, which, big surprise, calculates; and the potentially mystifying Mail program, which is used to send and receive e-mail—sort of.

# Palm Security

At the risk of sounding like a spy novel, listen up, 007, if your data falls into the wrong hands, it could spell disaster for M, Q, and lots of other letters of the alphabet. Fortunately, we've outfitted your Clié with foolproof security measures. Only you will have the access codes. Only you can view Heather Graham's phone number. (Can we have it? Please? Please?)

In all seriousness, it's not unlikely that you'll be storing some sensitive information in your Clié, information that should be kept private. Important passwords, account numbers, meeting locations, contact data—these are among the items you'd be loathe to let a stranger see. Fortunately, the Palm OS offers two very effective ways to protect your data: marking individual records as private, and locking your Clié every time you turn it off.

In both scenarios, you—or anyone who's trying to access your Clié—must supply a password in order to gain access. It's a bit of a hassle to have to enter it over and over again, but at least you have the comfort of knowing your Clié and data are totally secure.

# Security 101

To get started with Clié security, find and tap the Security icon. You'll see the screen shown in Figure 9-1. The first step is choosing a password. Notice that the Password box currently says "-Unassigned-"—meaning simply that you haven't entered your password yet. Before you do, read a little further.

## What You Should Know about Passwords

The password you choose can be any combination of letters, numbers, symbols and spaces. You can make it "Spock" or "H4T*Q" or "The quick brown fox." Ideally, it should be something reasonably short, as you'll probably wind up writing it frequently. Don't make it too obvious, like "123," but you could use something as simple as the last four digits of your social-security number or your spouse's initials.

**NOTE** *Capitalization doesn't matter. Even if you make a point to capitalize "Spock" when you enter it as your new password, you can write "**spock**" to unlock your Clié and it'll work just fine.*

**CAUTION** *Whatever password you decide on, it's vital that it be something you can easily remember. If you forget it, you could wind up unable to access certain records—or your entire Clié! Thus, if you have even the slightest concern that you might forget your password, write it down on a piece of paper and store it in a safe place. Better safe than sorry.*

## Working with Passwords

Okay, let's enter a new password on your Clié. Just tap the "-Unassigned-" box, then use Graffiti or the onscreen keyboard to enter your desired password.

**NOTE** *At this time you're also asked to supply a hint. If you use, say, your mother's maiden name as your password, you should put "mother's maiden name" in the hint field. This hint appears when an incorrect password is entered.*

**FIGURE 9-1** In Security, you select a password for use in hiding private records and locking your Clié.

Note the warning that's included here: "If you assign a password, you must enter it to show private records." This sounds a little scary, but don't worry—none of your existing records will immediately be affected by your selection of a password. Only when you mark one as private, as we explain later, does your password enter into play.

After you tap OK, you'll be asked to verify the new password by entering it again. And you'll see another warning about what'll happen if your password is forgotten. The moral of the story is *don't forget your password!*

Tap OK again, and notice that the Password box now reads "-Assigned-".

**TIP**    *You can tap this box again at any time to change or delete your password, but you have to supply the original one first.*

Now, when you mark records as private, they become hidden from view, requiring your password to reveal them. Additionally, if you use the "Lock & Turn Off…" option (as detailed shortly), you'll need to supply your password the next time you turn on your Clié.

**SHORTCUT**    *If you tap the "abc" button in the bottom-left corner of the Graffiti area, the onscreen keyboard will appear. You can use this to enter your password!*

## The "Lost Password" Button

Oh, the perils of the forgotten password. For the last time, just don't forget yours, okay? If you do, there's a scary but effective way to reestablish access to those records you've marked as private. In Security, when you tap the "-Assigned-" button under Password, you're prompted to enter your password. You'll also see a "Lost Password" button. Tap it and your password will be deleted—and all your marked-as-private records along with it. However, those deleted records will be restored on your Clié the next time you HotSync.

### Password-Protecting Your Entire Handheld

If you really want to secure what's stored in your Clié, you need to password-protect the entire thing, not just certain records. That's where "locking" comes into play. When activated, your Clié becomes "locked" the next time it's turned off. Translation: When the Clié is turned on again, a screen pops up requiring the password (see Figure 9-2). Without it, there's no getting past that screen.

**NOTE**    *You can modify the information that appears on this "locked" startup screen by going to Prefs | Owner (see Chapter 2 for a refresher). We recommend including your name and phone number, and maybe even a reward offer—so anyone who finds your lost Clié will have an easier time returning it (and an incentive to do so). What's a good reward? Considering how much a new Clié would cost you, we think no less than $20.*

**FIGURE 9-2**   When you "lock" your Clié, only the correct password will unlock it.

# Danger, Will Robinson, Danger!

The Palm Operating System's built-in security features are far too weak for the corporate environment. Consider the password, for instance. There's no mandatory length or required combination of letters or numbers: users can actually create a password from a single character, sure to send any system administrator into heart failure.

Passwords are also easy to bypass. A free utility called No Security, for instance, can easily circumvent the Palm security application, erasing the Palm's password and exposing all of the private records on the device. It's billed as a way to recover data if you've lost your password, but the reality is that such programs make it all too easy for thieves to retrieve sensitive data on a lost, stolen, or unguarded PDA. There's no need even to HotSync the device to install the application; No Security can be beamed from another handheld.

The moral of the story? Be careful what kind of data you store on your handheld, and take extra measures to protect it if it's valuable. Read on to learn about the software and techniques you need.

## Auto Lock Handheld

Palm OS 4.0 and later (which is found in nearly every Clié model) includes several automated locking options, all of them accessible by tapping the Auto Lock Handheld button in the main Security screen. Here's a quick rundown:

- **Never**   No automatic locking.
- **On power off**   The moment you turn your handheld off (or it shuts off after a few minutes of inactivity), it locks.

■ **At a preset time**   Set the handheld to lock at an exact time. For example, if you use it a lot during the day but rarely at night, you might set it to lock at, say, 6:00 P.M. That way, you won't have to keep entering your password all day.

■ **After a preset delay**   This is our favorite option. It locks the handheld after a period of inactivity—10 minutes, 3 hours, whatever you choose.

### The "Current Privacy" Menu

We've saved the Current Privacy option (see Figure 9-1) till last because it relates to the upcoming section on hiding and masking individual records. Simply put, when the "Hide" option is selected, all records you've marked as private will disappear from view. When you select "Mask," private records are hidden but still listed. When you select "Show," which you need your password to do, private records are made visible.

## Hiding and Masking Your Records

In the four main applications—Address Book, Date Book, Memo Pad, and To Do List—any record can be marked private, meaning it suddenly becomes masked or invisible and, therefore, inaccessible. Here's how:

**1.**  Select a record (just by tapping it) in any of the aforementioned programs.

**2.**  Tap the "Details…" button. (In Address Book, you have to tap Edit to get to the screen with the "Details…" button.) You'll see a window containing some options for that record—and a box labeled Private.

**3.**  Tap that box, noticing the checkmark that appears. This indicates that the record will become private after you tap OK.

**4.**  Tap OK.

Keep in mind that just marking a record as private has no effect unless you've chosen one of the two privacy options in the Security program. If it's set to "Mask Records," records you've marked as private will turn into solid gray bars. If you choose "Hide Records," records will just plain disappear. (Don't freak out—they're still in memory, just not visible.)

## Safety First—Well, Maybe Second

**Dave**: Call me a lazy, careless person, but I just don't get into most of these security precautions. Certainly, it's way too much trouble for me to enter a password every time I turn on my Clié. That defeats the whole idea of a PDA's instant accessibility. Instead, I've compromised. I put all of my most sensitive information in a program from Chapura called Cloak; when I need a program password or a credit card number, I enter one master password to access this encrypted area of my PDA. But if I ever lose my Clié, I need to hope for the best, because there's nothing to stop someone from getting all my address, calendar, and personal info.

**Rick**: Sadly, I'm just as lazy and careless as you—but at least I haven't abandoned showers. I use a similar program—Handmark's MobileSafe—to protect my passwords, card numbers, and so forth. But I don't bother to safeguard my entire device, which is just plain foolish. So here's my New Year's resolution (never mind that it's November): to install and use a program like OnlyMe (discussed a bit later in this chapter), which even a lazy person like me can handle. The "unlock code" can be a simple series of button presses, and the lockout won't engage each and every time I turn off my handheld—only after a predetermined amount of time has elapsed.

9

## The Difference Between Masking and Hiding

The Mask Records option provides a middle ground between the visibility of "shown" records and the total invisibility of "hidden" records (which appear to have been wiped from existence—great security but awfully inconvenient). Masked records still appear in your phone list, memo pad, and so on, but appear as solid gray bars (see Figure 9-3). This remains a less-than-stellar solution, as there's still no way to know what lies beneath until you tap the record and enter your password.

**FIGURE 9-3**   When you choose Mask Records, all records marked as private are hidden by gray bars.

The Hide Records option goes a major step further, removing marked-as-private records from view altogether. To make them visible again, you must return to Security and select "Show Records." Naturally, you'll need to supply your password at this time.

## Passwords on the Desktop

Security isn't limited to the Clié itself. It also extends to Palm Desktop, working in much the same ways. Thus, you can hide certain records, or password-protect the entire program. The same password you've selected for your Clié will automatically be used in Desktop.

> **NOTE**    *Only Palm Desktop is affected by masked and hidden records. If you synchronize with Microsoft Outlook or another third-party contact manager, records marked as private on your Clié will still be visible on your PC.*

### Hidden Records

Whenever you HotSync, any records marked as private on your Clié will become hidden in Palm Desktop—and vice versa. To change whether private records are visible or not, click the View menu, then select the desired option: Hide, Mask, or Show.

### Password-Protecting Palm Desktop

Just as you can lock your Clié, so can you lock Palm Desktop. When you do, and then exit the program, your password will be required the next time it's started—by you or anyone else. Here's how to activate this setting:

1. Make sure Palm Desktop is running, then click Tools | Options....
2. In the tabbed dialog box that appears, click the Security tab.
3. Click the box labeled "Require password to access the Palm Desktop data."
4. Click OK, then exit Palm Desktop.

> **NOTE**    *This security setting applies only to your data. If multiple users are sharing Palm Desktop on a single PC, they'll need to implement password protection for their own user profiles.*

## Other Security Software

While the Palm Operating System's built-in security features are fairly comprehensive, there's always room for improvement. Hence the availability of numerous third-party security programs, which generally offer greater versatility and/or convenience. We've spotlighted some of the more intriguing solutions in the next few subsections.

### MobileSafe

Your Clié can be a handy place to store account numbers, PIN numbers, passwords and other secret codes, but stuffing them all into a memo isn't really the most practical solution. HandMark's MobileSafe, one of Rick's personal favorites, is designed expressly to organize and protect your important numbers and passwords. You just need to remember one password (different from the one used by Palm Security) to access all this neatly categorized information. MobileSafe also has a Windows-based counterpart, so you can manage and access the information on your PC.

NOTE *While Rick is a fan of MobileSafe, Dave likes Chapura's Cloak—a similar product. It's worth checking out if you're interested in this kind of security.*

9

## How to ... Keep Others from Accessing Palm Desktop

Suppose you step away from your desk for lunch or a meeting. You don't want coworkers or corporate spies poking around through your records. Fortunately, there's an easy way to password-protect Palm Desktop for Windows (alas, the Macintosh version has no security features). Just choose Tools | Options, click the Security tab, and check the box marked "Require password to access the Palm Desktop data." Now, whenever someone starts Palm Desktop, they must input the correct password (which is the one you created on your handheld) to access their data.

### OnlyMe

Like Security on steroids, OnlyMe locks your Clié automatically whenever it's turned off. Your password is entered by tapping on a special six-button keypad, or by pressing the Clié's buttons in a particular sequence, or by entering certain letters or numbers in the Graffiti area. You can even create a password that's based on sliding your stylus over the special keypad. Best of all, OnlyMe lets you set a "lock delay," so your Clié doesn't lock until after a designated period of time.

## Sign-On

Passwords can be guessed or discovered, but it's a lot harder to duplicate your signature. Communication Intelligence Corp.'s Sign-On automatically locks your Clié when it's turned off, then requires you to sign your name—right on the Clié's screen—to unlock it again. This is a great choice for those concerned about forgetting their password.

# The Find Feature

The more you use your Clié, the more data you're likely to wind up storing. And the more data you have, the harder it can be to expediently find what you're looking for. Some examples:

■  A couple days ago, you set up a meeting for a few weeks in the future, and now want to check the details of that meeting. Must you page through your calendar a day at a time to find the entry?

■  You've got dozens of memos, and need to find the ones containing the word "inventory." Must you open each memo individually?

■  You have 1500 names in your address list, and want to quickly find the record for that guy named Apu whose last name and company you can't remember. How will you locate him?

Using the Palm Operating System's built-in Find feature, you can unearth all this information in a snap. True to its name, Find sifts through your databases to ferret out exactly what you're looking for, be it a name, a number, a word, a phrase, or even just a few letters.

As we showed you in Chapter 2, Find can be found in the lower right corner of the Graffiti area, represented by a little magnifying-glass icon. Using it couldn't be simpler: Tap it (at any time, no matter what program you're running), then just write in what you want to search for (see Figure 9-4).

**NOTE**  *Capitalization doesn't matter. Even if you're looking for a proper name like "Caroline," you needn't capitalize the first letter.*

**TIP**  *If you use your stylus to highlight a word or chunk of text (done much the same way you select text using a mouse), that text will automatically appear in the Find field when you tap the Find icon.*

The search process should take no more than a few seconds, depending on how many records you've got on your Clié and the complexity of your search criteria.

FIGURE 9-4    Looking for a specific word? Just write it in the Find box and the Clié will find it for you.

## How Find Works

When you execute a search, the Palm OS looks through all stored records (except those marked as private) for whatever text you've specified, starting with whatever program you were in when you tapped the Find icon. It looks not only in the main databases—those used by Address Book, Memo Pad, and so on—but also in the databases associated with any third-party software you may have installed.

> **TIP** *If you're looking for, say, a phone number, you can save a lot of time by loading the Address Book before tapping Find. That's because Find starts its search in whatever program is currently running.*

Keep in mind that Find searches only the beginnings of words. Thus, if you look up "book," it will find "bookcase" but not "handbook." There are third-party programs that can perform much more thorough searches—we talk about some of them a little later.

> **TIP** *You can make your data a bit more "Find friendly" by using special modifiers. For instance, you might use the letters AP to preface any memo that has to do with Accounts Payable. Then, when you do a search for "AP," you'll quickly unearth all the relevant records.*

### Running a Search

After you've written the desired search text in the Find box and tapped OK, the Clié will get to work. You'll see items appear in a categorized list as they're found. If you see what you're looking for, you can halt the search immediately by tapping the Stop button. Then, simply tap the item to bring up the corresponding record in the respective program.

If the Clié finds more instances of the desired item than can fit on the screen at once, it will stop the search until you tap the Find More button. This essentially tells it to look up another screen's worth of records. There's no way to return to the previous screen, so make sure you definitely need to keep searching before tapping Find More. (You can always run the search again, but that's a hassle.)

## Third-Party Search Programs

Many users discover that Find isn't nearly as robust as it could be. If you want to maximize the search potential of your Clié, one of the following third-party programs might be in order. They're a little on the advanced side, meaning they require the program X-Master (which we talk about in Chapter 14). That doesn't mean you should shy away from them, just that they might prove a little more complicated to install and operate.

### FindHack

The Rolls Royce of search programs, Florent Pillet's FindHack lets you specify whether to search all the installed applications, just the main applications, or only the current application. It also remembers the last six searches you ran, lets you preconfigure up to four "permanent" searches, and supports the use of wildcards. Best of all, it's faster than Find.

### Find Ignore Hack

This simple Hack lets you select applications that should *not* be searched during the Find process. Why would you want to do this? E-books are a great example: if you have a few of them loaded on your Clié, they can slow a search considerably. With Find Ignore Hack, you could exclude your e-book viewer.

### PopUp Find

One problem with Find is that it forces you to leave the application you're currently working in (when you open the "found" record). Bozidar Benc's PopUp Find puts the data into a pop-up window, thus allowing you to stay in your current program. It has viewers for the four main applications, and can transfer you to any of those programs with the tap of a button.

# The Calculator

What's an electronic organizer without a calculator? Not much, so let's take a quick peek at the Clié's. Activated by tapping the icon in the upper-right corner of the Graffiti area, Calculator operates like any other (see Figure 9-5). In fact, it's so self-explanatory that we're not going to insult your intelligence by explaining how to use it.

There are, of course, one or two features we feel obligated to point out. First, you can use the standard Palm OS copy option to paste the result of any calculation into another program. Second, you can review your last few calculations by tapping Menu | Options | Recent Calculations.

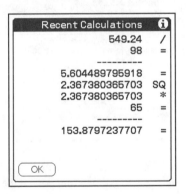

 *Calc's buttons are large enough that you can tap them with a fingernail, so save time by leaving the stylus in its silo. Just keep in mind that oil and dirt from your fingers will grubby-up the screen.*

## Third-Party Calculators

Whether you're a student, realtor, banker or NASA engineer, there's no debating the value of a good scientific and/or programmable calculator. Your Clié has ample processing power to fill this role, and the proof is in the dozens of third-party calculators currently available. Let's take a look at some of the best and brightest.

The Clié calculator functions like every other calculator you've ever used.

## FCPlus Professional and the powerOne Series

Aimed at financial, real estate, and retail professionals, Infinity Softworks' FCPlus Professional is one of the most sophisticated calculators around. It offers more than 400 built-in business, math, finance, and statistics functions, and includes memory worksheets for keeping track of various computations. If anything, FCPlus Professional might be overkill, but if you need this kind of power, you'll love the program.

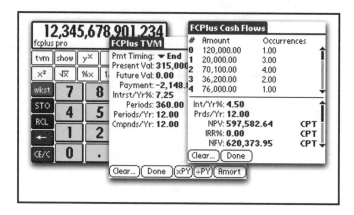

Infinity Softworks also offers a series of task-specific calculators: powerOne Finance, powerOne Graph, and powerOne Scientific. Don't be surprised to find powerOne Personal bundled with your Clié—it comes with most models.

## SynCalc

A fully algebraic calculator, Synergy Solutions' SynCalc offers a unique plug-in architecture that allows new functionality to be added. As it stands, SynCalc is already plenty powerful, with algebraic parsing of expressions, a full suite of trigonometric and logarithmic functions, and support for up to 100 macros that simplify the execution of complex calculations.

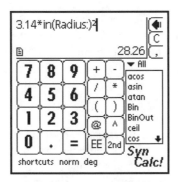

# The Mail Program

An underrated member of the Clié's supporting cast of characters—er, programs—is Mail. We're going to teach you to use it in Chapter 11, but a brief bit of explanation is in order now. Specifically, Mail allows you to read, compose, and send e-mail, but not in the traditional sense. That is, Mail is not capable of connecting to your Internet service provider via a Clié modem and conducting e-mail transactions. Rather, it merely synchronizes with your desktop e-mail program, such as Eudora or Outlook Express, absorbing copies of messages you've received and transferring outgoing messages you've written.

In practical terms, this means your Clié serves as a kind of portable e-mail viewer. Here's an example: In the morning, before heading off to work or the airport, you HotSync with your PC. All the e-mail messages you received the night before are transferred to your Clié. Throughout the day, you read through those messages, and reply to those that require it. You can even compose new messages if the need arises. Later, when you return home, you HotSync once again, and all the outgoing messages are transferred to your desktop e-mail program and then sent.

9

*If you own a Clié modem, you can HotSync from the road, but even this doesn't allow for real-time e-mail transactions. For that you need a program like Clié Mail, which comes bundled with certain models. Find out more about it—and third-party e-mail programs—in Chapter 11.*

# All about Expense

Expense is an often-overlooked but decidedly valuable addition to the Clié software arsenal. With it, you can track and manage all your expenses and mileage, whether for personal reconciliation or reimbursement from your company or clients. While a bit on the rudimentary side, Expense does afford quick and easy item entry and push-button synchronization with Microsoft Excel. Ultimately, it can create detailed and attractive-looking expense reports that are ready to print.

 *For whatever reason, Sony chose not to include Expense with latter-day models like the Clié NR70 and SJ20. If your model doesn't have it, skip ahead to the section "Alternatives to Expense." As you may have guessed by now, there are third-party applications for just about everything.*

Put simply, Expense is like an electronic folder for your receipts, and a logbook for your mileage. Whenever you buy something, you simply add it to your expense list. Whenever you take a business-related road trip, you do the same. On the Clié side, using Expense is a piece of cake. (Using it with Palm Desktop is even easier, but we get to that in the section "From Expense to Excel.")

## Creating New Expense Items

Adding new expense records is a snap. Here's the basic process:

1. Tap "New" to create a blank expense item. You see a line appear with the date, the words "-Expense type-", and a blank field next to a dollar sign. Note that your cursor appears in that field.

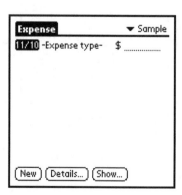

**2.** Write in the amount of the purchase or, if you're recording mileage, the number of miles driven.

**3.** Now tap the words "-Expense type-" to see a predefined list of expense categories, and choose the one that most closely matches your purchase. If you're recording mileage, select that option, noticing that the dollar sign changes to the abbreviation "mi."

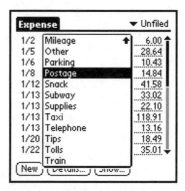

**NOTE**   *Unlike most lists that appear in Palm OS applications, the Expense list cannot be modified or expanded. In short, you're stuck with the categories provided. If you can't find one that fits the situation, there's always the "other" category.*

**4.** By default, any new expense is created with the current date. If, however, you're catching up on previous purchases, you can tap right on the date that's shown to bring up the calendar and select whatever date is appropriate.

There, wasn't that easy? You've just recorded a new expense. Now let's talk about recording the more specific details of that expense.

**TIP**   *You can save yourself a step when you create a new expense by not tapping the "New" button first. Instead, just start writing the dollar amount in the numeric portion of the Graffiti area. A new expense item is instantly created. This same practice also works in Date Book, Memo Pad, and To Do List.*

## Modifying Expense Details

Obviously, any expense report worth its salt needs to have more than just the date, expense type, and amount. As you've probably guessed, your next stop after entering these tidbits is the "Details…" button.

**NOTE**   *Before tapping it, make sure you select the expense item you want to modify. You know when an item is selected because the date is highlighted and a cursor appears in the "amount" field.*

The Receipt Details screen (see Figure 9-6) lets you specify the minutiae of your purchase, from the category to which it belongs to the type of currency used to the city in which it took place.

## From Expense to Excel

One key difference between Expense and most of the other core Clié programs is that the data you enter isn't replicated—or even accessible—in Palm Desktop. Certainly the data is transferred to your PC when you HotSync and backed up in a folder on your hard drive, but as for turning those raw numbers into an actual printed expense report, we've got good news and bad news.

The good news is it's a one-step procedure. In Palm Desktop for Windows, you simply click the Expense button on the toolbar. The bad news is you must have Microsoft Excel installed on your computer because the Expense data shoots directly into an Excel spreadsheet—and can't go anywhere else. (Okay, it's bad news only if you're not an Excel user.)

## Alternatives to Expense

Truth be told, Expense isn't the most robust expense-management program—especially relative to some of the software created by third-party developers. If your needs extend beyond what Expense has to offer—and for business people who rely heavily on reimbursement reports, and they probably do—you should definitely check out one of the many available alternatives.

We've spotlighted some of the major programs, but keep in mind these are designed for expense tracking only. There are other programs that manage billing as well as expenses, and that let you track your bank accounts and stock portfolios. (We talk about those in Chapter 14.) So don't be discouraged if none of these packages fit your particular bill. Chances are good there's a program out there that will.

**FIGURE 9-6**  You can record any or all of the crucial details of your expense in the Receipt Details screen.

## ExpensePlus

One of the most robust and versatile expense managers available, WalletWare's *ExpensePlus* uses an icon-based interface to simplify the selection of expense types, and automation to fill in dates and amounts for things like hotel stays and car rentals. More importantly, it can link directly to any existing company expense forms created in Excel or FileMaker (including the Mac versions), so you needn't contend with nonstandard forms. And, if your company's forms aren't based in Excel, WalletWare can design a custom link (for a fee) to other software programs.

## ExpensAble

*ExpensAble* began as a PC application and has migrated to the Palm OS. LandWare's software makes it a snap to record reimbursable, nonreimbursable, and personal expenses, and it supports split transactions. Also present is the ever-popular *AutoFill* feature, a Quicken staple that simplifies repetitive data entry.

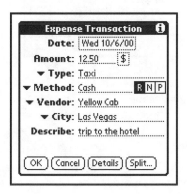

Naturally, the Palm version of ExpensAble integrates seamlessly with the computer version, the latter offering report submission via e-mail or the ExpensAble web site.

# All the Other Goodies that Came with Your CLIÉ

While writing this book, Sony kept us on our toes by changing and expanding the roster of applications that come bundled with the various models. The model you have now might lack some of the programs listed in this section, or it might have others that aren't listed here at all. Fortunately, the documentation that Sony provided should have all the information you need to learn the basics. In the meantime, here's an overview of the most common bundled applications, and leads to where in the book you can learn more about them.

- **gMovie** With gMovie, you can view video clips right on your Clié. The Sony software CD includes a few samples, which you have to manually install (see Chapter 4) in order to view. Find out more about Clié movies in Chapter 17.

- **Memory Stick Autorun** Memory Sticks are a kind of removable storage media that can hold extra applications, data, and even a backup of your Clié. Normally, when you insert a Stick into the handheld, all that happens is you get access to its contents. However, it's possible to automatically run a program stored on the card, and that's where MS Autorun comes in. Tap the MS Autorun icon, then choose which application (or database) you want to run the next time you insert the Stick.

- **Memory Stick Backup** As discussed in Chapter 2, you can create a backup of your entire Clié, storing all the applications and data on a Memory Stick card. With MS Backup, all it takes is a tap to start the process, and to restore everything if the need arises. Find out more in Chapter 22.

- **Memory Stick Gate** The Palm OS lets you copy files to and from Memory Sticks, but it's a wimp compared to MS Gate. With this utility, you can not only copy files, but also move and delete them. Yep, you guessed it: see Chapter 22 for more details.

- **Memory Stick Import**   As you learned in Chapter 4, you can install applications and other files directly to a Memory Stick using the Palm OS Install Tool. However, when you have big stuff like photos and MP3 files, it would take forever to HotSync them. MS Import, when used in conjunction with MS Export (a Windows utility), turns your Clié into another drive that's accessible from within Windows. This makes it faster and easier to move, copy, delete, and organize Memory Stick data. Pop back to Chapter 4 for a refresher.

- **PictureGear Pocket**   This is an image viewer that lets you view photos transferred from your PC or a digital camera, or see those taken with the NR70V's built-in camera or Sony's Memory Stick Camera. The full scoop can be found in Chapter 16.

- **PhotoStand**   If you're like us, your Clié probably spends a fair amount of time sitting on your desk in its cradle. Why not put the screen to good use? PhotoStand turns it into a kind of digital picture frame, running a constant slideshow of photos stored in PictureGear Pocket. See Chapter 16 if you're intrigued.

## Where to Find It

| Web Site | Address | What's There |
|---|---|---|
| Handmark | www.handmark.com | MobileSafe |
| Chapura | www.chapura.com | Cloak |
| Tranzoa | www.tranzoa.com | OnlyMe |
| CIC | www.cic.com | Sign-On |
| Florent Pillet | perso.wanadoo.fr/fpillet/ | FindHack |
| PalmGear | www.palmgear.com | Find Ignore Hack |
| Benc Software | www.benc.hr | PopUp Find |
| Infinity Softworks | www.infinitysw.com | FC Plus Professional, powerOne series |
| Synergy Solutions | www.synsolutions.com | Launch 'Em, SynCalc |
| WalletWare | www.walletware.com | ExpensePlus |
| LandWare | www.landware.com | ExpensAble |

# Chapter 10 Going on a Trip

## How to…

- Organize your Clié's categories and data for travel
- Pack smartly so you're prepared for trouble
- Make sure your Clié doesn't run out of power during the trip
- Prepare for HotSync opportunities away from home
- Enhance the core applications for life on the road
- View your coworkers' Date Book entries on your own Clié
- Load your Clié with essential travel phone numbers
- Use the Clié as an alarm clock
- Use the Clié as a subway map
- Communicate in a foreign language with your Clié
- Use your Clié as a compass
- Get star charts on your Clié

Some people find their Clié so useful that—imagine this—they put it in their pocket and take it on trips away from the home and office! Daring, we know, but it's well-prepared for these kinds of "away missions." Its batteries mean you needn't plug it in, and because it synchronizes with your desktop PC, you can bring important information with you wherever you go. The Clié even has a built-in clock in case you forget your watch. What could be better?

Seriously, we know you already carry your Clié around town. But, if you plan to take it on an extended trip, you might want to read this chapter. We have all kinds of suggestions for how to prepare your Clié for a grueling business trip, as well as what kind of software you might need to make the trip a little smoother. And how about camping? Your Clié might not be the first accessory that springs to mind when you consider roughing it in the Rocky Mountains, but your trusty little handheld has a lot to offer in the wilderness, too.

# Preparing Your CLIÉ for the Road

When we go on a business trip, it's usually such absolute pandemonium—running around at the last minute, throwing power cords and HotSync cables in the travel bag—it's a wonder we ever make it to the airport in time. Because of our experiences with forgetting data, bringing dead batteries, and being unable to connect to the Internet in strange cites, we offer the following checklist to you for bringing your Clié on trips.

## Setting Up Your Data

Make sure your Clié is ready for the details of your upcoming trip. Specifically, consider the kinds of data you need to create while you're on the road and prepare your Clié ahead of time. Here's how you can make sure you're ready:

1. In the To Do List, create a trip checklist and enter everything you need to do before you leave, plus what you need to bring with you. If you have a comprehensive checklist, you're less likely to forget something important before you go.

*You probably don't want to build your travel list from scratch each time. One solution is to create a comprehensive list of travel tasks and leave it in the Memo Pad. You can copy the entire memo and paste it into a new memo before a trip, and then erase individual lines as you complete them. The master list is still safely stored in a different memo entry.*

2. Create a new category in which you can store data related to your trip. If you're going to Chicago for a convention, for instance, create a category on the Address Book, the To Do List, and the Memo Pad called Chicago. (If you want to call it something else, that's okay too.) By using a special category on the road, you can find data related to your trip more quickly—both during the trip and after you return home. When you get back, you can recategorize the data any way you like.

3. Enter your itinerary in the Date Book. If you're flying, enter each flight's number, departure, and arrival time in your Clié so it's available when you need it. An easy way to do this is to enter the flight number in the Date Book at the scheduled departure time, and note the arrival time there as well. That way, you can check your Clié in flight to see how much longer you have to grit your teeth and eat cashews (warning: may contain peanuts). You might even want to try a travel-specific alternative like TravelTracker—check it out later in this chapter in "Itinerary Tracking." Here, you can see an itinerary in DateBk5, complete with icons to identify the kind of activities:

10

TIP *You can block out the dates of your trip on the Clié using an untimed event. The trip appears at the top of the Date Book and still lets you schedule actual appointments during those days.*

## Having a Backup Plan

Call us Luddites, but we don't like to rely 100 percent on a fragile piece of electronic gizmotry (and yes, that's a word. Don't look it up, just trust us.) What if you drop your Clié in the airport and it shatters on the nice marble floor? You'd better have a Plan B.

**Dave:** For me, the most important document to have access to on a trip is my flight itinerary. I always buy e-tickets—so I have no written record of my flight—and then I enter the flight information in my Clié. But, to be on the safe side, I also print a copy of my flight info and stick it in the back of my bag somewhere. That way, if my batteries die before I finish the trip or my Clié falls out of a five-story window, I can always refer to the piece of paper and get myself home.

**Rick:** For once I have to agree with Dave (despite the physical pain involved). I also recommend buying a Memory Stick. With just a few stylus taps, you can back up the complete contents of your handheld's memory. Then, in the event some catastrophe leaves you with a wiped handheld (it's been known to happen), you can restore everything in a matter of minutes. Well worth the money you'll spend for a memory card. See Chapter 13 for details on making backups on Memory Sticks, and Chapter 22 for information on where and what to buy.

# How to ... Get Your Hardware Ready

When you leave on a trip, you should make sure your Clié is fully prepared to go the distance. There's nothing like being a thousand miles from home and remembering you forgot to bring some data from your desktop PC, or discovering you forgot an important cable.

To save yourself from calamity, remember these tips:

1. Always bring a stylus with a reset pin. Every Clié we've used includes a reset pin in the stylus—just unscrew the tail end to get to it. If you don't have one, bring a paperclip or a thin pin instead. And test the pin before you go! Rick once traveled with a paperclip too thick to fit in the hole. D'oh! Bottom line: There's nothing worse than having your Clié crash when you're away from home and discovering you have nothing small enough to fit into the reset hole.

2. Perform a HotSync right before you leave. This way, you're sure to have the latest info on your Clié, and you also have a current backup in case something unfortunate happens to your trusty handheld while you're away.

3. Do you plan to do a lot of typing? If so, pack a keyboard for the Clié. You have several options to choose, from Sony's own fold-up Clié Compact Keyboard (also known as the Stowaway when sold by Think Outside) to the totally wireless Pocketop keyboard. See Chapter 23 for more details.

4. Be prepared to restore. Call us paranoid, but... hey, wait a minute, did you just call us paranoid? Sheesh, the nerve... Anyway, if your Clié should lose all its data for some reason, you might want the capability to restore it while you're on the go. The easiest solution? Get a Memory Stick and use the MS Backup program that's found on every Clié. Back up right before you walk out the door, and then daily while you're on the road so you won't lose much if the unthinkable happens.

10

## Real-Life Tragedy

Last year, Dave spent a week in sunny Florida in the dead of winter to see a photography trade show and do a bit of scuba diving. At the time, he was still using a Visor Prism that, like the Clié, also uses the Palm OS. While there, his trusty Visor Prism held all his data—contact info, schedules, even flight information for the return trip. Thanks to quirky hardware, two days into the trip, the PDA performed a hard reset, erasing all the data on the device.

"I had thrown caution to the wind," Dave reports. "I thought I could trust my Prism, and I had no backup of any kind—no laptop, no backup module, not even a printout of my schedule."

In fact, Dave had to call home repeatedly to be updated on his daily schedule and to know what time to show up to the airport at the end of the trip. He reports that he plans to follow his own advice in the future.

## Staying Powered

A dead Clié is no good to anyone. Take these steps to keep it working while you're away:

- Be power-smart. The vast majority of Clié models use rechargeable batteries, so you should top off your Clié right before you leave and bring some sort of charging solution with you. There are many options, from Electric Fuel's Instant Power system (available for some Clié models) to Sony's own Battery Adapter (which charges the PDA via a set of AA batteries). Sony also sells AC adapters and car chargers. Therefore, there's no excuse to run out of power, even if you're traveling for a week or two.

- If your Clié takes replaceable batteries, change them before you go. If you're going to be away for a week or more, bring a spare set of batteries with you—better safe than sorry. If you generally leave a spare set of batteries in your travel case, score ten points for preparedness. But use a battery tester before each trip to make sure your backup batteries are still in good shape.

- Remember to bring batteries for any accessories you might have. You might even want to add the batteries to your travel checklist so nothing gets overlooked.

## HotSyncing on the Go

You don't have to be satisfied with the last HotSync you performed at home before you jumped on a plane, of course. You can perform a remote HotSync to connect to your desktop PC from anywhere, or you can use the Clié's capability to perform an IR HotSync to connect your Clié to a laptop PC while you're on the go. Few people use these capabilities, but they're worth considering. Remember:

- If you plan to perform a Remote HotSync (see the Clié manual for details), be sure to test your connection before leaving home. You can never anticipate everything that might go wrong with a modem connection, but you can at least verify the system works before you leave.

- Check with your hotel concierge to see if the phone lines in your room are PBX or analog. PBX lines can damage your Clié's modem, so don't experiment with a connection unless you know for sure.

TIP    *If your room phone has a "data port" built in, the room is modem friendly and you needn't check with the front desk.*

- If you plan to perform either a Remote or an IR HotSync, perform a normal Local HotSync using the cradle first. Also, don't forget to turn your PC on before you go and leave it ready to receive incoming calls.

*Check what the room charge will be for each call. It can be as much as a dollar per call just to dial the phone, so those communication charges can add up.*

# Road Tips

We've done our share of traveling, and we've amassed a few handy tips for making the best use of your Clié on the road. Not all of these suggestions will appeal to you, but you're sure to find a few things to make your next trip a little more enjoyable.

- If you're in a different time zone, reset the time on your Clié. Otherwise, all your appointment alarms will sound at the wrong time and you'll show up late everywhere you need to be. To change the time, tap the Prefs application and choose the Time & Date page. Tap the Set Time Zone box and set it to your new location. The time will automatically update for you.

- Your Clié may set off the metal detector at the airport. To save yourself time and hassle, go ahead and pop it into one of those little trays, along with all your change, *Sliders*-style alternate universe teleporter, roll of aluminum foil, and other personal items, right at the outset when you go through a metal detector.

- The Clié is considered a "portable electronic device" and you shouldn't use it at the beginning or end of a flight. You probably already knew that, but your Clié can get you in trouble anyway if you're not careful. Specifically, don't enable any alarms for the start or end of the flight, or your Clié will come to life and start beeping during verboten moments.

- If you need to print something stored on your Clié while you're on your trip, there are several ways to do it. The easiest is to get a print driver for your Clié like PalmPrint, PrintBoy Anywhere, or IS/Print. If you do a lot of printing, get a portable printer and carry it with you. If you can get to a printer, but it isn't IR-capable, you still have options. The best solution? Carry the PrintBoy InfraReady Adapter from Bachmann Software. This is a little device that fits in your pocket (or travel bag) and plugs into the parallel port of any printer. Its infrared port lets you instantly convert any printer into an IR-ready printer for your Clié. When you're finished printing, remove the adapter and put it back in your travel bag. It's a very cool solution for printing anything anywhere you can find a printer when you travel. As a last resort, you might install a fax program like Mark/Space Fax. Equipped with a modem, you can fax to your hotel's front desk, and then pick up the printout.

# Software to Bring Along

Don't rely on the software that comes with your Clié to get you through extended trips away from home. Most of the software we discuss in this next section is available from **PalmGear.com**. Experiment and see what applications are useful.

 *Don't install a new application as you're walking out the door to go to the airport. Some applications might cause your Clié to misbehave. Others can change the way your Clié functions or make it hard to access data you've already created. You don't need to discover those kinds of things on an airplane bound for Topeka. Bottom line: install and experiment with new software well in advance of a trip.*

## Address and Date Book Enhancements

Sure, you love the Address Book and Date Book. But, by enhancing these core applications, you might find you can significantly improve the way you work when away from home.

### Synchronizing with the Web

Believe it or not, you can synchronize your Clié's Date Book and Address Book with web-based information managers. Why would you want to do that? Well, when you're on the road, you might want to access your schedule and contacts from a PC that isn't yours. And, if you can get to any web-enabled PC, you can log on to a Web-based calendar and address book. Here are some cool reasons to try this:

- Send e-mail from a Web-based e-mail system using contact information culled from your Clié.
- Add calendar appointments on the PC and synchronize it to the Clié later.
- If something happens to your Clié on a trip, access all your data from a PC that's connected to the Internet.

**Yahoo.com** offers the best synchronization support on the Internet. By installing a small utility on your home or office-based PC, you can sync the Clié's Date Book, Address Book, and To Do List with equivalent applications on the Yahoo! site. Because Yahoo! also offers free e-mail, you can use the Address Book to send messages without reentering any data.

## Sharing Your Appointments

Let's say you're meeting with coworkers at a trade show to review the newest, most innovative garden hoses. If your associates are as busy as you plan to be, how can you reconcile your schedules to meet for lunch? Or, if you're a little more business-minded, how can you find out where everyone is during the day and schedule meetings everybody can attend?

One solution is to use WeSync (see Figure 10-1). This web-based calendaring and contact tool lets you sync your Clié data with a Web-based information manager and share it with coworkers. The best part is WeSync takes the form of a new Date Book–style application on your Clié that can display multiple schedules side by side. So, you can visually evaluate free and busy times on two schedules on the same screen.

To try out WeSync, visit **www.wesync.com** and install the WeSync application. After you and at least one other person are using the application, you can share your calendar in this way:

**1.** Start by creating a private community. Visit the WeSync web site and log on with the username you selected. Then click Create A New Community.

**2.** Give the community a name and description, and then enter your username as the Member/Administrator Name. Now, click Create Community. After that, you should be in the My Community tab.

**3.** Click Manage Community, and then click Invite New Members. Enter the e-mail and username of the person you want to invite, then click Invite.

**4.** Now it's time to share your calendar with this private community. Start the WeSync Desktop Viewer and choose Edit | Calendar Manager from the menu. You should see the WeSync Calendar Manager dialog box.

**5.** Select your calendar (it should currently be configured as Local). Click the Published button, then click and Close.

**6.** HotSync your Clié. Your calendar will be transferred to the web calendar, ready to be shared with others.

**FIGURE 10-1**    WeSync lets you share your Clié data with others via the Internet.

After this setup process, any time you change your calendar, the data is updated on the WeSync web site at the next HotSync, and then updated on all the shared Cliés. Of course, if you're invited to join a community, as in Step 3, you need to accept the invitation before you can see a shared calendar. To join, click the Your Invitations link on the web site and place a check mark next to the community you've been invited to join.

To see calendars side by side on your Clié, start the wsCalendar application and choose +Cal | Calendar Manager from the menu. Check all the calendar entries you want to see onscreen at once, and then click OK.

### Getting Rental Car Phone Numbers

The Clié can hold lots of phone numbers, so why not take advantage of this? Several databases of phone numbers exist to services like rental car companies, airlines, and hotels. If you travel frequently, you probably want to try one of them:

| Application | Data Included |
| --- | --- |
| Travel Telephone Numbers | A smaller list (about 100) of the most popular hotels, car rentals, and airlines |
| Rental Car 800# | A database of rental car phone numbers in MobileDB format |
| Palm Rent-a-Car | List of rental car companies and their 800 numbers |

*These applications are all available from **www.palmgear.com**.*

## Itinerary Tracking

While you can certainly store your itinerary information in the Date Book, using a specialized program is more efficient for many people. There are many applications at a site like PalmGear that fit the bill. Some of our favorites include TravelTracker and Travel Pal, both shown next.

# The Ultimate Alarm Clock

You can set alarms with the Clié, but the somewhat-anemic alarm system built into the Date Book isn't terribly useful in a lot of situations. Instead, you should download a copy of BigClock (see Figure 10-2). This free application displays the time, and has a timer and four independent alarms. It also lets you easily change time zones.

BigClock's alarm is good enough to serve as your morning alarm clock, either on its own or as a safety backup to a hotel wake-up call. To use BigClock's alarm function, follow these steps:

**1.**   Start BigClock and tap on the Alarm tab at the bottom of the screen. You have four different alarms available. We'll set Alarm 1.

**2.**   Highlight the Alarm 1 title at the top of the screen and rename it "**Wake Up.**"

**3.**   Set the time you want to wake up. Tap the top half of a number to increase its value, tap the bottom half to decrease it. Do this for both minutes and hours.

**4.**   Make sure the A.M./P.M. indicator is set to A.M. for your morning alarm. Tap it to switch between the two.

**5.**   Tap the day or days you want the alarm. If the day is highlighted in black, it's selected.

**6.**   To enable the alarm, tap the large check box to the left. The alarm will now trigger at the designated time.

You should test your alarm before trusting it to get you out of bed the next morning. Specifically, be sure you haven't disabled system sounds in the Clié's Prefs application. If you did, then you'll never hear the alarm. Also, you want to be sure you remembered to set the alarm up for the right day of the week and the right half of the day.

## Other Clocks

There are quite a few timekeeping applications available for the Clié, so you might want to check out some of these others to see which you like the best:

- **WorldMate**   This cool program lets you compare four world clocks to your local time. It also synchronizes the Clié with an online atomic clock at each HotSync, retrieves weather forecasts, and includes a currency converter.

- **CityTime**   We like the gorgeous color display that graphically shows the day/night line as it moves across the globe. CityTime displays four world clocks and lets you change your location and time easily without entering the Prefs application.

- **Time 2.0**   For those who want a simpler, calendar-based view, Time 2.0 shows the time and a calendar along with a second time zone and upcoming appointments.

# Finding Your Way Around

Many Clié tools can help you find your way around in a strange place. In fact, Sony sells a Memory Stick–mounted GPS receiver that lets you navigate via satellite, but alas, it's only available in Japan right now. Most people need more mundane assistance, though, so we've collected a few interesting navigation aids for you here.

## Getting Metro and Subway Routes

Do subway routes leave you scratching your head? Those maps they put in the train stops aren't exactly intuitive, and finding the best route from one end of Paris to the other can be a nerve-wracking experience. That's why you should install Metro, a free utility that calculates the best

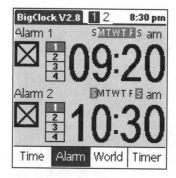

FIGURE 10-2    BigClock has multiple alarms and time zones—the perfect companion for life on the road.

route between any two stations in over 100 cities. The application comes with database files for cities like New York, London, Paris, Chicago, and Hong Kong, and you only need to install the files for cities you're visiting.

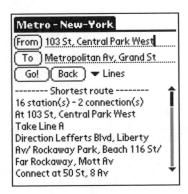

Many other travel guides specific to certain cities exist. Try some of these:

| Region | Service | Program Name |
| --- | --- | --- |
| 200 cities worldwide | Computes shortest route between any two subway stations | MetrO |
| Montreal | Map of the subway system | Montreal Subway Map |
| Moscow | Metro guide to the city of Moscow, including maps | TealInfo Moscow Metro Guide |
| New York | Enter a Manhattan address and program provides the nearest cross street | X-Man |
| Paris | Metro paths between monuments, museums, and stations | Paris |
| Southern California | MetroLink schedule | MetroLink |

## Language Translators

In the past, traveling abroad often resulted in serious communication difficulties. Do you know how to ask for the bathroom in French? If not, try one of these applications:

- **Small Talk**  This program is a real-time, two-way translator. Hold the Clié up to the person you want to communicate with. Small Talk presents you with complete sentences organized into situation-based categories such as Basics, Lodging, Emergency, Food, and Entertainment. Select a phrase in English and it's translated into the target language, as you can see in Figure 10-3. The person you are communicating with can then select a response from a menu, which is translated back into English. Small Talk supports French, Italian, Spanish, German, and Japanese.

10

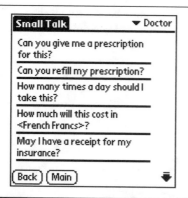 

**FIGURE 10-3** Choose a phrase from a list, divided by topic (left), and your associate can choose a response (right) that is translated back into English for you.

- **TourMate** Available in several versions (including English-Spanish, English-Italian, English-French, and English-German), *TourMate* is easy to use. Choose a common greeting, expression, or question in English, and read the phonetically spelled foreign-language equivalent expression to the person with whom you're trying to communicate.

- **Translate** This application enables you to enter a word and instantly translate it among 18 languages. The translator works in both directions, so you can go from English to Italian or Italian to English, for instance.

## Unit Conversions

If you're an American in Europe, you need to contend with an alien set of measurements. Not only is the currency different, but even the length, weight, and volume of common items are unusual. Heck, unless you're a scientist or an engineer, you may not know if 40 degrees Celsius is hot or cold. Try Conversions (see Figure 10-4), a calculator utility that lets you instantly make conversions among measurements like currency, temperature, length, area, and volume.

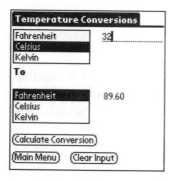

**FIGURE 10-4** Conversions makes it easy for an American to get by in a metric world.

# Wilderness Survival Tools

It's not surprising to walk into a fancy hotel and see a dozen executives standing around in fancy suits, checking their schedules via the Cliés. But how often do you go camping in the middle of the woods and see people bring their PDAs? Not that often, we're willing to bet. And that's too bad, because the Clié is a handy survival tool. It does almost everything, except open cans of beans or start campfires.

## Using Your CLIÉ as a Compass

While we're quite sure you know a Clié won't open a can of beans, we suspect you wouldn't believe it could be a compass, either. But you'd be wrong. Using a program like Sun Compass, you can get an immediate onscreen indication of north any time, anywhere (during daylight hours).

Unfortunately, Sun Compass comes with virtually no documentation, which may make it confusing for new users. To use Sun Compass, all you need to do is input a few pieces of information:

- **Tz** This is the time zone you are in currently. Time zones are calculated from –12 to 0, and then on up to +12. Your time zone value is simply the number of hours away from Greenwich, England (home of Greenwich Mean Time) you are located. GMT is a time zone of 0. New York is –5, and California is –8. You can find a complete list of time zones in Windows by opening the Date/Time Properties dialog box (in the Control Panel) and looking on the Time Zone tab.

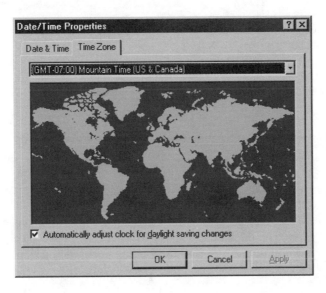

- **La**    Enter your latitude. Latitude is measured from 0 degrees (the equator) to 90N and 90S.
- **Lo**    Enter your longitude. Longitude is commonly measured from 0 (at the longitude line that cuts through Greenwich, England) to 180E and 180W.

**TIP**    *Looking for your latitude and longitude? Visit **www.census.gov/cgi-bin/gazetteer**. Enter your city or ZIP code to find out your lat/long.*

- **DSI**    DSI stands for daylight savings time, and it needs to be set either on or off, depending on the time of year. Daylight savings time is used between the first Sunday in April and the last Sunday in October.

**TIP**    *A few locations in the United States don't observe daylight savings time at all. These include Arizona, Hawaii, and parts of Indiana.*

Once you enter these values, point the front of your Clié at the sun (keep the Clié level with the ground) and the compass indicates which way is north. That's all there is to it!

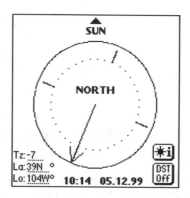

## Did you know?

## The CLIÉ Can Be A GPS Receiver

Sony sells a GPS Memory Stick that uses a constellation of navigation satellites called GPS to show your exact position on the earth. Using the GPS Memory Stick, you can see your position on a map and follow turn-by-turn directions to reach a new destination. Unfortunately, Sony has only released this gadget in Japan. Someday, hopefully, it'll appear in the U.S. and we can navigate with our Cliés as well.

## Finding Stars

You can also use Sun Compass to find the North Star. Choose Misc | Polarstar from the menu and you see a dark screen with the Big and Little Dipper constellations. By aligning them with what you see in the sky, you can find the North Star, and thus get a northerly orientation even at night.

That's great, but you can also use your Clié for some real star gazing. Here are a few programs you can try the next time you're far away from city lights with your Clié:

- ■ **Planetarium**   This program calculates the position of the sun, the moon, the planets, and over 1,500 of the brightest stars and deep sky objects in the sky. You can enter any location and any time period—you needn't use the present system clock. In addition to using this program for stargazing, it can also be used as a compass when the sun or moon is visible (much like Sun Compass).

- ■ **Star Pilot**   This program lets you specify your location, and then see the planets, moon, and 500 stars in a compact star map. You can identify objects by clicking them and searching for celestial objects by name.

## Reading Late at Night

When all of your tent buddies are trying to sleep while wondering if that odd sound is an approaching bear, you can relax in your sleeping bag and read a good book—with your Clié. The Clié's efficient backlighting makes it easy to read both in total darkness and in bright sunlight. What you need is a document reader. While you can see Chapter 21 for details on electronic books and document readers, we think it's worth pointing out right now that there's nothing like curling up with a good e-book on a camping trip. You can store lots of reading on one Clié, so you can travel light and still have a lot of things to read on those quiet, lonely nights.

## Where to Find It

| Web Site | Address | What's There |
|---|---|---|
| Electric Fuel | www.instant-power.com | Instant Power Charger |
| BigClock site | www.gacel.de/palmpilot.htm | BigClock |
| Mark/Space | www.markspace.com | Mark/Space Fax |
| Stevens Creek Software | www.stevenscreek.com | PalmPrint |
| Bachmann Software | www.bachmannsoftware.com | PrintBoy |
| IS/Complete | www.iscomplete.com | IS/Print |
| Yahoo! | www.yahoo.com | Web-based information management that HotSyncs to the Palm |
| WeSync.com | www.wesync.com | Side-by-side calendaring |
| SilverWare | www.silverware.com | TravelTracker |
| LandWare | www.landware.com | Small Talk |

**10**

# Chapter 11

## CLIÉ Communications

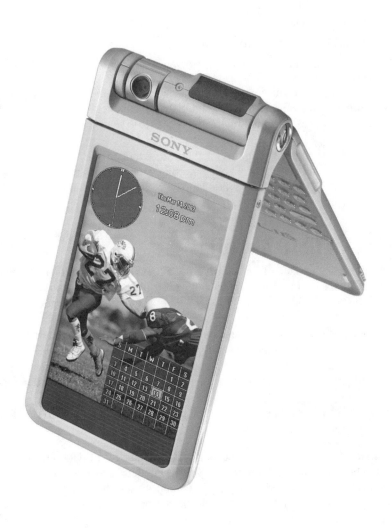

## How to...

- Send and receive e-mail with your Clié
- Connect your cell phone to your handheld
- Configure your handheld for Web and e-mail access
- Work with the Palm Mail program
- Use the Clié Mail program
- Send sketches and drawings with RiteMail
- Access America Online
- Use AvantGo to take the Web with you
- Wirelessly connect an NX-series Clié to your LAN

Someday, probably in the very near future, you'll be able to buy a Clié that doubles as a cell phone or wireless communicator. Several other Palm OS–based handheld devices do that already. In the meantime, surely there must be some way to use your Clié to send and receive e-mail, maybe even surf the Web?

In fact, there are several ways. In this chapter, we introduce you to the e-mail software that comes with your Clié, and to the process of connecting your Clié to a cell phone for wireless Web browsing and e-mail. We also give you the scoop on a couple cool web browsers, some of which don't require an Internet connection at all—at least, not in the traditional sense.

# An Overview of CLIÉ E-mail

Omniscient authors that we are, we can tell what you're thinking right about now. "E-mail on a Clié? No way! It doesn't have a modem or antenna or carrier pigeon, so how could mail possibly get into or out of the thing?" Silly reader—don't you know better than to ask such doubtful questions by now?

In fact, your Clié can transact e-mail a number of different ways. For starters, all Clié models come with a Palm OS application called, aptly enough, Mail. You'll get the scoop on that a little later. Many newer models also come with Clié Mail (see Figure 11-1), which is simply a more powerful e-mail program. If yours doesn't, there are several third-party e-mail programs you can leverage.

That's the software side of the equation. But the question remains: how to get messages to and from your Clié? We have three answers:

- **With a modem**   As of press time, Sony was continuing to manufacture the PEGA-MD700, a 56 Kbps modem "sled" for N- and S-series models. The modem clips onto the bottom and back of the handheld, then plugs into an ordinary phone jack (just like the modem inside your computer). You can then dial into your Internet service provider (ISP) to check and send mail (and browse the Web, as discussed later in this chapter). Unfortunately, Sony doesn't offer a modem for any other Clié models, and has no immediate plans to so.

```
┌─────────────────────────────────────────┐
│ ▐Edit▌                                    │
│    To: dave@bydavejohnson.com             │
│    CC: _____     │
│   BCC: _____     │
│  Subj: CLIE Mail_____      │
│                                           │
│ │Dave,                                    │
│ I've attached the latest property         │
│ photos for your review.                   │
│                                           │
│ Best,                                     │
│ Rick                                      │
│                                           │
│ (Send)(Draft)(Attach)(Cancel)       ☎     │
└─────────────────────────────────────────┘
```

| **FIGURE 11-1** | With Clié Mail, you can send and receive e-mail—complete with photos and attachments. |
|---|---|

What's more, the N- and S- series have been discontinued, so the modem is likely to follow before long. If you can't get one from Sony, try eBay. You may also want to try an infrared modem which doesn't require a physical connection to your Clié, and therefore guarantees compatibility. Check out the Psion Travel Modem and 3Jtech PP2I-5600B.

■ **With a cell phone**   This is a potentially ideal option for many users, as it allows you to use your existing mobile phone as a wireless modem for your Clié. Read on to learn more about this.

■ **With your computer**   This is one of our favorite Clié e-mail options because it's just so darn clever. Basically, new e-mail received on your PC gets transferred to your Clié when you HotSync, while messages composed on your Clié get transferred to your PC—and sent. Read on to learn more about this.

In the rest of this section, we tell you how to use Palm Mail and Clié Mail. If you want to learn about connecting a cell phone so you can use Clié Mail to send and receive messages wirelessly, see the section titled "Connecting Your Clié to a Cell Phone for E-mail and Web Browsing" later in this chapter.

## Working with the Palm Mail Program

It's hard to remember life before e-mail, isn't it? Imagine having to actually pick up the *phone* every time you wanted to communicate with someone. Now we just fire off e-mail messages. And with Mail, we needn't wait till we're sitting at our PC to conduct e-mail business.

What Mail does, in a nutshell, is link to the e-mail program on your desktop computer. Just as Memo Pad, Address Book, and other applications synchronize with Palm Desktop (or Outlook), Mail synchronizes with Outlook Express, Eudora Pro, and various other e-mail programs. The end result is that Mail becomes a portable extension of that program, allowing you to view, delete, and reply to messages and write new ones.

Mail is not a stand-alone e-mail client. That is, it works only when it's linked to desktop software. You'd think if you purchased a modem for your Clié or connected it to a cell phone, you could use Mail to dial into your ISP and transact messages. In reality, Mail has no use for a modem whatsoever (unless you're dialing into your PC for a remote HotSync).

*This is one key area where Clié Mail differs from Palm Mail. Clié Mail adds support for live Internet connections, so you can indeed get directly to your ISP without the need for a computer.*

This is not to say that Mail is an underpowered or valueless piece of software—quite the opposite. It comes in very handy when you're on the road and suddenly think of a message you need to send—presto: you can compose it on the spot, knowing it'll be sent the next time you HotSync. Additionally, if you take the train to work every morning, you can HotSync before you leave and read all your e-mail from the night before.

Mail also sports some reasonably advanced features, such as blind carbon copies, signatures, and delivery confirmation. And because it's a Palm OS program, the interface is streamlined and familiar. Let's get you up and running with this great little e-mail manager.

## Setting Up Palm Mail

Although Mail comes preinstalled on most Cliés, you must set it up for use with your desktop e-mail program. It's possible you did this already while installing the Palm Desktop software, which gives you a choice of configuring your e-mail settings then and there or skipping it till later. If you chose the latter (or need to change your settings), you can access the Mail Setup program in Windows by clicking Start | Programs | Sony Handheld | Mail Setup.

The only real step involved in this setup procedure is choosing which e-mail program you use, as shown here:

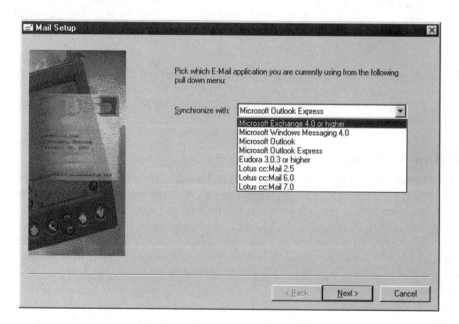

## Which Desktop E-mail Programs Does Mail Support?

Mail doesn't work with every e-mail manager on the planet, but it does work with the most popular ones:

- Lotus cc:Mail, versions 2.5, 6.0, and 7.0
- Microsoft Exchange 4.0 or later
- Microsoft Outlook (all versions)
- Microsoft Outlook Express (all versions)
- Microsoft Windows Messaging 4.0
- Qualcomm Eudora 3.03 or later

For the sake of continuity, most of our explanations will center around Outlook Express, one of the most popular e-mail programs. There may be some slight differences if you're using an enterprise-based program like Lotus cc:Mail. Consult your IT manager if you need assistance.

NOTE *Due to a Windows-related issue, you cannot sync your e-mail with Outlook Express if you sync everything else with Outlook. You can, however, use Outlook for outbound HotSync e-mail. And depending on which version of Windows you use, there may be a solution. Visit* **support.microsoft.com** *and search for Fixmapi.exe.*

## Palm Mail and HotSync Manager

After you run Mail Setup, check your HotSync Manager settings to make sure they're properly configured. To open HotSync Manager, click the HotSync icon in your Windows System Tray and choose Custom. (You can also access it from within Palm Desktop by choosing HotSync | Custom.) You will see a dialog box listing the installed conduits (which handle the actual synchronization for each program) and the setting (that is, action) for each one.

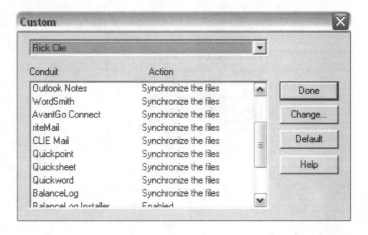

If the action for the Mail conduit reads Synchronize the Files, you're all set. (But don't HotSync yet! We still have to configure the settings on the Clié side.) If, for some reason, it still reads Do Nothing, click the conduit to highlight it and then click the Change button. In the resulting dialog box, choose Synchronize the Files, then check the box that says Set as Default.

**TIP** *If you ever decide to stop using Mail, you can simply return to this setup screen and select Do Nothing. Regardless of how you've configured your Clié, this single HotSync Manager setting overrides all others.*

## Configuring Mail Settings on the CLIÉ

Synchronizing your desktop mail with the Mail applet is not an all-or-nothing proposition. For instance, you can elect to pull only unread messages into your Clié, or create filters so that only messages tagged as "high priority" will be synchronized. The settings for such options are found in the HotSync Options screen on your handheld, which is accessible by choosing Menu | Options from within the Mail program.

Note that you can configure Mail settings for both local and remote HotSyncs, just by tapping the Settings For arrow at the top of the screen. If you do plan to HotSync remotely, you may indeed want to have different synchronization settings in order to minimize the connection time.

Figure 11-2 shows the HotSync Options screen. Let's take a look at the five choices therein.

**All**   This option forces all messages to be synchronized between your Clié and your desktop e-mail program. Take caution when selecting this option—if you have more than a couple dozen messages in your PC's Inbox, your HotSyncs may take quite a bit longer (a few minutes instead of a few seconds), and you'll eat up that much more of your Clié's memory.

**Send Only**   This one-way solution sends any messages composed on your Clié, but doesn't retrieve messages from your desktop mailbox. Use this if you don't wish to view your mail on your Clié.

**FIGURE 11-2**   The HotSync Options screen contains important settings for use with Palm Mail.

**Filter**    The most complex of the e-mail options, Filter lets you choose to ignore messages that meet certain criteria, or retrieve messages that meet certain criteria. Suppose, for instance, you want to retrieve e-mail that comes only from your coworkers. Or you want to ignore messages that originate from a specific address. Filter makes such options possible, all in the interests of giving you greater control over the mail that's retrieved from your desktop mailbox.

NOTE    *If you plan to use filters, expect to experiment a bit to get them set up right. There's always the concern that you might accidentally miss an important message if, say, the sender misspells the subject name or sends the e-mail using a different-than-expected account. So use them with caution.*

**Unread**    Rather than transferring all the e-mail from your Inbox to your Clié, this option transfers only those messages marked as unread. This is an excellent choice if you tend to retain mail on your PC after reading it, as it won't download your entire Inbox.

**Truncate**    If you find that HotSyncs are taking too long because you often receive lengthy e-mails, or you're just concerned about messages eating up too much of your Clié's memory, you can instruct Mail to truncate (that is, trim) messages that exceed a certain size. By default, Mail truncates messages longer than 4,000 characters, but you can change the value by tapping the Truncate button in the HotSync Options screen.

NOTE    *This has nothing to do with file attachments, which Mail never downloads. If an e-mail in your Inbox has an attachment, it is simply ignored during HotSync.*

## The Relationship Between CLIÉ and Desktop

It's important to understand that Mail and your desktop e-mail program are not just mimicking each other; they're actually linked together. Thus, when you delete a message on your Clié, it gets deleted on your desktop the next time you HotSync. When you mark a message as read on your desktop, it subsequently gets marked as read on your Clié. Keeping that in mind, consider the following as well:

- It's not uncommon to have a variety of different mailboxes set up in whatever e-mail program you use on your PC. You might have one marked "personal," another for "work," and so on. This helps you keep inbound messages better organized, rather than lumping them all into a single folder. However, regardless of how you've configured Mail's options or filters, the only place it will retrieve messages from is your main Inbox. Hey, we never said the program was perfect.

- When you compose or reply to a message, the resulting outbound e-mail is sent via Outlook Express (or whatever desktop program you use). Unfortunately, you don't have any control over which desktop e-mail account is used—it's automatically sent via your default account. This might pose a problem if you use multiple accounts and need to send messages using one that's not the default. Again, we never said the program was perfect.

11

## Mail's Mailboxes

Like all e-mail programs, Mail uses mailboxes to keep messages organized. Thus, it has the standard Inbox and Outbox, plus folders for draft, deleted, and filed items (see Figure 11-3). Alas, you can't edit the names of the mailboxes or create new ones, but you can still meet most of your basic organizational needs.

## Composing New Messages

Okay, so you've configured Mail to your liking, and now you're ready to start writing messages. There are two ways to go about this: tap the New button, or choose Menu | Message | New. You can't simply start writing in the Graffiti area, as you can with most other core Clié applications.

The New Message screen consists of four fields, which should be quite familiar to anyone who's worked with e-mail on a PC.

- **To** Enter the address of the recipient here. You can send the same message to multiple recipients simply by writing more e-mail addresses, separating them with a comma. Tap the To field button for access to a larger address-entry screen (and the Clié Lookup function, should you care to pull e-mail addresses from your contact list).

- **CC** Want this message to reach additional recipients? Enter their e-mail addresses here in the "carbon copy" field. Tap the CC field button for access to a larger address-entry screen (and the Clié Lookup function, should you care to pull e-mail addresses from your contact list).

- **Subj** Enter the subject of the message here. Tap the Subj field button for access to a larger data-entry screen.

- **Body** Enter the full message here. Tap the Body field button for access to a larger data-entry screen.

## Replying to and Forwarding Messages

Hey, wait a second. Mail has a Reply button, which is used to answer e-mails. But what if you want to forward a message to someone else? Where's the Forward button?

```
┌─────────────────────────────────┐
│ Mail 15 Msgs, 15 Unread  Inbox   │
│                          Outbox  │
│ zotnet.net  Re: freelan  Deleted │
│ Karmendy... How to Do..  Filed   │
│ Andrew Eis.. FW: Mobile. Draft   │
│ freemerch.. "Welcome...          │
│ Daniel Pesi. RE: Tap's A..  12/1 │
│ mspeir@fc.. Re: Freelan..   12/1 │
│ Didier Diaz  RE: Palm V..  11/30 │
│ Andrew Eis.. Tap Magaz..   11/30 │
│ Andrew Eis.. RE: Please a.. 11/30│
│ Andrew Eis.. RE: SFPUG     11/30 │
│ Andrew Pe.. Re: Tap We..   11/30 │
│                                  │
│  ( New )  ( Show )               │
└─────────────────────────────────┘
```

| FIGURE 11-3 | Tap the arrow in the upper-right corner of the screen to access Mail's message folders. |
|---|---|

Surprise—there isn't one, at least not where you'd expect it to be. Though most people would agree that replying and forwarding are two very different animals, Mail inexplicably buries the Forward option in the Reply Options menu. Let's take a look at that menu, as shown in Figure 11-4.

- **Reply to** To whom should this reply go? The person who sent it? Everyone else who received it? Maybe you just want to forward the message to someone else. Choose the desired option by tapping Sender, All, or Forward, respectively.

- **Include original text** It's a common courtesy to include a copy of the original message when replying to or forwarding one. By checking this box, Mail will do exactly that, as you see in the body of the new message that appears.

- **Comment original text** Of course, it can be difficult to distinguish the old text from the new, which is why it's a good idea to "comment" the original message. Translation: the old text is marked and indented using > symbols. Mail even adds a descriptor ("So and so wrote on 12/2/01 at 12:30 P.M.") before the commented text, as illustrated next:

**FIGURE 11-4**   When you reply to a message, Mail lets you specify who gets the reply and whether or not to include the original message.

## Working with CLIÉ Mail

In creating Clié Mail (see Figure 11-1), Sony must have looked at Palm Mail and said, "We can do better." The result is an e-mail program that is indeed an improvement, and not just in the looks department. Though Clié Mail can send and receive messages via HotSync, it also supports live Internet connections for e-mail on the go. Translation: if you have a modem or cell-phone connection for your Clié, you needn't be at your computer to transact mail. What's more, Clié Mail lets you attach certain items to outgoing messages: an Address Book contact, a memo, a program or database (specifically, a PRC or PDB file), or a photo from PictureGear Pocket.

> **NOTE**   *Clié Mail 2.0, included with the NX series, also lets you attach voice and movie files.*

Because only the newest Clié handhelds come with Clié Mail (and, alas, it's not available to users of older models), we're not going to devote quite as much space to it as we did Palm Mail. Suffice it to say, it operates in a pretty straightforward fashion, and Sony's instructions (found in the Add-on Applications Guide included with your Clié) are quite comprehensive. However, we would like to share the following tidbits of information.

### Installing CLIÉ Mail

Clié Mail doesn't come preloaded on your handheld; rather, it's on the Clié Installation CD-ROM in the section titled "Clié Add-on Applications." Insert the CD-ROM into your PC, then navigate to that section and you'll find Clié Mail listed. Install it…but don't yank the CD-ROM just yet. Your next step is to install the Clié Mail Conduit, found in the Clié Utilities section.

> **NOTE**   *If you don't plan to synchronize Clié Mail with your desktop e-mail program, you needn't install the Clié Mail Conduit.*

The Clié Mail Conduit does exactly for Clié Mail what the standard Mail conduit does for the Palm Mail program: synchronizes e-mail between your desktop PC and your Clié. Thus, the settings for the Clié Mail Conduit can be found in HotSync Manager's Custom dialog, as shown here:

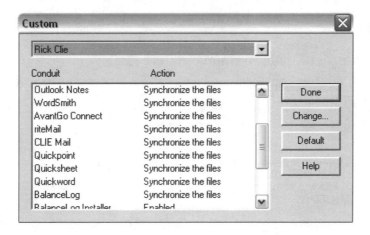

The rules for these settings are exactly the same as for Palm Mail. Therefore, skip back to the "Palm Mail and HotSync Manager" section to learn what you need to know.

## Working with Attachments

After you compose a new message, you can elect to attach one or more items that will be sent along with the e-mail. It's a pretty easy process: just tap the Attach button at the bottom of the screen, then choose the "Attach Type" from the pull-down list. Your choices are as follows:

- **PG Pocket**   A photo stored in your Clié's internal memory
- **Address**   A contact from your Address Book
- **Memo**   A memo from Memo Pad
- **PRC**   A program installed on your Clié
- **PDB**   A database (e-book, spreadsheet, or some other kind of data file) stored on your Clié
- **MS (DCF)**   A photo in DCF format that's stored on a Memory Stick
- **MS (PG Pocket)**   A photo in PGP format that's stored on a Memory Stick

So, just what happens when you attach, say, a contact to an outgoing e-mail? In that instance, the record is automatically converted into a ".vcf" file, so the recipient can easily import the listing into Palm Desktop or Outlook. Memos become ".txt" files, suitable for viewing in any text editor or word processor. As for photos, if you want to send them in industry-standard JPEG format (suitable for viewing on any PC, usually within any e-mail program), you must first copy them to a Memory Stick in DCF format (see Chapter 16 for details) and choose that option from the

Attach Type list. If you choose one of the two PG Pocket options, the recipient will have to load the photo into his/her own Clié in order to view it—probably not the best solution.

 *You can receive these kinds of file attachments just as readily as you can send them. Clié Mail gives you the option of previewing attachments and saving them to the appropriate "destinations" on your Clié (but only addresses, memos, and photos).*

### Setting Up Internet E-mail Accounts in CLIÉ Mail

Planning to use Clié Mail with a modem or cell phone? You'll need to set up your e-mail account first. Here's how:

1. Tap Menu | Options | Accounts, then tap the New button.

2. Follow the instructions on the screens that appear, entering your name, e-mail address, and POP/SMTP server info. If you don't know these last two bits of info, contact your ISP.

3. Enter your account name and password, which are the same ones you use to retrieve mail on your desktop PC.

4. On the Network Setting page, you'll be asked to choose the network settings you want to use with this e-mail account. When you tap the Blank box, you're taken to the Palm OS Network screen, which is normally accessible via the Prefs icon on your Home screen (see Chapter 2 for a refresher). This is where things get a little complicated. Depending on what method you plan to use to connect to the Internet (modem or cell phone), you'll want to have those settings already configured (and tested) in the Network screen. That way, when you get there from within Clié Mail, all you have to do is select the desired service, then tap Done.

## Sending Sketches and Drawings with RiteMail

Whereas Clié Mail lets you attach items like photos and memos, RiteMail goes a step further. It's designed expressly for sending handwritten notes, sketches, maps, or whatever else you care to scribble on your Clié's screen. Indeed, envision your Clié as a blank sheet of paper (or one with gridlines, a feature RiteMail offers), and you get the idea. The software provides some basic tools for writing, erasing, and creating basic shapes.

Just address your note as you would any other e-mail, then tap the Send icon. RiteMail works much like Clié Mail in that it can send mail when you HotSync or via a live Internet connection. Take it from us: it's a pretty cool product.

## Accessing America Online

At last count, America Online (AOL) had something like 70 billion subscribers. Okay, we may be off by a few billion, but there's no debating the popularity of the service. With AOL for Palm OS, you can access your e-mail account(s) as well as some of the service's more popular areas. Get it from within AOL at keyword **Anywhere**, or on the Web at **www.aol.com/anywhere/index.html**. You will, of course, need a means of dialing into AOL, via either a Clié modem or your cell-phone connection (see "Connecting Your Clié to a Cell Phone for E-mail and Web Browsing" later in this chapter).

# An Overview of CLIÉ Web Browsing

Did we pique your interest with our discussion of Clié e-mail? As the saying goes, "You ain't seen nothin' yet." Your Clié can also double as a portable web browser, though you'll need more software than what comes in the box. (Actually, if you own an NX60, NX70V, or any other Palm OS 5-based Clié, you'll find a web browser—called Netfront—included with the device. However, at press time we didn't have one available for testing.)

To get on the Web with your Clié, here's what you'll need:

■ **A landline or wireless connection to the Internet** See the previous section for information on the Clié modem and cell-phone options. Or, you can use products like AvantGo and Mobipocket to engage in "offline" web browsing, which uses your computer's Internet connection to pull down web pages that are then transferred to your Clié. More on that later in the chapter.

■ **Web-browsing software** Most Clié users will need to investigate third-party browsers, which can be found on sites like ClieSource, Handango, and PalmGear. Among the options: Blazer, PocketLink, and Xiino.

## The Browsers

Typically, Clié-powered PDAs don't come with any built-in web browsing software (the exceptions are the NX60 and NX70V, which come with Palm OS 5 and, therefore, a built-in browser).

That's okay—you can add your own. There are several Palm OS browsers available for the Clié, including AvantGo, Blazer, Eudora, PocketLink, and Xiino. AvantGo and Eudora are free, but the others offer more features.

### Surfing Limitations

Once you have a browser installed and some sort of modem (either wired or wireless) attached, you're ready to start surfing. Surfing with your PDA is radically different than surfing with your PC, though. Keep these limitations in mind as you start exploring the Internet with your Clié:

- **Graphics are much more limited**    It doesn't take a rocket scientist to deduce this one, but you don't have a lot of room to work with. Most browsers can squeeze large graphics to fit on the small screen, but it can make them hard to see clearly.

- **Color**    Unless you have a color model, you'll be looking at everything in shades of gray. The good news? Most browsers support color, so armed with the right handheld, you can surf the Web in full color.

- **Connection speeds are much lower**    Your overall web surfing experience may be a lot more sluggish than you're used to, especially if your desktop PC has a broadband connection. It can take minutes, not seconds, for a web page to display.

- **Don't download**    The Clié isn't equipped to handle ordinary Windows applications or data files, so don't bother trying to download anything. (Actually, you can download Clié applications using the Xiino browser.)

## Essential Web Sites

There are a bunch of web sites dedicated to the Palm OS family of handheld devices. If you're surfing for good Clié-related content, give some of these sites a try:

■ The best collection of downloadable Clié software on the Internet can be found at **www.palmgear.com**. The second-best is at **www.cliesource.com**.

■ There are lively discussion forums, news, feature stories, and reviews at **www.pdabuzz.com**, a site that caters to all kinds of handheld PCs.

■ The only magazine that covers handheld devices exclusively, **www.hhcmag.com** is a good source for news about your Clié.

## Channel Surfing with AvantGo

Buy all the modems you want—the Web just doesn't fit on a 2- or 3-inch screen. Enter AvantGo, a free service that not only delivers web-based content to your Clié, but also formats it to look pretty (and readable). With every HotSync, the software downloads your preselected channels—everything from news and stock reports to driving directions and movie showtimes—using your computer's modem to ferry the data. Pretty slick—and did we mention it's free?

### Setting Up AvantGo

To get started with AvantGo, visit the AvantGo web site and download the software. Install it per the instructions—you'll need to set up an account, complete with username and password.

To set up the channels you want to transfer to your Clié, go to the AvantGo web site and log in. The site should look something like Figure 11-5, in which your currently selected channels appear in a box called My Account. You can browse the AvantGo web site and click any channel you like to add it to your personal AvantGo hot list.

**FIGURE 11-5** AvantGo lets you transfer web "channels" to your Clié for offline reading.

## Editing Your Channel Content

Most AvantGo channels are configured to work well on a handheld device with limited memory. Sometimes, however, you might want to customize the way channel content is delivered to your Clié. Take *The Onion*, for instance—Dave loves to read this news parody each week, but the site

## Wireless Channels

AvantGo is mainly known for its offline browsing capabilities, but it also supports wireless channels and real-time web browsing. Visit the Wireless section of the AvantGo site and you'll find a collection of channels that are interactive when used with a wireless connection (like your cell phone). You can request real-time stock quotes, find movies playing in your area, get map data, and more. In fact, here are some of our favorite wireless channels:

- **White Pages and Yellow Pages** The "killer app" for wireless handheld devices! You can look up people and companies using this channel—just enter their name and city to get an address and phone number. Or, if you already have a phone number but need the street address, you can search that way, too.

- **Hollywood.com** This channel lets you find movie listings, theaters, and show times for movies wherever you happen to be.

- **Trip.com** Want to know details about a flight—like its' airspeed, flight path, and arrival time? This channel lets you find that data.

is so large that many of the stories often aren't downloaded to the Clié in their entirety. The solution? Dave increased the Maximum Channel Size from the default of 100KB to 500KB so it all fits on his Clié. To edit your channels as cleverly as Dave, open the AvantGo web page, log in, and click a channel in the My Account box. You should see the Channel Properties page, as in Figure 11-6. Make your changes and click the Save Channel Changes button.

## Using AvantGo on Your CLIÉ

While we've spent a lot of time talking about configuring AvantGo channels in your desktop's web browser, all the fun stuff really happens on your Clié. Tap the AvantGo icon and you should see all the channels you selected and configured on the Web.

<table>
<tr><td>**NOTE**</td><td>*If you don't see any channels in AvantGo, it's probably because you haven't HotSynced yet. Remember, with AvantGo installed, channel updates are downloaded and transferred to your Clié every time you HotSync. That means you must be online before you press the HotSync button.*</td></tr>
</table>

**11**

To use AvantGo, just tap one of the channels in the My Channels list. You can read text, view pictures, and drill deeper into the channel by tapping links. There are two navigational tools built into each and every channel page:

■ Tap the navigational arrows to move forward and backward through the current channel.

■ Tap the Home icon to return to the My Channels list.

In addition to reading cached channels on your Clié, AvantGo can also be used to open live web pages if you have a cell phone attached. To do that, follow these steps:

**1.** Start AvantGo.

**2.** Choose Channels | Connect from the menu. This tells AvantGo to activate your modem.

**3.** Choose Channels | Open Page from the menu. Enter the URL you would like to visit and tap OK.

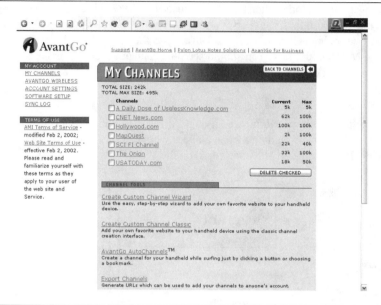

FIGURE 11-6　You can modify the amount of data contained in each channel from this page.

　*Some users prefer using a program called Plucker (available at **PalmGear.com**, of course) instead of AvantGo. Another program, Mobipocket, offers functionality that's similar to AvantGo, but doesn't have nearly as many channels. It does, however, double as an e-book reader, as detailed in Chapter 21.*

# Connecting Your CLIÉ to a Cell Phone for E-mail and Web Browsing

You probably already own a cell phone—most people do. And it's already wireless, so wouldn't it be great if you could link it to your Clié for web browsing and e-mail? You can, and it's easier than you might think. Here's what you need:

- A phone that supports data calls. Most modern phones do (those that work with CDMA and GSM networks), but check with your service provider to be sure. You may also have to pay a little extra per month to make data calls, though some companies build the cost into their standard service plans. Some phones also have a "modem" mode (or something similar) that connects you to the Internet via the carrier's own network, thus eliminating the need for the phone to actually dial into your ISP.

■ Two cables: a serial cable that plugs into your Clié, and a data cable that plugs into your phone. The two meet in the middle. (It may be possible to find a single-cable solution—see the next section for details.) If, on the other hand, your phone has an infrared port (found almost exclusively on GSM phones, and only a handful of those), you may be able to link phone and handheld wirelessly. We think a cable is the best bet, as it gives you greater flexibility in positioning the two devices. (With an IR connection, the phone and handheld need to lay on an even surface so they can communicate.) However, it could cost you upward of $100 for the two cables.

### Finding Connection Cables

Unless you're lucky enough to have an IR-equipped phone, you'll first need a serial cable to make the connection to your handheld. We know of two good sources:

■ **PN Technologies**   www.pcables.com

■ **SupplyNet**   www.thesupplynet.com

Next, you need a so-called "data cable" that's compatible with your phone. You may be able to find one at your local office-supply,  computer, or cell-phone outlet store. If not, try these web resources:

■ **Amazon.com**   www.amazon.com

■ **Cell-Phone-Accessories.com**   www.cellphones-accessories.com

You should also visit **www.syncablesolutions.com**, which carries a limited variety of cables designed to link your phone directly to your handheld.

11

# Another Way to Go Wireless: WiFi

If you're lucky enough to own a Clié NX60 or NX70V—which at press time were just rolling off the production line—then you have the option of wirelessly connecting to the Internet via an 802.11b (or "WiFi") network. Put simply, if your Clié is in range of one of these networks (which have become extremely popular in homes, offices, and even public places), you can enjoy high-speed Internet access—and wireless HotSyncing—in the palm of your hand.

To make this happen, you need an accessory for your Clié: Sony's PEGA-WL100 Wireless LAN Card, which costs $150.

TIP

*It may be possible to use a third-party CompactFlash WiFi card instead of Sony's. It depends on whether the manufacturer—or some enterprising software developer—writes the necessary drivers. Check the message forums on sites like ClieSource and **PDABuzz.com** to see if non-Sony options exist.*

# All about Bluetooth

Bluetooth is a short-range wireless technology that allows devices to communicate with each other up to a distance of about 30 feet. That's really just a fancy way of saying that Bluetooth is a technology designed to replace connection cables. By using Bluetooth, handheld gadgets like your Clié and cell phone can communicate with each other without wires and without even getting in line-of-sight with each other.

That said, Bluetooth is a new technology just starting to hit the streets. When we wrote this chapter, no Cliés were yet shipping with Bluetooth built in, and the only available Bluetooth accessory—Sony's own Memory Stick Bluetooth module—was limited to customers in Europe and Japan. With any luck, it will be available in North America by the time you read this.

## Where to Find It

| Web Site | Address | What's There |
|---|---|---|
| ClieSource | www.cliesource.com | All manner of software for the Clié |
| Handango | www.handango.com | Palm OS e-mail programs and web browsers (and lots of other software) |
| PalmGear H.Q. | www.palmgear.com | Palm OS e-mail programs and web browsers (and lots of other software) |
| RiteMail | www.ritemail.net | RiteMail for Palm OS |
| Psion | www.psion.com | Psion Travel Modem |
| 3JTech | www.3jtec.com | PP2I-5600B infrared modem |

# Chapter 12

# Your CLIÉ as a Total PC Replacement

## How to...

- Use your Clié as a complete business application computer
- Read and edit Word and Excel documents on your Clié
- Distinguish between Palm Doc and Word .doc files
- Import Clié documents into Microsoft Word
- Generate graphs and charts on the Clié
- View Adobe Acrobat files
- Print to wireless printers
- Print to serial and parallel printers

The core applications that come with your Clié are fine for many people—they offer all the basic functionality you need to stay on top of contact information and schedules while on the go. But, as you've already seen in this book, your Clié can do so much more. In fact, it's possible to use your Clié as a full-fledged alternative PC, capable of running applications as varied as a word processor, a spreadsheet, and a database program.

Why on Earth would you want to do that? Well, which would you rather carry around—a Clié that fits in your pocket or a seven-pound laptop? Which is easier to store in a hotel room? Which is more easily stolen? Which lasts longer on a set of batteries? We think you get the idea. Obviously, using a suite of "office" applications on your Clié isn't for everyone, and it won't work all the time. After all, a Clié has a limited amount of storage space and a much smaller screen than a laptop. Most PDA-sized document editors don't support an extremely extensive array of formatting options, so even if you exchange documents with your desktop applications, your text and format options may be somewhat limited. But if you're intrigued by the thought of leaving your PC at home and traveling only with a Clié, then read on. This chapter is all about creating the perfect Clié office.

# Building the Perfect Beast

No, we weren't really big fans of that Don Henley solo album either. But that does describe your Clié if you want to outfit it to be a mobile office, complete with office applications.

The name of the game when it comes to creating a Clié office is convenience and compatibility. What good is it, for instance, to generate documents on your Clié if they're not readable by the word processor on your PC? And why bother trying to do office-style work on your Clié if you can't do it easily, efficiently, and in all the formats you're used to on your desktop? With this in mind, here's a checklist of things to consider if you plan to do serious work on your Clié:

- **Your Clié**    Have plenty of memory. Word documents, databases, and spreadsheets soak up memory, so you should invest in a beefy Memory Stick so you can store large documents.
- **A keyboard**    As much as we love Graffiti, the fact remains you'll hate writing long documents or entering data in a spreadsheet with the stylus alone. Invest in a keyboard.

There are several compact, yet comfortable keyboards available for your Clié; see Chapter 23 for a rundown of the best ones.

■ **Office suite**    If you want to create new documents or edit files you made in Microsoft Word, then a simple document reader like Palm Reader won't be enough. You should try an office suite instead. Though these applications are not quite full-featured suites—at least not in the sense that Microsoft Office on the desktop is—a number of them deliver sophisticated tools like spell checkers, rich text formatting, charting for your spreadsheets, and more. Most importantly, these programs break through the file-size limit imposed by the Memo Pad and let you edit documents of almost unlimited length that can be shared with Word and Excel.

■ **Adobe Acrobat**    If your office makes extensive use of PDF files, you should have an Acrobat reader on your Clié so you can view those documents on the go.

■ **Database**    Yes, database applications are available even for Palm OS PDAs like the Clié. There are a slew that let you create new databases from scratch, and most even let you import existing databases from programs like Access, FileMaker, and other ODBC-complaint applications. Some of the most popular database engines for the Clié include HanDBase, JFile, MobileDB, ThinkDB, and dbNow. FileMaker also has its own PDA "companion" to FileMaker, called (not too surprisingly) FileMaker Mobile. If you're a FileMaker user, FileMaker Mobile may be all you need.

## Top Ten Reasons to Use a CLIÉ

**Dave:** With all the really neat office-like applications available for the Clié, it got us thinking. What are the top ten uses for a handheld computer? So, here goes (and if you imagine us reading this off blue cards at your local book store, you've pretty much experienced a *How to Do Everything with Your Clié* book signing):

**10.** New excuse for the office: I was writing the weekly status report, but I dropped it and it broke.

**9.** Too old for a Game Boy, but can still play Pac-Man on your Clié.

**8.** The digital camera and headphones for the NR70 make you look like a spy.

**7.** As a *Star Trek: The Next Generation* fan, you like to pretend you're an Enterprise crewmember on an away mission.

**6.** As a *Star Trek: The Original Series* fan, you like to pretend you're an Enterprise crewmember in a landing party.

You know, for me, the funny thing is you have to be a *Star Trek* fan to even appreciate the difference between those last two items.

**12**

**Rick:** For me, it's humorous to hear Dave describe any of *his* half of the list as "funny."

**5.**    Gives you a great pickup line: "Hey, let's HotSync!"

**4.**    When tipping the pizza guy, now you can calculate 15 percent of $16.87 to the exact penny.

**3.**    No one can tell you're reading Monica Lewinsky's autobiography.

**2.**    You can look busy in a board meeting when you're actually playing a game of *SimCity*.

**1.**    They don't put a single penny into Bill Gates's pocket!

# Dealing with Documents

If you're like most business travelers, you're used to carting a laptop around with you to edit Word documents. If you have a 14-inch or 15-inch display, then you know what it's like trying to get the laptop screen open in the cramped space on an airplane seat. Heck, sometimes we can't get it open far enough to read what we're typing.

Thankfully, there's an easier solution. Your Clié—combined with a keyboard—can take the place of your laptop for text entry. You can even synchronize specific Word documents with your Clié, edit them on the road, and update your desktop PC with the latest versions of your work when you get home.

## Understanding the Doc Format

All Doc files are not created alike. Specifically, when Clié users talk about Doc files—text documents in the Doc format—they're not gabbing about Microsoft Word's .doc format but, instead, about a text format originally popularized by a program called, unfortunately, Doc (we say "unfortunately" because it created confusion that lasts to this very day). These days, programs like TealDoc and Palm Reader are generally considered the de facto standard among text readers. While any Doc file can be read by almost any Doc reader/editor for the Clié (and vice versa), the Doc format is totally incompatible with the version used by Microsoft Word. On the plus side, you can generally get converters for most of these readers that convert desktop .doc files to Palm Doc files and back again.

## Using an Office Suite

Pocket PC users have one teeny-tiny advantage over Clié users: a Microsoft-branded office suite that includes Pocket Word and Pocket Excel. People can trust those applications to be very compatible with Microsoft Office on the desktop.

What a lot of people don't realize, though, is that there are several excellent Office-compatible suites for the Clié as well. Most Cliés come with one right in the box, such as Documents to Go, Standard Edition, from DataViz. If your Clié didn't come with an office suite—or you want to try another, you'll be happy to know there are three popular suites to choose from:

■ **Documents To Go (www.dataviz.com)**   Documents To Go is quite popular by virtue of the fact that Palm, Sony, and other Palm OS companies put it in the box of every new PDA they sell. The standard version works with Word and Excel files, and you can upgrade to the 5.0 Professional Edition, which includes additional support for PowerPoint, Adobe Acrobat, and other office tools. Documents To Go supports the full-screen mode on Clié models with a collapsible Graffiti area.

 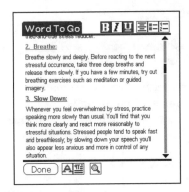

■ **iambic Office (www.iambic.com)**   Composed of FastWriter and TinySheet, these programs offer Word and Excel connectivity for your Clié. In addition, the suite includes iambic Mail, an e-mail client that lets you synchronize messages with your desktop e-mail program or check mail on the go with a modem. iambic Mail uses FastWriter and TinySheet to let you read Word and Excel attachments in e-mail.

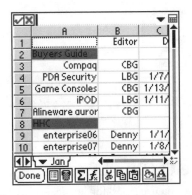 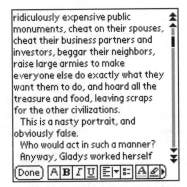

■ **Quickoffice (www.cesinc.com)**   This suite includes Quickword and Quicksheet for reading and editing Word and Excel documents. Quickword has its own thesaurus and spell checker, and you can install custom fonts as well. Quickoffice supports the full-screen mode on models with a collapsible Graffiti area, and is Dave's choice for all-around document work on the road.

- **WordSmith (www.bluenomad.com)**   Not really a full office suite, we couldn't neglect mentioning WordSmith here anyway. This word processor for Palm OS PDAs is one of the very best, ranking right up there with Quickword—it even supports the Clié's HiRes+ mode and can use the entire screen on models that allow the Graffiti area to disappear. The only downside is the lack of a spreadsheet—but if you don't need one, consider WordSmith.

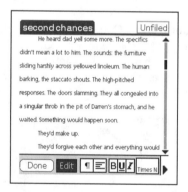

**TIP**   *If you don't want the entire suite, you can usually buy the word processor and spreadsheet separately by visiting the vendor's web site. For instance, Cutting Edge Software sells Quickword all by itself if you don't need Quicksheet.*

## Transferring Documents Between the CLIÉ and Desktop

No matter which suite you choose, they all work similarly: you use a desktop application to manage the documents you want to work with on the Clié. Just drag the document you want to move into the suite manager (you can see several of them in the following illustration), and it'll be copied to the Clié at the next HotSync. When you make a change to the document on either the Clié or the desktop, it'll be synchronized after the following HotSync, keeping the two documents exactly the same.

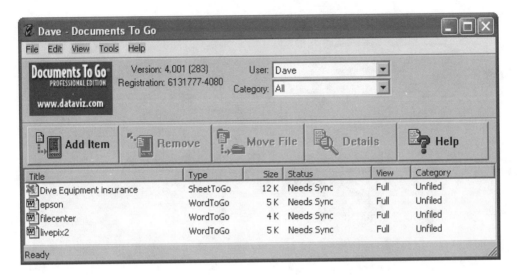

## How to ... **Work with Documents on the CLIÉ**

To create or edit long documents on your Clié, you first need a program like Documents To Go, Quickoffice, iambic Office, or WordSmith. Once you have that, here's what you need to do to work with text documents on the Clié:

1. On the desktop, open your office suite's manager application.

2. Click the button to add a file, or just drag-and-drop a document into the suite's manager window.

3. Close the program and then HotSync to transfer the files to the Clié.

4. Edit the files on your Clié.

5. HotSync to carry the changes you made to the Clié back to the desktop versions of the affected files.

If you prefer not to synchronize your Clié documents with their cousins on the desktop, that's fine as well. In each suite manager, you can disable synchronization and select familiar options like Handheld Overwrites, Desktop Overwrites, and Do Nothing:

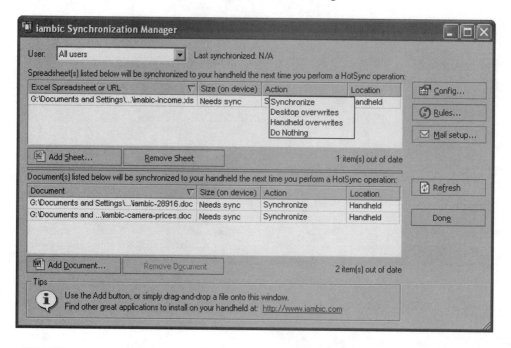

What if you create a new document from scratch on the Clié? No problem. On the next HotSync after you create it, you'll find it has been synchronized with the desktop. To find it, just open your suite manager software and double-click the new file; it'll automatically open in Word.

## Working with Documents and Spreadsheets

If you want to leave your laptop at home and just carry a PDA, it's absolutely essential to be able to read and edit Word and Excel files on the go. Any of the suites we've already mentioned will work, and if all you care about is text, you have a fourth excellent option as well—a program from Blue Nomad called WordSmith. WordSmith doesn't come as part of a suite with a spreadsheet. Instead, it's a stand-alone word processor for the Clié that, like Quickoffice, includes font support, a spell checker, thesaurus, and sophisticated formatting controls. Many users choose WordSmith as their word processor of choice, especially if they don't also need a spreadsheet.

While most Clié word processors try very hard to preserve all of the formatting in your document, keep in mind that these programs do it with varying levels of success. You may find, for instance, that group annotations or graphics like "boxes" around text may be stripped out when the files are synchronized back to the PC. As a consequence, word processing on the PDA is often best reserved for documents that have fairly conservative amounts of formatting. In addition, some word processors have more formatting features than others. Documents To Go, for instance, may be popular, but it can't hold a candle to WordSmith and Quickword when it comes to features like offering a spelling checker and thesaurus.

Bottom line: since all office suites have a free trial period, we recommend installing each and seeing which you like best.

## Better Software for Bigger Screens

If you feel constrained by the anemic size of the Clié display and can't imagine word processing on such a small screen, you're not alone. That's why some new Cliés offer dramatically higher resolutions. When you try out office suites, be sure to look for software that takes advantage of the higher resolution in your new handheld. When we wrote this chapter, WordSmith, Documents To Go, and Quickoffice all took advantage of higher-resolution Clié screens. And because these applications also support a variety of fonts and font sizes, you can pack a lot more data on the screen—provided you have strong enough eyesight to see all those little letters.

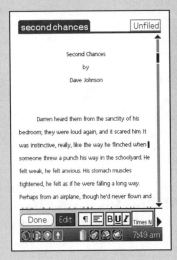

## Charts and Graphs on the CLIÉ

Spreadsheets are often reported to be the most popular PC-based application in the history of computers (we're not sure who they talked to—personally, we'd vote for games). And like milk and cereal or guitars and rock 'n roll, nothing goes with spreadsheets quite like charts and graphs. It makes sense, then, that you might want to view your spreadsheet data visually in the form of charts and graphs even on your Clié. You're in luck: both iambic Office and Quickoffice come with their own spreadsheet graphing tools. As you can see next, you can make some very attractive graphs using these programs.

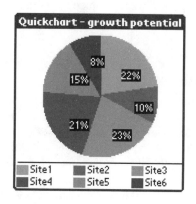 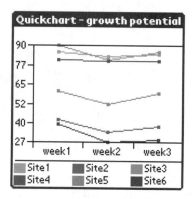

Neither of these programs is particularly intuitive, though, since they run from within their parent spreadsheet application; you won't get anywhere by tapping on TinyChart or Quickchart directly. Nonetheless, getting started with these graphing applications is easy. If you use iambic Office, just open TinySheet, select a range of cells to graph, and choose Cell | Chart from the menu. If you want to embed a chart within the spreadsheet, tap an empty cell and choose Cell | Insert Chart instead. Then select a range of cells and draw the Enter gesture with Graffiti. Double-tap the inserted chart to view it in TinyChart.

In Quickoffice, open a spreadsheet in Quicksheet and tap an empty cell. Then choose Chart(Range) from the list of functions. Select a range of cells for your chart, and tap another cell or use the Enter gesture. Your chart is created. To see the finished chart, double-tap the cell that now says *CHART*. QuickChart launches, and you can modify the chart and see it in all its grayscale glory.

## Adobe Acrobat on the CLIÉ

In most offices, Word and Excel pop up pretty often—but Adobe Acrobat files, also known by their file extension as PDF files, are incredibly popular as well. That's because PDFs are self-contained, fancy-looking text-and-graphic documents that display exactly the same no matter what kind of computer you view them on. They also can't be edited, so you can distribute a PDF secure in the knowledge that some clown in room 234 won't make changes to your handiwork.

That's great, but until recently you couldn't view them on the Clié. Here are two of the most popular ways to display Adobe Acrobat files on your PDA:

- **Documents To Go Professional**　This program has its own PDF viewer. On the downside, this viewer strips out graphics, so it's only useful for text-based documents.

- **Adobe Acrobat Reader for Palm**　A free program from Adobe that lets you download PDF files to your Clié. You can choose to strip out non-essential graphics, allowing you to save memory on your PDA.

# Printing from Your CLIÉ

The ultimate handheld PC would probably look a lot like the Clié, but with one important difference: it would have a paper-thin printer embedded inside, enabling you to print anything you see on the screen. While that's mere science fiction—like Rick having the ability to beat Dave at any game of skill—this doesn't mean you can't print stuff from a Clié. Quite the contrary: armed with a print driver, you can send a wide variety of documents from your Clié to a desktop printer or a portable, pocket-sized printer.

In order to print anything from your Clié, you need to add a print driver. There are several available, and selecting one isn't as easy as it sounds. You need to consider these ingredients:

- **What you want to print**  Some print drivers only print data from the Clié's four core applications, while others can print documents from certain office suites.

- **What kind of printer you want to print to**  If you have your eye on a compact, battery-operated portable printer, you'll need to find a print driver that works with it.

This table outlines some key data for the most common Clié print drivers:

| Print Drivers | Applicable Printers | Software |
|---|---|---|
| IrPrint | Prints to almost all portable and desktop printers via IR | Supports Documents To Go, WordSmith, and other applications |
| BtPrint | A version of IrPrint that works with Bluetooth printers | Supports Documents To Go, WordSmith, and other applications |
| InStep Print | Almost all portable and desktop printers via IR | Works with Documents To Go, Quickoffice, iambic Office, and Wordsmith—very versatile |
| PalmPrint | Supports most portable and desktop printers | Prints from the Clié's core applications as well as a few third-party programs, including Quickword |
| PrintBoy Anywhere | A versatile print driver that works with IR, Bluetooth, and cable connections. | Largely prints only from the Clié's core applications |

As you can see, getting a good match between your Clié device, the software you want to print, and the printer you want to use can be tricky. If you're looking for the best all-around compatibility, it's probably InStep Print. Be sure to visit the web site of each of these print driver vendors to check their latest list of compatible programs and printers.

## Infrared Printers for Your CLIÉ

The easiest way to print from your Clié to a nearby printer is via infrared. Your Clié's IR port (the same one you can use to beam applications and data to other PDAs) can communicate directly

12

with compatible printers. A small handful of lightweight portable and IR-enabled printers are around. If you like the idea of printing wirelessly from your Clié, or if you travel frequently and want to print from wherever you happen to be, look into one of these:

| Manufacturer | Printer | Description |
| --- | --- | --- |
| Canon | BJC-50 | Lightweight mobile printer |
| | BJC-80 | Lightweight mobile printer |
| Datamax | E-3202 | Desktop thermal printer |
| Hewlett-Packard | LaserJet 2100 | Desktop laser printer |
| Pentax | PocketJet 200 | Lightweight mobile printer, compatible with IrDA adapter |
| Sipix | Pocket Printer A6 | Handheld portable printer |

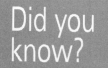

# Palms Speak "Laptop"

Technically, IrDA stands for the Infrared Data Association, which is just a bunch of companies that make IR-enabled products. More important, though, IrDA represents the industry-standard infrared port you can find on most laptops, handheld PCs, and printers with IR ports. If you find a printer with an IrDA port, chances are excellent it'll work with one of the Clié's print drivers.

## Bluetooth Printing

When we wrote this chapter, Sony was reluctant to release its Bluetooth adapter for the Clié in the United States (something that annoyed Dave to no end). If, after this book is published, you manage to get a Bluetooth adapter for your Clié (or if you buy a model with Bluetooth built in), you may be able to print wirelessly to a Bluetooth-enabled printer.

We've found two Bluetooth options for desktop printers. First, you can use Epson's C80 inkjet printer. It's Bluetooth-compatible, and by adding the Epson Bluetooth Adapter (a small gadget that plugs into the back of the printer), you can send print jobs to the printer from up to 30 feet away. Additionally, HP sells a similar Bluetooth adapter for several of its printers, including LaserJets like the 1100, 1200, 2100, 2200, and the 4000-, 5000-, 8000-, and 9000-series. It also works with a grab-bag collection of other printers, including the Business InkJet 2250, a few Color LaserJets, and some printers in the PhotoSmart series.

## Where to Find It

| Web Site | Address | What's There |
|---|---|---|
| Stevens Creek | www.stevenscreek.com | PalmPrint |
| DataViz | www.dataviz.com | Documents To Go |
| Blue Nomad | www.bluenomad.com | WordSmith |
| Cutting Edge Software | www.cesinc.com | Quickoffice |
| Iambic Software | www.iambic.com | iambic Office |
| IS/Complete | www.iscomplete.com | IrPrint and other print drivers |
| Bachmann Software | www.bachmannsoftware.com | PrintBoy Anywhere |
| Instep Group | www.instepgroup.com | InStep Print |

12

# Chapter 13

# Hacks and Other Utilities

## How to...

- Install and use Hacks
- Make capital letters the easy way
- Automatically correct spelling errors
- Expand the Clié's clipboard
- Drag and drop text
- Use the Clié buttons to load multiple applications
- Automatically remove duplicate entries from your databases
- Access "hidden" Clié memory
- Manage and beam applications
- Choose a launcher
- Protect yourself from Palm OS viruses
- Create your own Palm OS software
- Speed up your handheld
- Dress up your NR or NX with Graffiti skins

When you hear the word "utilities," you probably think of your monthly electric bill or those four worthless Monopoly properties (hey, $150 isn't gonna break anybody's bank). In the world of computers and Cliés, however, utilities are software programs that add capabilities and fix problems. They're power tools, though not necessarily limited to power users.

In this chapter, we tell you about some very cool and worthwhile Palm OS utilities. When we're done, you'll find yourself with a reliable backup that can overcome any data-loss disaster, a way to drag and drop text (which you can't normally do in the Palm OS), a time-saving way to write capital letters, and lots more. Utilities may sound boring and technical, but they're actually fun, easy to use, and extremely practical.

# X-Master

The mother of all Palm OS utilities, X-Master, is what separates the men from the boys, the women from the girls. It is a tool Tim Allen would love, as it allows Cliés to reach beyond their limits, to achieve "more power!" And, it's a tool many users come to find indispensable.

 *Hacks (and the programs that run them) won't work in Cliés equipped with OS 5. Software developers will no doubt introduce new versions of their products that support the new OS, but be sure to investigate compatibility before you install a Hack on your handheld. An unsupported bit of code could wreak serious havoc.*

## What X-Master Does

Technically speaking, X-Master is an "operating system extension manager." By itself, it serves no function. But it enables the use of *Hacks*—little programs that extend the capabilities of your Clié. Forget the negative connotations usually associated with "hacking"—these programs are here to help, not harm.

If you want to run them, you must first download and install X-Master. See Chapter 4 for information on installing programs like this—it's applicable to the Hacks you'll be downloading as well.

*Because Hacks tinker directly with the Palm OS, they can create the occasional glitch. And the more Hacks you have installed and running, the greater the likelihood of some sort of problem. The most common is your Clié crashing, which is usually more of an annoyance than anything else. But we encourage anyone who's working with X-Master to perform regular backups, preferably with a utility like BackupBuddy (discussed later in this chapter). This way, if the unthinkable happens (such as a total loss of data), you're protected.*

As you venture out into the world of Palm software, you may discover other Hack managers. For instance, there's HackMaster, the granddaddy that started this whole crazy Hack business. There's also TealMaster, the most robust and feature-rich of all the Hack managers. But we're partial to X-Master because we've used it extensively and it has just the features we need. Plus, it's freeware—unlike TealMaster, which costs $9.95 (still a great deal).

## How to Use It

Launching X-Master is no different from launching any other program—you just tap its icon. But, as previously noted, the software is useless without any Hacks loaded. Therefore, to help you learn to use this utility, we're going to walk you through the installation of one of our favorite Hacks.

It's called *MiddleCaps*, and it saves you from having to write the Graffiti upstroke every time you want to create an uppercase letter. Instead, you simply write the letter so it crosses the invisible line between the letter and number sides of the Graffiti area. We find this enables us to write much more quickly and naturally.

*MiddleCaps does not work with the NR and NX series. However, there's a Graffiti enhancement called TapPad that offers the same capability. Learn about it in Chapter 15. In the meantime, you can still follow this tutorial to learn how to install and activate Hacks.*

MiddleCaps is freeware, as many Hacks are, so you can download and use it free of charge. (A note of appreciation e-mailed to the author is always nice.) You can find Middle Caps at PalmGear.com, among other sites. Let's get it running on your Clié.

13

1. Download MiddleCaps and install it on your Clié. You won't find an icon for it in the Applications screen; the only real evidence of Hacks appears in X-Master.

2. Tap the X-Master icon to load the utility; you'll see MiddleCaps listed.

3. Notice there's an empty box to the left of the name. Tap it with your stylus, and you'll see a check mark appear. That means the Hack is now enabled. Should you wish to disable it, just tap the box again. (For purposes of our tutorial, please leave it enabled.)

4. Notice the Configure button at the bottom of the screen. Tap it to set up MiddleCaps (a one-time procedure).

5. You're now in the MiddleCaps Preferences screen, where you can tweak a few of the program's settings. For now, check the box marked "Caps on crossing." This means a capital letter will appear whenever you write a character that crosses between the letter and number sides of the Graffiti area. You can test it out by tapping to place your cursor on the line near the bottom of the screen, then doing some sample writing.

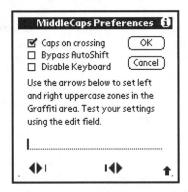

6. Tap OK to return to the main X-Master screen. That's it! MiddleCaps is now enabled and will work in all Palm applications—even third-party ones.

What about those other two buttons at the bottom of the X-Master screen? You can tap Details to get version information and other notes about the Hack, or tap Info to get the Hack's "splash screen."

## Beam Hacks to Other Users

X-Master has the enviable capability of beaming Hacks directly to other users (see Chapter 4 for more information on beaming). But before you start, make sure the recipient has X-Master (or HackMaster or another Hack manager). If he doesn't, you'll need to beam a copy of X-Master before you beam any Hacks. However, X-Master doesn't include the option of beaming itself; for that, you must return to the Home screen, then tap Menu | App | Beam. Choose X-Master from the list, then tap the Beam button. Now you can return to X-Master and beam some Hacks. Just highlight the one you want to share, then tap Menu | Extensions | Beam.

## Important Notes about X-Master

There are a few rules of thumb important when using X-Master on your Clié, all of them intended to keep things running smoothly:

- If you ever decide to delete a Hack from your Clié, make sure you disable it first! If you try to delete a Hack while it's still running, it could cause errors, crashes, or even data loss.

- If you install two or three Hacks on your Clié, don't enable them all simultaneously. Instead, enable one at a time, making sure each works properly before enabling the next.

- If you have to reset your Clié for any reason, a message pops up asking if you want to "reinstall your formerly active collection of system Hacks." Tap Reinstall (the equivalent of "yes") only if you're sure it wasn't a Hack that forced you to have to reset in the first place. Otherwise, tap Cancel. Then you can go back into X-Master and manually enable your Hacks again.

## The World's Greatest Hacks

If you were impressed by what MiddleCaps did for your Clié, wait till you get a load of some of our other favorites. Rather than list them by name, which doesn't always describe what they do, we're going to list them by function. You can find all these Hacks at PalmGear.com.

**13**

## Automatically Correcting Spelling Errors

Giving Graffiti a helping hand, CorrectHack works like the AutoCorrect feature in Microsoft Word, automatically correcting words you frequently misspell. Alas, it doesn't have a database of its own; you have to supply both the words and their correct spellings. But as you compile your list over time, you wind up with far fewer mistakes. And you can also use CorrectHack as shorthand for commonly used words. For instance, you write your initials, and the software automatically plugs in your full name.

## Fonts…Lots and Lots of Fonts

The Palm OS comes with a whopping three fonts: regular, bold, and large. That's not nearly enough for those of us who grew up with Arial, Century Gothic, Times New Roman, and other font faves. You can have access to a boatload of typefaces if you install FontHack 123, which lets you replace the system fonts with fonts of your choosing. FontHack comes with just one—you'll find 20 more in the Alpha Font Collection 1.71. Both products are freeware. Beat that!

## Drag-and-Drop Text

While you can select snippets of text by tapping and dragging your stylus, you can't drag that text to another spot and drop it in (as you can with any word processor). TextEditHack adds that capability to text-oriented applications like Memo Pad, and even makes it easier to select text. You can double-tap to select a single word, triple-tap to select a sentence, and quadruple-tap to select all the text on the screen. Very handy.

## Launching More than Four Programs with the Application Buttons

The more software you have loaded on your Clié, the harder it becomes to hunt for the desired program icon. Enter *AppHack*, which uses two sequential presses of the application buttons to launch up to 24 programs. You needn't remember the combinations you set up—AppHack displays a cheat-sheet when you press the first button, so you can see which program will load when you press the second one. This Hack is a little confusing to work with, especially because no instructions are provided, but it sure can save time.

## Enhancing the Find Feature

*FindHack* turbocharges the Clié's Find function, remembering the last six searches you performed, and letting you define up to four default searches. What's more, you can choose whether to search all installed applications, just the core applications, or only the currently loaded program. It even supports the use of "wildcards." For instance, searching for "book*" would return "book," "bookmark," "bookstore," and so forth.

## Looking Up a Contact Without Switching Programs

While the Clié makes it easy to switch back and forth between programs, it can be a hassle to have to quit what you're doing just to look up, say, a phone number or address. *PopUp Names* pulls up your address book "on top" of the program that's currently running—and with a handy two-paned window. Thus, it's not only a timesaver, it's also a more practical way of accessing your contact list.

## Improving Your Graffiti Accuracy

One of our all-time favorite hacks is TealEcho, which lets you see your Graffiti strokes as you write them. This "visual feedback" helps you improve your writing speed and accuracy, as it allows you to see how your characters really look, as opposed to the way they're supposed to look. TealEcho (**www.tealpoint.com**) costs $11.95, but we think it's well worth the money.

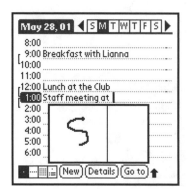

NOTE *If you have an NR- or NX-series model, you don't need TealEcho because your pen strokes are already displayed in the Graffiti area as you make them.*

### Liven Up Those Sound Effects

Getting tired of your handheld's boring old beeps? TechSounds comes with a handful of nifty audio snippets you can assign to various system functions, and allows you to download even more sound effects (**www.ecamm.com**). It also supports startup and shutdown screens, if you're into that sort of thing.

# Other Utilities

X-Master works minor miracles, but it isn't the only tool you should consider owning. There are no Hacks that create reliable backups of your data, or give you greater flexibility in beaming software to other users, or remove duplicate entries from your databases. And there's certainly no Hack that digs up 800KB of extra memory for you to use. So read on to learn about some of the other highlights of the Palm OS utility world.

NOTE *Most of the utilities listed here can be purchased and downloaded from sites like Handango and PalmGear.com.*

### "Free" Extra Memory with JackFlash

Psst! Don't let this get around, but your Clié has been holding out on you. It has extra, hidden RAM that's just sitting around doing nothing. You see, in addition to its 8–16MB of main memory, it has a few megabytes of Flash memory (a.k.a. the Flash ROM) where the operating system is stored. But the OS occupies only some of that space, leaving idle a few hundred kilobytes. The actual amount varies depending on your model—the NR70V has about 384KB available, the T615C about 128KB. Brayder Technologies' JackFlash lets you tap into that memory, using it to store programs, data, even backups of your primary databases.

Indeed, if you use JackFlash's sister program, JackSplat, you can delete unused files from your Clié's Flash memory. For instance, don't need the demo files that came with your PDA?

Delete them—and get a megabyte or two for extra program storage. It's all perfectly safe, since JackSplat makes a backup of all the files it deletes on your PC. If you ever want them back, it's as easy as clicking a button.

```
 JackFlash          ▼ Apps In RAM
 Name           Size  ▼
 FontHack123     9K  ▼ RAM
 Graffiti ShortC... 1K  ▼ RAM
 HostFS         10K  ▼ RAM
 McPhling       13K  ▼ RAM
 PhotoSuite    115K  ▼ RAM
 Spy Hunter    108K  ▼ RAM
 TapPad Hack    43K  ▼ RAM
 TomeRaider     95K  ▼ RAM
 X-Master       41K  ▼ RAM

 ( Update )    Free RAM:  5279K
               Free Flash:   n/a
```

## The Problem with Prequels

Clié, schmié…let's talk about the really important stuff—namely, treasured sci-fi franchises that have been ruined by prequels.

**Rick:** First there was the colossal disappointment of *Enterprise*, the blandest, most uninteresting Star Trek series ever. Now, George Lucas continues to make a mockery of the Star Wars trilogy by serving up pablum like *Attack of the Clones*. Maybe I'm too old, maybe I'm jaded, maybe I just expect fresh writing and decent acting, but these prequels have left me colder than a polar bear in January. They're just not *fun*. The magic is gone. And I think this is a problem inherent to the prequel formula—when you know the outcome, there's no suspense. I *know* Anakin will turn into Darth Vader in Episode III; for me there's no excitement in watching it happen. And don't get me started on all the ways Enterprise has violated Star Trek canon…

**Dave:** You, my friend, have been abducted by mind-controlling body snatchers. First, Enterprise: It's fresh, fun, and engaging. I enjoy the show immensely, though I'm sometimes disappointed that the stories are too "Next Generation-ish." It's always with the time travel, and there's often not enough "Gee whiz, Batman! We're in outer space!" I know that if I were one of the first people to travel into deep space, you'd have to follow me around with a towel to clean up the drool. As for Lucas' Episode II, you're just off your rocker. Are you too cool to like stuff anymore? Have all the million-dollar book royalties gone to your head? What do you expect? To be knocked off your feet like you were watching Star Wars when you were 12? Not going to happen—that film is a classic, and you were lucky enough to see it for the first time at the perfect age. Episode II is a good film in its own right, though, and it may eventually be judged as the second best of the lot... unless Episode III really knocks our socks off, that is. Read whatever book Rick and I write next year to see what we thought of that movie.

**13**

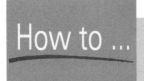

# Beam Software to Another Palm User

Suppose you're enjoying a game of *Vexed* (one of our favorites), and a fellow Clié user says, "Hey, I'd like to try that!" Generous sort that you are, you agree to beam a copy of the game (which is perfectly legal, as *Vexed* is freeware). To do so, return to the Home screen, then choose Menu | App | Beam. Find *Vexed* in the software list, tap to highlight it, then tap the Beam button. Point your Clié at the other person's Clié, then wait a few seconds for the transfer to complete. Presto! You've just shared some great software—wirelessly!

## Backup Utilities

One of the really cool things about the Palm OS is the way it keeps a complete copy of your data on your PC. Every time you HotSync, it's like you're making a backup of your important info. Should something terrible befall your handheld—it gets lost, stolen, run over, sat on, or inexplicably wiped clean—at least you know your data lives on your PC.

That said, consider working with one or more backup utilities. Some of them are designed to improve the HotSync-backup process, while others leverage your Clié's expansion slot to make bulletproof backups using memory cards.

### BackupBuddy

BackupBuddy creates a backup of every bit of data on your Palm, programs and preferences included, every time you HotSync. Doesn't the Palm OS do that? Well, yes and no. While the Palm OS does back up most of your programs and data, it doesn't necessarily catch everything. Technical details aside, if you want a 100-percent backup, BackupBuddy does the job. And should your handheld ever get completely wiped, a regular old HotSync is all it takes to restore everything.

Version 1.5 of the program includes support for Virtual File System (VFS) media, meaning it can back up software and data stored on Memory Sticks. That's a nice perk, because if your handheld gets lost or stolen, everything stored on a Stick would normally be gone forever.

### Memory Stick Backups

In Chapter 22, we tell you about some of the really cool things you can do with your Clié's Memory Stick slot. But forget cool for the moment—we're here to discuss practical. The hands-down best use of a Memory Stick is making a backup. As it happens, there's a perfectly good backup utility that comes bundled with most Cliés: *MS Backup*.

```
MS Backup
       Date          Size  DBNum
1. 2002/08/13 12:44   3478k   42
2.                    ----
3.                    ----
4.                    ----
5.                    ----
                            ( Delete )

     ➡◆                 ◇⬅

     Backup            Restore
```

As you can see, there's not a lot to this utility. You simply insert a Memory Stick into your Clié, then tap the Backup button on the screen. The backup process—which copies everything in your Clié's memory to a unique folder on the stick—usually takes no more than a few minutes. When it's done, you'll see the date, time, and size of the backup listed in the box in the upper portion of the screen. While MS Backup doesn't allow for incremental backups—that is, it doesn't back up only those items that have changed since last time; it backs up *everything*—it does let you store multiple backup sets on your Memory Stick.

However, because you can't see the contents of any given backup, there's not much point in keeping multiple backups. After you make your second one, it's safe to delete the first one. Tap it so it's highlighted in the list, then tap the Delete button.

Hopefully, you'll never have cause to use the Restore option. This wipes whatever is currently in your Clié's memory and replaces it with whatever's stored in the backup, so you should use it only in the event of a disaster—like if you're traveling and your Clié crashes hard and gets totally erased.

TIP     *You don't need a special Memory Stick just for backups. MS Backup simply creates another folder on the card, so you can use just one for extra programs, data, MP3 files, and your backups. Just make sure you have a card that's large enough to accommodate everything. At press time, the sweet spot for Memory Sticks was 64MB, which were selling for about $35 at Buy.com. That would give you more than enough room for all your stuff—backups included.*

**MS Backup Alternatives**   Don't get us wrong: we like MS Backup. It gets the job done simply and efficiently. But if you're more of a power user and would like a more robust backup solution, consider a third-party alternative. We're partial to *PiBackup II*, which is just as easy to use, but has the added benefit of supporting individual files. In other words, you can choose which files to back up and which files to restore—it's not an all-or-nothing proposition. It also enables you to make backups automatically, either at a certain time of the day or week, or whenever you turn your Clié off. Best of all, it copies itself to your Memory Stick after a backup, so you won't lose the capability to restore data if your Clié gets wiped.

13

## Extending the Clipboard with Clipper

Like most computers, Cliés make use of a "clipboard" for copying-and-pasting text. And, like most computers, Cliés can hold only one selection of text at a time in that clipboard. *Clipper* turns it into a repository for multiple selections, thereby expanding your copying and pasting capabilities. Everything you copy is retained in Clipper (where you can even go in and edit the text). When you want to paste something, you simply make a special Graffiti stroke to bring up the Clipper window, and then choose which snippet of text to paste.

This can come in extremely handy if you frequently write the same lengthy words or phrases. Doctors could use Clipper to create a little database of diagnoses, lawyers to maintain a selection of legal terms, and so on. Sure, you could use the Clié's own ShortCuts feature (see Chapter 9) to do much the same thing, but you'd still have to remember the shortcut keys.

## Removing Duplicate Entries with UnDupe

If you routinely work with ACT!, Outlook, or some other third-party contact manager on your computer, it's not uncommon to wind up with duplicate entries on your Clié. This can also happen if you import additional databases into Palm Desktop. Whatever the cause, the last thing you want to have to do is manually delete these duplicates from your records. *UnDupe* does it automatically, ferreting out duplicate entries in Address List, Date Book, Memo Pad, and To Do List, eliminating them in one fell swoop.

 *Palm Desktop 4.1 duplicates this capability on your PC, and it doesn't cost a penny. If your Clié didn't come with it (at press time, version 4.0 was standard), you can download it from Palm's web site at **www.palm.com**.*

## Managing (and Beaming!) Your Files with Filez

The more you work with software, the more you need a good file manager. Filez lets you view, edit, copy, move, delete, and beam virtually any file on your handheld. It's not the most user-friendly program of its kind, but it does have one feature that makes up for it: it's free.

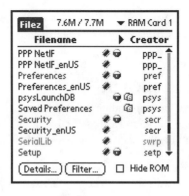

Beaming is one of Filez's most admirable capabilities. As you may recall from Chapter 4, beaming programs and data to other Clié users isn't only practical, it's just plain fun. But the Palm OS is a bit limited in terms of what it can beam. Specifically, it can't beam Hacks or e-books or certain kinds of databases. That's where Filez comes in—it can beam just about anything.

# The Wonderful World of Launchers

As you know from poring over Chapter 2 (you did pore, didn't you?), the Palm OS allows you to assign applications to different categories, the idea being to help keep your icons organized and more easily accessible. However, a variety of third-party programs take this idea to a much higher level, and with much better results. In this section, we introduce you to a few of our favorite launchers—programs that organize your applications, simplify certain features, and, in some cases, slap on a much prettier interface.

What should you look for when choosing a launcher? Here are a couple of key features to consider:

- **Support for memory cards**   Because your Clié has an expansion slot, your launcher should have direct support for memory cards. That means you can install applications on a card, but still organize them as you see fit from within the launcher.

- **Support for color and/or high-res screens**   A good launcher should take full advantage of your screen's capabilities, meaning it should offer a colorful visage and let you tweak the colors to your liking. If your Clié has a high-resolution screen, choose a launcher that supports it directly. You'll be able to fit more icons on the screen at a time (should you desire to) and enjoy a nicer-looking interface.

- **Support for themes**   Part of the fun of using a launcher is the ability to customize your handheld's interface. Some launchers let you install themes (or "skins," to use MP3 parlance) that dramatically alter their appearance (while maintaining the same basic layout and functionality). The standard Palm OS interface looks downright stark in comparison to these nifty themes, which are usually free to download (though the launchers themselves cost a few bucks).

- **Support for Jog Dials**   The Jog Dial is one of the Clié's best assets, so make sure to choose a launcher that supports it. That way, you can still enjoy the benefits of one-handed operation.

13

*As with most Palm software, you can try demo versions of these launchers before plunking down your hard-earned cash. We recommend you use each one for at least a week so you can really get to know it.*

## A Few of Our Favorite Launchers

We've tried most of the launchers out there, including the one that attempts to re-create the (horrors!) Windows desktop on your handheld's screen. Rest assured, that one is not among our favorites (but if the idea intrigues you, by all means check it out—it's called GoBar). These are

■ **Launch 'Em**   It's not the most stylish-looking launcher we've seen, but Launch 'Em does have simplicity and flexibility in its corner. The software uses a tabbed interface to organize your icons, so you can switch categories with a single tap of the stylus. It costs $14.95, but doesn't yet support high-resolution screens.

■ **MegaLauncher**   When Rick made the move to a Sony Clié N760C, this is the launcher he chose to go with it. In addition to its crackerjack support for memory media and high-resolution color screens, MegaLauncher offers a wealth of advanced features (including one-tap beaming, deleting, and copying) and comes with a handful of attractive themes. It costs $19.95.

■ **SilverScreen** Dave's launcher of choice, SilverScreen offers the most glamorous interface of any launcher, and a growing library of way-cool themes. It's also the only launcher to replace the core-application icons with icons of its own, thus creating an even more customized look. In short, if you're big on bells and whistles, this is the launcher for you. However, we should point out that it's a bit on the slow side—the unfortunate by-product of its graphics-laden interface.

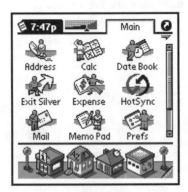

■ **LauncherX** Another of our favorites, LauncherX employs a tabbed-based interface for easy organization and navigation. At the bottom of the screen, a row of "gadgets" provides quick access to commonly used functions like beam and delete. LauncherX also features a built-in file manager, which saves you from having to invest in separate programs like McFile (see Chapter 22).

**13**

■ **YiShow** Its strange name notwithstanding, YiShow is among the most popular launchers for Clié users. That's because it not only supports all the Clié's advanced features, but also enables you to view photos and Doc files, use colorful background "wallpaper," and manage files.

# CLIÉ Antivirus Utilities

Unless you've been living under a rock, you know that computer viruses can wreak havoc on a PC and even propagate from one system to another without the users' knowledge. Viruses are an unfortunate fact of computer life. They aren't, however, a part of Clié life, at least not at press time. While a few Palm OS viruses are known to be floating around out there and several companies have introduced virus-protection software, do yourself a favor and don't bother wasting money or energy on them.

## The Great Virus Scam

Although no fewer than five companies (including heavyweights like McAfee and Symantec) have released virus-protection software for the Palm OS, at press time there's no known record of a virus ever harming a Clié or its data. If you want our humble opinion on the subject, these companies have acted irresponsibly, creating fear to create sales and in effect challenging programmers to design Palm OS viruses.

# Creating Your Own CLIÉ Programs

Ever wonder why there's so much third-party software available for Cliés? Maybe because it's so easy to write programs for the platform. While the more sophisticated applications do require programming experience and professional development tools, utilities are available that enable you to design basic Palm OS software with ease. Indeed, if you're willing to tackle a short learning curve, you can create customized applications for your personal or business use.

NOTE    *If you're looking for software to create databases, see Chapter 12.*

Here's a quick rundown of some of the tools available to budding Palm OS software developers:

- **AppForge**    A powerful development tool (available in Standard and Professional editions) that lets you write for the Palm OS, using Microsoft Visual Basic 6.0.

- **CodeWarrior**    Reputed to be the most popular Palm OS development package, CodeWarrior (available for both Windows and Macintosh) requires extensive programming knowledge. It's based on the C and C++ programming languages.

- **NSBasic/Palm**    Remember that BASIC programming class you were forced to take in high school or college? Now you can put the knowledge to practical use. NSBasic/Palm lets you create Palm OS applications with everyone's favorite programming language. Okay, show of hands: who remembers what BASIC stands for?

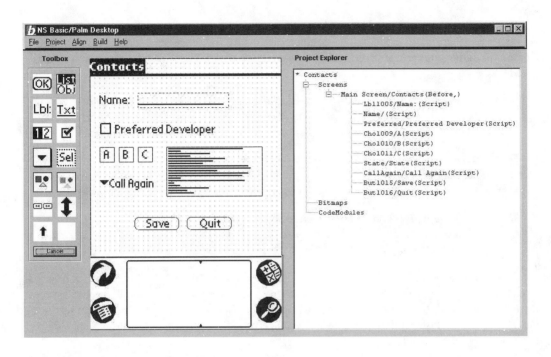

- **PDA Toolbox**    Formerly known as PalmFactory, PDA Toolbox doesn't require much in the way of programming knowledge. Rather, the software employs a graphical interface and makes software design as easy as dragging-and-dropping elements on to a simulated PDA screen. You can even create your own icons for your programs.

- **Satellite Forms MobileApp Designer**    Suppose you have an idea for a Palm OS program and want to create a prototype before hiring a programmer. Or, you want to design a special order form for your outside-sales team, one that links to your company's inventory database. PumaTech's Satellite Forms can handle all this and more; it's a robust software-development package that can create sophisticated programs. Although it uses a graphical environment—not unlike PDA Toolbox's—some database and programming knowledge is necessary.

- **SuperWaba**    Okay, we don't pretend to understand Java but if, you do, this program is a "Java Virtual Machine" that runs on the Palm OS (among other platforms).

# Making Your CLIÉ Run Faster

Like any computer, a Clié runs only as quickly as its microprocessor allows. If you're working with a particularly large database or spreadsheet, or if you're running a search and have a large number of records, you may find your Clié a bit more sluggish than you prefer. Oh well, not much you can do about it, right?

**13**

Wrong. Thanks to so-called *overclocking* software, it's possible to turbocharge your device. A popular pastime among speed-hungry computer users, overclocking is the technique of forcing a processor to run at faster-than-rated speeds. Assuming all goes well, the result can be a significant speed boost.

**CAUTION**    *Overclocking is a try-at-your-own risk technique, one that can result in crashed Cliés, lost data, possibly even a fried processor. One guaranteed side effect is shortened battery life. Overclocking is recommended neither by Sony nor the authors of this book.*

Given the possible disasters associated with overclocking, why bother with it? Shaving a few seconds off certain operations is certainly a plus, but the more likely answer is some users like to tinker, to push the envelope. If you're one of them, check out Daniel Wee's Afterburner 3.10.

**TIP**    *If you're going to run the risk of overclocking, at least do it sensibly. Don't jack up the clock speed to maximum—increase it gradually, starting with a small increment. Then use your handheld for a few days to see if any adverse effects result.*

One final note: If you really want better performance, buy a Clié NR, NX, or T650C. These models have 66 MHz processors—quite a step up from the 16 MHz chips found in the earliest Palm handhelds and the 33 MHz chips in most other models. In-the-wings handhelds that run Palm OS 5 will run faster still, so if you're really concerned about performance, consider upgrading to a newer, speedier model.

# Souping Up Your NR or NX with Graffiti Skins

In case we haven't made ourselves perfectly clear on this, we love the software-based Graffiti area used by the NR- and NX- series. And not just because it's collapsible, either. No, what really makes us all tingly are Graffiti "skins"— user-created artistic replacements for the Graffiti area. Here are a few examples (and just imagine what they look like in color!):

As you can see, these skins can dramatically change the look of your Clié, allowing you to customize it in a very personal way. There are hundreds of skins available, so you're sure to find something you like.

To install a skin on your Clié, you first need a "skin manager"—a utility that allows you to swap in the new skin in place of the old one. Our favorite by far is the aptly named SkinManager, which gives you an onscreen preview of the skin before you switch to it. (When you do make the switch, your Clié will reset itself, a process that takes about 30 seconds to complete. That's why the preview is such a nice feature.) SkinManager also enables you to rename and delete skins.

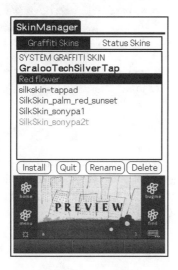

The shareware version of SkinManager allows you to work with five skins. If you want more, you'll have to pony up the $5 registration fee (a definite bargain). So, where can you find the skins themselves? They're scattered around the Web, but we've got links to some spots with great collections:

- **www.cliesource.com**  Look in the Skins section under Clié Files.
- **www.jalbrant.com**  Also includes a tutorial on creating your own skins.
- **www.sonipa.net**  The "Sonipa series" includes some really attractive designs.
- **www.graphicbliss.com/GraffitiSkins/graffitiskins.html**  Some absolutely beautiful photographic and fractal skins.

## What about the Status Bar?

Why stop with just the Graffiti area? You can also load up a customized "status bar"—the row of icons at the very bottom of the screen.

Just as users have created some beautiful skins for the Graffiti area, so have they designed some nice alternatives for the status bar. Very often, they're designed to match the Graffiti area, as shown in this nifty Sonipa skin/status bar set:

You can use SkinManager to change status bars just as easily as skins. However, there is a more practical status bar alternative you may want to consider. It's Stand Alone's NR Buttons, which doesn't change the design of the status bar, but instead adds more functionality to it:

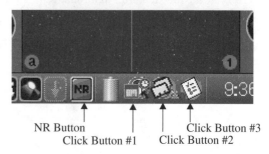

NR Button
Click Button #1
Click Button #2
Click Button #3

As you can see, it adds application buttons to the status bar so you can quickly launch up to four of your favorite programs. This is great for when you have your Clié "twisted" so that just the screen is showing, as it saves you having to tap the Home button and search for your desired application. It's well worth the $8.95.

## Where to Find It

| Web Site | Address | What's There |
| --- | --- | --- |
| PalmGear.com | www.palmgear.com | Afterburner, Clipper, SuperWaba, and virtually every other Hack and utility under the sun |
| Linkesoft | www.linkesoft.com | X-Master |
| Blue Nomad Software | www.bluenomad.com | BackupBuddy |
| AppForge, Inc. | www.appforge.com | AppForge |
| PDA Toolbox | www.pdatoolbox.com | PDA Toolbox |
| Puma Technology | www.pumatech.com | Satellite Forms |
| NS Basic Corp. | www.nsbasic.com | NSBasic/Palm |
| Metrowerks | www.metrowerks.com | CodeWarrior |
| Brochu Software | www.skinmgr.com | SkinManager |
| Stand Alone, Inc. | www.standalone.com | NR Buttons |
| NoSleep Software | www.nosleep.net | FileZ |

# Chapter 14

# Time and Money Management

## How to...

- Track your finances with the Clié
- Keep up with Quicken data entry on your Clié
- Calculate loans using your Clié
- Calculate restaurant tips and divide dining bills with the Clié
- Track your investments on the Clié    .
- Manage projects and clients with the Clié
- Keep up with time zones
- Calculate the time between any two dates

There's a saying where Dave grew up: you can never have enough time or enough money. Actually, we're pretty sure that this expression is common to most places, but Dave tends to ramble on and on about New Jersey. And because there's no reasonable way to discuss authentic New York pizza in this book, we've covering this topic instead.

No gadget that we know of is going to give you more time or money just as a happy consequence of owning it. But many Clié applications are designed to maximize what time and money you have by helping you manage it better. Project management systems help you track your jobs and clients, financial programs manage your checkbook, and portfolio systems let you stay on top of your investments. In this chapter, we round up a few of the best of each.

# Managing Your Money with the CLIÉ

"Money," the Swedish rock band ABBA once said. "Money, money," they continued. In all, they said it three times, as in, "money, money, money." Then they sang some other stuff. We couldn't agree more. Your Clié is an ideal pocket-sized tool for keeping track of your money. You can use it as an extension of your desktop financial management program or as a stock tracker—and a lot of little applications in between.

## Keeping Up to Date with Quicken

You know who you are. No sooner do you get home from dinner and a movie, than you rush to the PC and enter your receipts in Quicken. It's a habit, it's an addiction. Well, your Clié, together with the right software, can now save you the agony of waiting until you get home: relax and enjoy the movie, because Pocket Quicken lets you enter your expenses into your Clié as they happen.

Pocket Quicken isn't a PDA-based replacement for the entire Quicken application on your desktop. Instead, it's a handheld companion that lets you store payments, deposits, and account transfers in your Clié and synchronize the transactions with Quicken on the desktop at your next HotSync. You can also review your account balances and analyze old transactions. If you're a Quicken user and you methodically enter all your receipts into the program, then this is a program you should try.

## Rock Bands to Live By

We need to make a strong caveat at this point: neither Dave nor Rick is particularly fond of the recently mentioned ABBA (anymore—Rick boogied to "Fernando" every night through his formative years). Since you're relying on this book for advice anyway, we humbly give you our top choices for music to listen to as you troubleshoot your PC or surf the Web with your Clié:

**Dave:** The dual art forms of Electric Blues and '60s Rock really constitute the height of Western culture. For the most part, it's all been downhill since then, made painfully obvious by whatever that stuff is that Rick forces me to listen to when I visit his office or ride in his car. No, I say, stop the madness. Don't listen to music just because it's popular—you know, like Rick does. Instead, try adding come class and culture to your life. Listen to The Beatles, Pink Floyd, the Velvet Underground, Kristin Hersh, Throwing Muses, and The Call, and you're pretty well set. If you have a few dollars left over, pick up some Peter Himmelman, B. B. King, Dire Straits, and Eric Clapton. You won't be disappointed. And, whatever you do, don't buy anything Rick is about to recommend.

**Rick:** Not unless you have good taste and want to *enjoy* what you're listening to. With the exception of The Beatles, Dave feels all music should be weird or depressing—or both, ideally. Give me Billy Joel, Green Day, Smash Mouth, Simon and Garfunkel, Alanis Morrissette, Big Bad Voodoo Daddy, and, of course, the *Blues Brothers* soundtrack. Yes, that's right, I don't listen to artists or bands just because they're unpopular or unknown. That's Dave's job. Oh, and for the record, Dave doesn't even like jazz—proof positive that he's a few sandwiches short of a picnic.

Before you begin using Pocket Quicken, you should perform a HotSync. This transfers your accounts and categories from the desktop version of Quicken to your Clié. Be sure to do this before you take your Clié on the road expecting to enter any transactions!

Once you have a chance to synchronize the applications and get Pocket Quicken configured with your desktop settings, look at the Pocket Quicken interface. Pocket Quicken has two views: the display toggles between the Accounts view (which lists your accounts and current balance) and the Register view, where you enter and review transactions (both seen in Figure 14-1).

When you want to enter a new transaction, tap the New button at the bottom of the screen and choose whether you're creating a payment, a deposit, or a cash transfer. Then fill out the resulting dialog box as appropriate. Pocket Quicken includes Quicken's AutoFill tool (which completes the transaction for you when it recognizes what you're entering). You can also choose to use a "memorized" transaction from a pick list to speed your entry.

14

**TIP** *You can lock prying eyes out of your records with a four-digit PIN. To protect your Quicken data, start Pocket Quicken, and choose Options | Security from the menu. Then create your PIN.*

| **Accounts** | | |
|---|---|---|
| **Name** | **Type** | **Balance** |
| Savings | Bank | 14,492.15 |

**Balance Total:**           14,492.15

[ Edit... ]  [ Register ]

| **Register** | | ▼ All |
|---|---|---|
| **Date ▼ Ref & Payee** | | **Amount** |
| 12/19 | Rick | -130.00 |
| 12/19 DEP | Cbrt | 1000.00 |
| 12/19 DEP | Tap | 258.00 |
| 12/19 | Kris | -15.00 |
| 12/19 DEP | Zd | 250.00 |

▼ New Transactions           14,492.15

[ New... ]  [ Accounts ]

**FIGURE 14-1**   Pocket Quicken's two major views

If you use your Clié frequently to store transactions, the data can add up. It's easy to keep it in check, though, and preserve your Clié's memory. To trim your transactions to a manageable size, choose Actions | Trim History. Then delete old transactions based on date or by the oldest set of entries. Remember, though, don't delete any entries that haven't yet been HotSynced.

## Using Other Cash Management Tools

If you aren't a Quicken user or you don't want the capability to synchronize your Clié with a desktop finance program, there are other applications you might want to try. Specifically, these:

- **PocketMoney**   An outstanding alternative to Pocket Quicken, PocketMoney is a comprehensive personal finance program that interfaces with a handful of other applications and a number of desktop financial programs (including Quicken and Microsoft Money).

- **BankBook**  Another great personal finance program; the interface is simple enough that you can enter transactions as they happen. You can later synchronize with your desktop finance program.

- **Personal Money Tracker**  This is a popular finance package for your Clié that's ideal for non-Quicken users. It has a conduit that synchronizes the Clié's data with a standard CSV file on the desktop. You can then import that data into a spreadsheet or personal finance software.

- **Accounts and Loans**  This program lets you track your bank account balances and loan information in one application. The program is easy to use and lets you export your financial data to the Memo Pad.

## Did you know?

# PayPal's PDA Roots

These days, everyone knows PayPal and the way it makes buying stuff electronically on the Internet easy. You probably even have your own PayPal account to make eBay purchases. But we bet you didn't know that PayPal started as a way to exchange money using PDAs like Palms and Cliés. We used to love "beaming" money to each other at restaurants to settle bar tabs, for instance. Alas, PayPal discontinued PDA-to-PDA cash transfers a few years back, so only the true handheld pioneers remember those golden days.

## Streamlining Your Day with Other Financial Tools

What is the Clié if not convenient? That's why we love to load up the Clié with tools that make it easier to do mundane tasks like pay bills and calculate loans. Real estate and loan professionals use the Clié to calculate amortizations, and you can too. In truth, there are dozens of these kinds of programs floating around, and you can try them all quickly and easily from PalmGear.com.

*Financial Consultant*, for instance, turns any Palm-powered PDA into a business calculator that includes many of the most useful features of Hewlett Packard and Texas Instruments calculators. The program comes with 90 pre-programmed functions including loan payments, interest rate conversions, and onscreen amortization schedules. *Loan Pro*, from Infinity Software, is a similar loan analysis calculator that can be used by professionals or consumers for any kind of amortized purchase—like houses, cars, and boats (if you can afford a boat, by the way, give Dave or Rick a call. We have some business ideas we'd like to run past you.) Finally, *Triloan* takes a different approach to the problem of real estate calculations by displaying up to four loans at once on the same screen, allowing you to visually compare several different financial profiles side-by-side. There's also *LoanUtil*, a small application that tells you monthly payments, total amount of loan, or interest rate, depending on what data you enter. Tap the icon marked three at the bottom of the screen and you're taken to a Compare screen that lets you directly compare two different loan offers based on the same principal.

Have we whetted your appetite for handy financial tools? Here are a few other kinds of programs you might want to try:

- **Shopping Assistant** At the top of this little heap is a program called *HandyShopper*. This cool little program is designed, quite simply, to help you shop more efficiently and to save money in the process. It lets you maintain lists of products you want to buy, and you can even tell HandyShopper in which store (and what aisle) you found it. Then, you can later go back and track down the products more easily. For us, one of the most interesting features is its capability to compare the actual price of two similar products. Suppose you're buying tissue paper that costs $4.99 for 10 ounces, while another brand sells 12 ounces for $5.49. Which is the better deal? Find out by choosing Record Best Buy from the menu, and then enter the price and quantity in the Best Buy dialog box. For the record, you should buy the second item because it's cheaper by about 4 cents per ounce.

- **Tip Calculator**   Let's be honest—no one really needs a program to help them calculate a restaurant tip or divide a bill among a few people. And to add insult to injury, there must be a hundred tip calculators floating around PalmGear.com. But if you really want to try one, give EZTip a spin. It enables you to enter the total amount of a bill, add a tip, and then evenly divide the total among a number of diners.

- **Currency Conversion**   Traveling? You may want to know what $50 is worth in yen, euros, or rubles. There are a few programs that can retrieve current exchange rates when you HotSync, and other programs can pull the rates down in real-time via a wireless connection. We suggest you check out Travel Pal.

- **Car Maintenance Tracking**   If you want to stay on top of your car's routine maintenance, try TealAuto (on the left) or TotalCar (on the right). These programs also track your gas mileage—or, if that's all you care about, try a program called MPG.

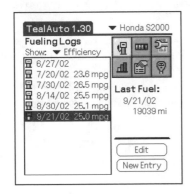   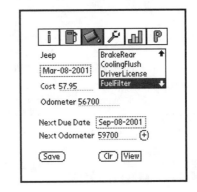

# Tracking Your Investment Portfolio

One of the Internet's biggest killer applications, it turns out, seems to be investment web sites. Then the Internet crashed, we all lost our money, and no one really wanted to know what our investments looked like anymore. If you're one of those few people that still have a few stocks with a non-zero balance, you might want to track your portfolio on the go.

That's where your Clié comes in. You can use any one of a number of portfolio management packages to monitor your investments. Most investment programs for the Clié let you check your portfolio's health anywhere, anytime. Suppose you don't get a chance to check the paper's business pages until you get on the subway in the morning. You can update your portfolio right from your seat on the train and instantly know your new positions.

If you like the idea of using your Clié for portfolio management, give either one of these programs a shot:

■ **Stock Manager**   One of the most complete portfolio managers for your PDA, Stock Manager is a color application that retrieves your current stock prices as well as the day's high, low, change, and volume. It also lets you set alerts on all your stocks based on current price, profit, and profit percentage. The program allows you to categorize your stocks into different portfolios, and a conduit lets you export your portfolio to an Excel-compatible CSV file.

| Stock Manager | ▼ All | | | Stock Manager | ▼ All | |
|---|---|---|---|---|---|---|
| 📁 Active ⚠️ 🔴 🌐 🗒 (New) | | | | 📁 Active ⚠️ 🔴 🌐 🗒 (New) | | |
| ▼ Name | ▼ Price | ▼ Profit | | ▼ Name | ▼ Price | ▼ Profit |
| Adobe | 60.8125 | 3932.99 ↑ | | Adobe | 60.8125 | 3932.99 ↑ |
| AMD | 30.5 | 75.05 ↑ | | AMD | 30.5 | 75.05 ↑ |
| Dell | 45.0625 | -1.16 ↓ | | Dell | 45.0625 | -1.16 ↓ |
| Extreme | 71.9375 | 27.86 ↑◻ | | Extreme | 71.9375 | 27.86 ↑◻ |
| IBM | 115.9375 | 128.86 ↓ | | IBM | 115.9375 | 128.86 ↓ |
| Tut Systems | 41 | -84.95 ↑ | | Tut Systems | 41 | -84.95 ↑ |
| Wind River | 37.9375 | 835.03 ↓◻ | | Wind River | 37.9375 | 835.03 ↓◻ |
| Profit: | 4913.68 | USD 🖼️ 🖥️ ⛰️ ▼ | | Profit: | 4913.68 | USD 🖼️ 🖥️ ⛰️ ▼ |
| Profit %: | 45.30% | Cost: 10845.12 | | Profit %: | 45.30% | Cost: 10845.12 |
| Profit PA: | 2.30% | Value: 15758.81 | | Profit PA: | 2.30% | Value: 15758.81 |

■ **StockPilot**   Do you love to see your holdings in lots of different ways? Then you'll love StockPilot. While we prefer Stock Manager, this is a good alternative, and it's a little cheaper ($19 instead of $25). StockPilot tracks a lot of details about your holdings, including dividends, profits, fees as a percentage of stock value, and total value. StockPilot lets you "watch" a stock even if you don't own it. The elegant display shows your portfolio in three columns, each of which is customizable to show different details, like stock symbol, shares, profit, and more.

# Streamlining Your Day

Time management isn't only about getting that spreadsheet to your client on time or tracking how many hours you were on the road delivering two tons of fertilizer to a nearby town. Time management can be little things—like knowing how many days are between two project milestones. Here's a small collection of utilities we think you might appreciate having on your Clié:

■ **Time Traveler**   This program is a fairly comprehensive time zone manager that lets you find the time difference between your current location and major cities around the world. One of its most interesting features is in the Time Travel screen, where you can specify your flight itinerary (including your departure location and time, followed by your arrival location and time), and the program calculates the actual travel time, taking time zone changes into account. This way, you know how many magazines to buy for your upcoming flight.

■ **BigClock**   We mentioned this program elsewhere in the book, but it's a winner and deserves mention here as well. Use BigClock to display the time (if your Clié recharges in the HotSync cradle and you set it to stay on while recharging, it can be turned into a desktop clock), play up to four different sets of alarms, and serve as a counter or countdown timer.

■ **BlueMoon**   When was the last time you changed the filter in the furnace, checked the oil in your car, or called your mom? These are tasks that don't always lend themselves to regular To Do List or Date Book entries, largely because they happen infrequently and not always on a predictable schedule. But BlueMoon is designed to accommodate just those kinds of recurring tasks.

■ **Timeout**   Do you take enough breaks during the day? If not, you might be heading down the road to stress and heart failure, like our friend Rick. Timeout is a simple program that pops a reminder on the Clié screen randomly throughout the day to tell you to take a short break and relax.

■ **Date Wheel**   This clever program lets you calculate the number of weeks, days, or business days between any two dates. You can also specify a duration, like ten business days, and find the necessary start or end date. This program is essential for any manager who needs to assign deadlines or determine if there's enough time between two dates to get a job accomplished.

**14**

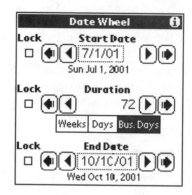

## Outlining Your Ideas

We all have a million great ideas every day—and promptly forget them minutes later. What you need is an outlining program that can help you get a handle on all the great ideas flowing through your head. It'll make you more efficient, more productive, and save you valuable time every day.

Typically, outliners use a hierarchical approach to data management. This might sound imposing, but the basic idea is that your ideas are generally related to each other. So, start with a single note, and then nest subnotes within it, as if you had a data tree with branches that grew off the main topic. By grouping related ideas together, it's easier to stay organized and arrange your data in a format that works for you.

The Clié has several excellent idea organizers with which you can experiment:

■ **BrainForest**   This program is perhaps the most complete organizer for the Palm and serves as an action item tracker, checklist manager, outliner, idea keeper, and project planner. BrainForest uses Tree, Branch, and Leaf metaphors to enable you to nest notes within each other, thus grouping items in a logical manner. Items are numbered using traditional outlining notation (like 1.2.3, for the third leaf in the second branch of the first tree of data). In addition, you can export specific items to the Palm's To Do List and Memo Pad. BrainForest also enables you to prioritize, sort, and rearrange items by dragging-and-dropping.

■ **MindManager Mobile**   "Mind maps" are non-linear outlines that show the relationship between related topics. They often look like cascading groups of thought bubbles, with spider-like connections holding them together. They let you take notes or brainstorm in a free-form way, without being restricted to a rigid format. The leading mind mapping software for the Clié is MindManager 2002 Mobile Edition. MindManager lets you create original mind maps on the Clié or synchronize with the desktop version of MindManager. Either way, you start with a central hub concept and branch out from there, adding ideas, tasks, and data in radiating branches. Branches can be nested, long-form notes can be attached, and the program makes use of graphic icons and color to highlight certain areas of a map. Though the program can stand on its own, its real power comes when you synchronize a map made on the Clié and feed it back to the desktop for inclusion in PowerPoint presentations, e-mails, or web pages.

# Where to Find It

| Web Site | Address | What's There |
| --- | --- | --- |
| PalmGear.com | www.palmgear.com | Applications, including those discussed in this chapter |

**14**

# Chapter 15

# Graffiti Enhancements and Alternatives

## How to...

- Turn the Graffiti area into a keyboard
- Make the Graffiti area more functional
- Replace Graffiti with a different handwriting recognition engine
- Replace the built-in keyboard with other keyboards
- Write anywhere on the Clié's screen
- Take advantage of "digital ink"
- Write faster with word-completion software
- Tweak Graffiti so it's more responsive to your handwriting
- Improve Graffiti recognition without third-party software

Many of us have a love/hate relationship with Graffiti, the handwriting-recognition software used by Palm OS devices like the Clié. Some users take to it right away, finding it a speedy and convenient method for entering data. Others just plain don't like it or can't get the knack. For those folks (who have absolutely nothing to be ashamed of, really), we present this chapter on Graffiti enhancements and alternatives.

Suppose you don't mind Graffiti, but find it too slow to keep up with your thought processes—or too inflexible to recognize your particular style of handwriting. The answer could lie in one of many available "Graffiti assistants," which can not only speed data entry, but also make your handwriting more recognizable.

Maybe you've been using the onscreen keyboard as an alternative to Graffiti, but find it too small or cumbersome. There are keyboard alternatives as well, some of them quite radical. And maybe you're just ready to give Graffiti the old heave-ho and try some other means of data entry. Full-blown replacements are out there, and they let you say goodbye to Graffiti forever.

We divided all these products into four categories: overlays, which actually cover the Graffiti area; assistants, which give Graffiti a helping hand; keyboards, which substitute for the stock onscreen keyboard; and replacements, which send Graffiti packing.

NOTE *In this chapter's discussion of keyboards, we're talking about software options. We look at actual keyboards in Chapter 23. Of course, the NR and NX series have a built-in keyboard already—but you may still appreciate learning about these Graffiti enhancements and replacements.*

# Overlays: Wallpaper for the Graffiti Area

One of our favorite tips for Clié users is to apply a piece of Scotch 811 Magic Tape to the Graffiti area. This not only protects the area from scratches, it also adds a tackier writing surface that many people find preferable to the slippery screen. A new breed of plastic overlays takes this idea several steps further, redefining the Graffiti area's functionality and protecting it at the same time.

*With one exception, none of the products in this section applies to the Clié NR and NX series, which use a software-based Graffiti area you certainly wouldn't want to cover with an overlay.*

## How Overlays Work

The entire Graffiti area—buttons and all—is sensitive to pressure. That's why when you tap a button or write something with your stylus, your Clié responds. The overlays simply take advantage of this fact, using special software to reprogram the Clié's responses to your taps and strokes. The products take different approaches to this, as you will see in our overview of each one.

### An Introduction to FitalyStamp

Before we unveil Textware Solutions' FitalyStamp, we have to tell you about Textware Solutions' Fitaly Keyboard—a replacement for the built-in Clié keyboard discussed later in this chapter. It's a fairly unusual product, but with practice it can increase your data-entry speed.

The problem with pop-up keyboards like Fitaly (and the standard keyboard, for that matter) is they occupy a major chunk of the viewable area of the Clié's screen. FitalyStamp offers a solution: an overlay that moves the keyboard from the screen to the Graffiti area.

As you can see, the key layout is quite unusual. The idea is to minimize the distance your stylus needs to travel (more on that later in this chapter when we look at the Fitaly Keyboard). But FitalyStamp also provides cursor-control buttons, numbers, and symbols—even the Clié's ShortCut and Command functions. Thus, while there's a learning curve involved with the keyboard itself, there's also a lot of convenience. Plus, FitalyStamp is a colorful, attractive addition to your Clié—an important consideration for those who prize aesthetics.

### Having Your Keyboard and Graffiti Too

If you often hop between Graffiti and the built-in keyboard, and wish you had an easier way to do so, Softava's Silkyboard is the answer. This overlay covers the Graffiti area with a large, easy-to-read QWERTY keyboard that enables full-time tap-typing, but also lets you use Graffiti without having to change modes.

**15**

Silkyboard's key advantage is it provides access to a keyboard without sacrificing any screen estate. Its secondary advantage is protection of the Graffiti area. Working with the overlay is as simple as tapping on the letter or number you want to enter, and holding down your stylus for a "long tap" when you want a capital letter or punctuation mark. Accessing Applications, Menu, Calc, and Find requires a stroke instead of a tap, but that's just a matter of simple memorization. Indeed, Silkyboard's learning curve is slight. And, if you get mixed up, you can go back to using Graffiti just by drawing the strokes on top of the letters. (The overlay even has the two little arrows that divide the letter and number areas.)

Given that different handhelds have slightly different Graffiti areas, Silkyboard is available in several varieties. Make sure you order the right one for your model. A simple calibration routine is all that's required to set up the driver software, and a handy applicator strip is provided to make sure the overlay is applied without any air bubbles.

If you prefer to write with a keyboard but don't want to give up Graffiti entirely, Silkyboard is a great best-of-both-worlds solution.

## Making Graffiti Smarter

One of the most ingenious overlays is TapPad, which doesn't try to replace or revamp Graffiti, but merely gives it a boost. TapPad extends the full length of the Graffiti area, thus providing total protection.

TapPad's benefits include:

■ Protection of the Graffiti area and a tackier surface that makes handwriting more comfortable.

■ The addition of a keypad in the numeric half, thus enabling you to enter addresses and phone numbers much more quickly (and more easily, in our opinion).

- One-tap buttons for six commonly used commands: undo, cut, copy, paste, delete, and backspace. The Undo button alone is worth the price of admission ($19.95 for five overlays—enough to last you a year).

- Left-right and up-down scroll buttons for easier cursor movement and document navigation. If you've ever tried to place your cursor in between two letters or at the beginning of a line, you know what a struggle it can be. The left-right buttons move your cursor one space at a time, greatly simplifying its placement. And the up-down scroll buttons are a major improvement over the Clié's skinny scroll bars and tiny arrows.

- A host of shortcut and pop-up tools designed to simplify data entry. Space doesn't permit us to list them all, but we think they're outstanding.

If you want superb protection for the handwriting area along with some Graffiti-related perks, you're likely to love TapPad.

**TapPad for the NR/NX Series**    In Chapter 13, you learned about "skins" you could apply to the NR/NX Graffiti area to dress it up. There's also a TapPad skin, which reproduces the overlay and all the capabilities therein. (The only thing you don't get is screen protection.) You have to pay $19.95 for the software, but TapPad still delivers the best of all possible Graffiti areas.

## Our Favorite Graffiti Aids

**Rick:** While I never travel without my Stowaway Keyboard, most of the time I prefer to use plain old Graffiti. But my accuracy could always use improvement, which is why I've become a big fan of TealEcho. It reproduces my Graffiti strokes in digital ink as I make them, so I can see what my characters look like (and make sure they're drawn correctly). Best $11.95 you can spend on your Clié, if you ask me. Of course, my Clié NR70V has the same functionality built right in, which is another reason I love that model.

**Dave:** Personally, I never used to use any Graffiti enhancements (my Jedi Master won't allow me to take the easy way out of any situation, lest it weaken my mind and allow the Dark Side to gain a foothold). Recently, though, I discovered the joy of TapPad. Since I use an NR70, I used a TapPad skin for the virtual Graffiti area instead of a plastic overlay. Best of all, there are at least a dozen variations of the TapPad skin, so I can change the look of my Graffiti area anytime I like—and still have access to the convenience of TapPad.

# Graffiti Replacements: A Software Solution

Love the idea of Graffiti, but don't like Graffiti itself? We understand—some of those special characters are just plain tough (Dave can't make a *j* to save his life, and who can remember the stroke for the percent sign?). Fortunately, there are two utilities that do away with Graffiti altogether, replacing it with a more natural—and familiar—character set.

The first, CIC's *Jot*, was born for Windows CE handhelds but eventually ported to the Palm OS. The second, ART's *SimpliWrite*, shares a similar heritage. Both programs have the added benefit of freeing you from the Graffiti area, enabling you to write anywhere on your Clié's screen. Even better, they leave a trail of "digital ink" beneath your stylus tip, so you can see what you're writing as you write, just like with a pen and paper. Finally, both Jot and SimpliWrite recognize a variety of cursive characters (see Figure 15-1 for a sample of Jot's character set), handy for those who mix script with print. Tricky Graffiti letters like *q*, *v*, and *y* are much easier to make.

# Keys, Please

Like to tap-type? Many users prefer the built-in keyboard to Graffiti, if only because it has no real learning curve. Of course, some software developers think they can do the keyboard one better, as evidenced by Textware Solutions' Fitaly Keyboard and a few interesting Hacks.

## QWERTY, Meet Fitaly

The *Fitaly Keyboard* (so named for the layout of its keys, like QWERTY) proceeds from the assumption that the Clié's own built-in keyboard requires too much hand movement. Because it's so wide, you have to move your stylus quite a bit, leading to slow and often inaccurate data entry. The Fitaly Keyboard arranges letters in a tightly knit group designed to minimize stylus travel. Hence, you should be able to tap-type much more quickly.

Clearly, Fitaly represents a radical departure from the standard QWERTY keyboard, and therefore has a high learning curve. Make that practice curve: it could take you several days to master the layout, and even then you might decide you don't like it. The moderate speed gain may not offset the difficulty in learning an entirely new keyboard.

**FIGURE 15-1**   Jot can recognize five versions of the letter *A* alone, meaning it's more accommodating to your style of writing.

On the other hand, Fitaly is much more practical than the stock built-in keyboard, in part because it makes most common punctuation marks readily available, without the need to shift modes or even tap the SHIFT key. And when you do access the Numeric mode (done by tapping the 123 button, as with the standard keyboard), you gain access to a number of extended characters (including fractions, the Euro symbol, and more).

If you like the idea of Fitaly but hate sacrificing a big chunk of the screen, check out FitalyStamp—a plastic overlay that moves the keyboard right on top of the Graffiti area. It was covered earlier in this chapter.

## Keyboard Hack

In Chapter 13, you learned all about X-Master and the little OS enhancements (Hacks) that work with it. Let's talk about one that's expressly related to the Clié's onscreen keyboard: *Keyboard Hack*. If you've spent any time with the Clié's standard onscreen keyboard, you've probably been frustrated at having to switch modes to access numbers and punctuation. Horace Ho's Keyboard Hack solves the problem by replacing the standard keyboard with a slightly modified one. His keyboard sports 69 keys, including a numeric keypad and a row of punctuation keys. It also has left/right keys for moving your cursor a space at a time.

**15**

*The latter feature, the cursor-control keys, was suggested by a user of an earlier version of Keyboard Hack. The author of the program incorporated it into his next update. This is part of what makes the Palm OS community so great: so many software developers are just regular folk who are happy to hear from regular users. You, too, can have a voice in the evolution of Palm OS software!*

# Giving Graffiti a Helping Hand

Here's a novel idea: Rather than trying to build a better Graffiti than Graffiti, why not simply cut down on the number of letters necessary to write a word? Or make it so you can write anywhere on the screen, instead of just in the Graffiti area? How about tweaking the recognition engine so it's more accommodating to your handwriting? These are among the goals of Graffiti assistants—software tools that just make life with Graffiti a little easier.

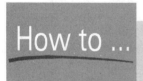 ## Improve Graffiti Recognition

For all its quirks, Graffiti is actually an excellent handwriting-recognition tool. If you plan to stick with it, you can use these tips to improve accuracy. You already learned some of them in Chapter 4, but we think they bear repeating.

- Write big. If your characters fill up the bulk of the Graffiti area, they're more likely to be accurately recognized.

- Don't write on an angle. Many of us do just that when writing with pen and paper, but that's poison to Graffiti. Keep your strokes straight.

- Take advantage of the built-in Graffiti Help application, which provides a graphical cheat sheet for all Graffiti strokes. Go to Prefs | Buttons | Pen, then choose Graffiti Help from the list of available options. Now, whenever you draw a line from the Graffiti area to the top of the Palm's screen, the Help applet appears.

- Having trouble with the letter *V*? Draw it backward, starting from the right side and ending with the left. You needn't add the little tail (as with the standard Graffiti *V*) and the letter will come out perfect every time.

- Having trouble with the letter *B*? Forget trying to draw it Graffiti's way—write the number 3 instead. Similarly, writing the number 6 gives you a good *G* every time, while the number 8 creates the perfect *Y*. Naturally, you should still make these characters on the letter (that is, left) side of the Graffiti area.

- Start your *R* at the bottom of the letter instead of the top. That initial downstroke often produces the ShortCut symbol instead of an *R*.

# Was This the Word You Were Looking For?

Remember the old game show *Name That Tune*? The host would describe a song, and the contestant would say, "I can name that tune in three notes." Imagine if Graffiti could adopt that precept, guessing the word or phrase you're writing as you write it. By the time you entered, say, the *e* in "competition," the software would have figured out the rest of the word, thereby saving you six additional pen-strokes.

That's the appeal of CIC's WordComplete, a Clié utility that helps you write faster by helping you write less. As you enter characters, a box containing possible word matches appears. If you spy the word you're after, just tap it. The more letters you enter, the closer you get to the correct word (if it's in the software's database).

Obviously, for little words like "the" and "to," the program won't help much. But for longer words, it can indeed save you some scribbling. And WordComplete lets you add your own words and/or short phrases to its database, which can definitely save you time in the long run. Let's look at its features and operation.

Once you install WordComplete on your Clié (it's compatible with all models), run the program and tap the Enable WordComplete check box. You'll see a number of options appear:

- **Suggest words after** After how many letters should the software start suggesting words? The default is two, but you can make it anywhere between one and four.

- **Display at most** How many matches should the software display at a time? You have to experiment to decide your preference. Obviously, more matches means a greater likelihood of your desired word appearing, but it takes a tiny bit longer to glance through a longer list.

- **Show word box near** Where should the suggestion box pop up—next to the cursor or near the bottom of the screen? We think the former is the most practical, as it cuts down on stylus travel.

- **Words with at least** What's the minimum word length WordComplete should attempt to guess? Three letters? Four? You can make your selection here.

15

■ **Insert a space after word**   Leave this box checked if you want the software to automatically add a space after you tap a word. Most of the time this is quite helpful, except when you're about to end a sentence with a punctuation mark. Then you have to draw a backspace stroke.

■ **Add words by double tap**   WordComplete supports the use of a custom dictionary to which you can add your own words. With this option checked, it's as simple as double-tapping a word with your stylus, then tapping the Add option from the little box that appears. (You hear a beep confirming the word has successfully been added.)

■ **Custom Dictionary**   Tap this button to manually add words to the software's dictionary. Although the aforementioned double-tap method limits you to adding one word at a time, here you can add multiple words (such as proper names) or even short phrases.

   *If you do add proper names to the dictionary, take note that they're case-sensitive. This means if you add "Rick Broida," you have to use a capital R if you want WordComplete to show the name while you're writing.*

## Goodbye, Graffiti Area!

Part of the challenge in learning and mastering Graffiti is that you can't see your characters as you write them. (Actually, if you have an NR or NX model, you can—their virtual Graffiti areas leave a trail of "digital ink" beneath your stylus. Very cool.) Plus, the Graffiti area is kind of, well, small. Most of us aren't used to writing in such a confined space, and that alone can be a source of Graffiti contention. Fortunately, CIC's RecoEcho can liberate your stylus from that tiny box, effectively turning the entire Clié screen into one big Graffiti area.

   *As you learned earlier in this chapter, programs like Jot and SimpliWrite offer the same capability—but you have to ditch Graffiti in the process. RecoEcho keeps Graffiti alive.*

RecoEcho enables you to write—using Graffiti characters—anywhere on the screen. What's more, like the Clié NR and NX models, it leaves a trail of "digital ink" beneath your stylus tip, which goes a long way toward helping you produce more accurate characters. Thus, you see what you write as you write it.

After you launch the program, you simply tap a check box to enable it. Then you set three simple options:

- **Write in full screen**   If, for some reason, you don't want to write on the screen itself (but only in the Graffiti area), uncheck this box. You still see your pen strokes as you write, provided the next option is still checked.

- **Show ink**   If you prefer not to see the trail of "ink" as you write, uncheck this box.

- **Ink width**   Choose 1 for a thin trail of ink, 2 for a thicker trail. This is simply a matter of personal preference.

When RecoEcho is activated, you see a large arrow at the top of the screen. This designates an invisible line separating the letter and number sides, just like in the standard Graffiti area. Now, write on the screen as you normally would, and presto! You're free to write as large as you like.

We'd be remiss if we didn't mention a similar product: TealPoint Software's TealEcho, which costs a couple of bucks more but offers a few more features.

## Graffiti, Your Way

Finally, we come to the one product that really manhandles Graffiti, that says, "Look, can't you just learn to understand *my* writing?" It is TealPoint Software's TealScript, a utility that lets you tweak Graffiti so it's more responsive to your hand, or replace it altogether with a customized character set.

If you're willing to battle one of the steepest learning curves we've encountered in a piece of Clié software, the benefits are truly worthwhile. TealScript works its wizardry through the use of custom profiles, which contain the Graffiti character set as you define it. In other words, you teach TealScript how *you* like to write, and it teaches Graffiti to accommodate *your* penmanship.

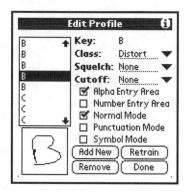

The letter *v* is a good example of how this works. Your profile can include the standard character—the one with the little tail we always forget to add—and a regular *v* you added yourself. Similarly, instead of always having to write capitalized versions of letters like *R* and *B*, you can add lowercase versions.

As confusing as TealScript can be, it's not totally out of the question for novice users. That's because it comes with an already-built profile that helps you overcome the most commonly miswritten Graffiti characters. So, right out of the box it's useful. And while TealScript may not be the friendliest program around, it's by far the best way to make Graffiti an ally instead of an obstacle.

## Where to Find It

| Web Site | Address | What's There |
| --- | --- | --- |
| Textware Solutions | www.fitaly.com | Fitaly Keyboard, FitalyStamp |
| Link Evolution Corp. | www.thumbtype.net | ThumbType |
| Softava | www.silkyboard.com | Silkyboard |
| TapPad | www.tappad.com | TapPad |
| Communications Intelligence Corp. | www.cic.com | Jot, RecoEcho, WordComplete |
| Advance Recognition Technologies, Inc. | www.advancedrecognition.com | SimpliWrite |
| Horace Ho | www.horaceho.net | Keyboard Hack |
| TealPoint Software | www.tealpoint.com | TealScript, TealEcho |

# Chapter 16

# Showing Digital Photos and Movies on Your CLIÉ

## How to...

- Use your Clié camera's settings
- Set white balance
- Prepare Clié photos for the desktop
- Transfer images from the Clié to the PC
- Watch movies on your Clié
- View photos on your Clié

Digital cameras have been around for less than ten years, but they have already dramatically changed the way we think about photography. Almost everyone we know, for instance, owns a digital camera and uses it to take snapshots at family outings. The pictures can be immediately e-mailed to friends and relatives, posted at an online photo site, or mailed out on CD-ROM. Even people who would never haul around a 35mm camera embrace the simplicity and convenience of a digital camera.

What does all that have to do with your Clié? Plenty. A few Cliés—namely, the NR70V and NX70V—come with a built-in digital camera; most others can accept Sony's Memory Stick Camera—a digital camera mounted on a Memory Stick. Even if you don't have a built-in or MS digital camera, you can load your handheld with pictures from an ordinary digital camera and use it like a digital album, filled with your favorite images.

# Taking Pictures on a CLIÉ

There are two ways to take pictures with your Clié. You can use a model that has a built-in digital camera—like the NR70V or NX70V—or purchase Sony's add-on Memory Stick Camera (you can see both in Figure 16-1). If you have the option of using a Clié with a built-in camera, do that. It's better than the Memory Stick camera for a few reasons:

- Newer models, like the NX70V, take better photos at resolutions as high as 640×480, while the Memory Stick camera (and older Clié models) limit you to 320×320.
- The built-in camera doesn't occupy the Memory Stick slot, so you can store pictures and other data on a Memory Stick even while you use the camera.
- The Memory Stick Camera is yet another small gadget that's easy to lose. If it's built in, it isn't going anywhere.

## Configuring Your Camera

The Clié camera is quite easy to manage. Depending upon which model you have, your options may vary, but you essentially have control over the resolution, storage location, white balance, and color effect of your photos. To see these options, tap the wrench icon on the digital camera screen—it opens your options.

Here's a rundown of your key options:

- **Save to location** If you have an integrated camera, you can save your pictures to the Clié's internal memory or Memory Stick. The Memory Stick is a good place if you want to keep a lot of images around—you won't consume precious system memory—but you can't rename or annotate images stored on a Memory Stick, nor can you include them in the Address Book (see Chapter 6 for details).

- **Size** How large do you want your pictures to be? Tiny 88-pixel images are good only for the Address Book, but you may also (depending on the camera) be able to store images in resolutions that include 160×160 (the ordinary Palm OS screen resolution), 320×320 (the Clié hi-res screen size), and 640×480 (VGA resolution).

- **Date** Some Clié cameras can record the current date in the picture. We recommend leaving this feature turned off, since there's nothing uglier than seeing the date in the corner of a photo.

**FIGURE 16-1**    Clié cameras typically rotate in their housing, which lets you take self-portraits.

16

- **Sound** You can turn on a realistic "shutter sound" that helps identify when the picture has been taken. Some cameras have a simple on or off control; others let you choose from among several sound options.

- **Effect** Many digital cameras offer you color effect options, and the Clié camera is no different. You can shoot your picture in ordinary color or switch to black and white, sepia (an old-fashioned, brown-tinted variation on black and white), negative (just what it sounds like—a cool artistic effect) and solarize. Solarization decreases the number of colors in the photo, and is commonly used in '80s rock videos and other artistic films. Since the Clié's pictures are kinda low-res to begin with, we generally ignore these fancy options and just take standard color pictures. You can always enhance them later in an image editor on your desktop PC.

- **White Balance** White balance lets you correct the colors in your photo based on the kind of light in the scene. Sony offers you four options: auto, indoor A, indoor B, and outdoor. See the sidebar "Adjusting White Balance," for more info.

- **Brightness** You can dial in the brightness of your photo to correct for an unusually dark scene (keeping in mind that the Clié has no flash). The Memory Stick camera puts the brightness control on the main screen, under the image preview, while the built-in models put brightness in Settings.

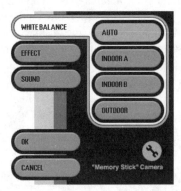

## Prepping Your Photos for the PC

If you've experimented a bit with your digital camera, you've no doubt seen that the Clié uses two mysterious file formats for its digital images: PGP and DCF. PGP is Sony's own format for the Clié, while DCF is just the JPG format under a different name. In order to transfer images from the Clié to your PC, they must be stored on a Memory Stick in the DCF format. Once there, you can use a Memory Stick reader on your desktop or the PictureGear application (a Windows application that comes on your Clié's installation CD-ROM) to copy them to a computer; see the "Moving Pictures to the PC" section later in this chapter for details.

## Adjusting White Balance

Your Clié camera has a four-setting control called "white balance." Your old 35mm film camera didn't have anything like it. So what the heck is white balance? In a nutshell, different light sources have different color temperatures, meaning that a scene will appear to have a different color tone depending upon how it's illuminated.

You can get a sense of this yourself. Candlelight appears more yellowish than sunlight, for instance. And other sources—like tungsten lights—can cast strange, greenish glows around a room. But in general, our brains automatically adjust for different color sources and make the color correction for us. We usually don't even notice.

Your camera's white balance control works like the human brain. It adjusts the exposure so your pictures have the same color cast no matter what light source you use. When properly balanced, your camera won't apply strange color casts to your pictures even if you shoot indoors, outdoors, in florescent lighting, or in candlelight.

Most of the time, your Clié is fine if you leave it set on auto (as in the previous image). If you notice your camera is taking pictures with a weird color cast—everything is coming out greenish or bluish, for instance—try one of the preset white balance settings and see if that improves your shots.

NOTE    *Some of Sony's newest Cliés actually save files in true JPG format and make it much easier to copy files to the PC. If you have one of those models, you're in luck, and can skip most of this section!*

To make the needed conversion, do this:

1. Open the application called PG Pocket on your Clié and make sure you're in the thumbnail view. If you only see a single image, tap the Return button in the lower-left corner to see the thumbnails. Make sure you're currently looking at pictures stored internally by selecting Internal from the menu at the top of the screen.

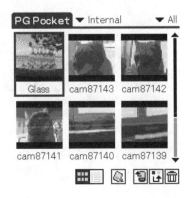

16

**2.** Tap the Import/Export button at the bottom of the screen. The button looks like a PDA with an arrow in it.

**3.** Select the images you want to move to the Memory Stick by tapping the selection boxes.

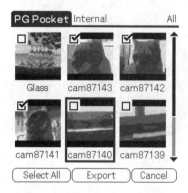

**4.** After you've selected your images, tap Export.

**5.** On the Import/Export dialog box, choose the DCF format and tap OK. After a short conversion process, the images will be copied to the Memory Stick, ready for the big move to your PC.

It's also possible that you have images on your Memory Stick in PGP format. You won't be able to copy these to your PC until they're in DCF format. To make the change, import the images back to internal memory, then export them back to the Memory Stick, being sure to choose the DCF option.

## Watching Movies on Your CLIÉ

Why would anyone want to watch a low-resolution movie on a screen barely larger than a matchbook? This question has been a source of much debate between Dave and Rick. Rick, who dismissed the idea of movies on a Clié out of hand without ever really trying it, recently had a change of heart when he found that he could watch TV shows on his Clié while traveling by plane. Now he's sold—yet another example of Dave being proved right.

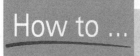 **Move Your Pictures to the PC**

You'd expect that Sony would include some sort of conduit to automatically transfer your pictures from the handheld to the PC, but that's not the case—at least not in any of the models that the company had shipped as of when we wrote this book. One of the most common questions people ask us is "How on earth do I get pictures from the Clié to the computer?"

Good question. And the answer is that it's actually pretty simple (though not particularly obvious). You have two choices. If you have a Memory Stick reader for your desktop PC, just pop the Stick out of your Clié, put it into your reader, and open the DCIM folder on the Memory Stick to see and copy the images.

If you don't have a Memory Stick reader at your disposal, follow these steps instead:

1. Start by moving your digital images to a Memory Stick and converting them to DCF format. See the section "Prepping Your Photos for the PC" earlier in this chapter for info on how to do that.

2. Place the Clié in its HotSync cradle and turn it on.

3. Start the MS Import on the Clié. Wait until you're connected, like this:

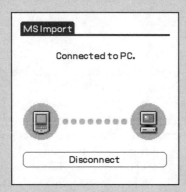

4. On the PC, start PictureGear Lite, which came on your installation disc.

**5.** In the folder list on the left side of the screen, find the Clié's Memory Stick and open the folder. You should see a folder called DCIM; this is where you'll find your photos.

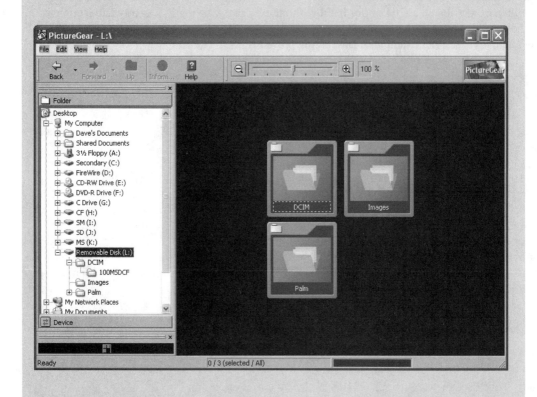

**6.** Drag the photos to the Windows desktop or to another folder on your PC. They'll be in good-old JPG format.

There are a whole bunch of ways to get movies into your Clié. The NX70V, for instance, comes with software that lets you capture movies right from the Clié's built-in camera. A more practical solution, though, especially if you have your sights set on copying a few episodes of *Seinfeld* or *The Simpsons* to your Clié for long commutes, is a third-party video player and encoder.

Third-party programs like FireViewer and TealMovie make it possible—but without a doubt, our favorite video tool is a program called Kinoma. Why Kinoma? Because it has an easy-to-use desktop converter program and supports the 480×320-pixel HiRes+ mode in the NR- and NX-series Cliés. That means you can turn your Clié on its side and watch widescreen video.

## Watching Movies on Your CLIÉ

**Dave**: Personally, I love the idea of watching a TV show I saved off of my VCR on plane trips. But you, Mr. Blows-in-the-Wind, what's your opinion of PDA movies now? For years you told me that it was silly to watch movies on a small handheld screen, and even when I suggested that faster processors, better screens, and improved sound would someday make watching a movie on your PDA commonplace, you poo-poo'd the idea as insane. But I know you're using Kinoma to watch SpongeBob episodes on your Clié, so what's your excuse? What made you decide that video on a Clié was a good idea? I expect to hear a lot of groveling, with the words, "You were right, Dave."

**Rick**: The day those words escape my lips is the day I've been drugged, beaten, and threatened with having to see Kristin Hersh in concert. Years ago, when you were going ga-ga over postage stamp–sized slideshows playing on your Palm without sound, I did indeed poo-poo the notion of handheld video. And on most Palm-based handhelds, the experience is still extremely lame. But on a Sony Clié—especially one with a high-resolution color screen and enhanced sound—mobile movies are pretty cool. There are still plenty of obstacles, like making space for the video files (a mere half-hour show can eat up over 64MB). But we're getting there, and I can't wait for the day when I can walk into an airport and download Moulin Rouge to my Clié from a kiosk.

Even if you don't want to watch a movie in widescreen, the sideways 480×320 format is great for ordinary television shows. TVs have a 4×3 aspect ratio, making them slightly wider than they are tall. That means you'll get a slightly bigger image if you encode it sideways than if you pack it into the usual 320×320-pixel space on screen.

Making a movie with Kinoma Producer is a drag-and-drop affair. It accepts video in a wide variety of formats, including QuickTime, MPEG, and AVI, and lets you tweak the movie's specs, like frame rate and audio format. You can also rotate the file to play in widescreen mode on compatible devices, and set other details like the background color or still image that frames the movie. Dave has used Kinoma extensively to copy music videos downloaded from the Internet, home movie clips transferred from a digital video camcorder, and even complete TV shows.

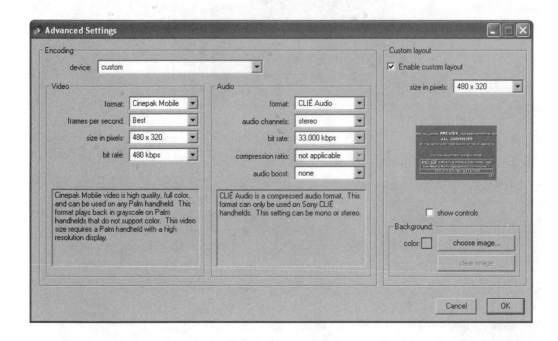

Of course, you'll want to have a lot of memory for videos. A 128MB Memory Stick is the bare minimum you'll need to get a television show or movie onto your Clié, and you might need to break it up onto more than one Stick. As of press time, larger Memory Sticks weren't yet available—but we've got our fingers crossed for 256MB, 512MB, and even 1GB Memory Sticks to appear soon.

# Build an Electronic Photo Album

Even if you're not interested in taking pictures with your Clié, you may still want to use it as a digital photo album to show off images you took with a different camera. With the right photo viewer software, you'll never be without a picture of your spouse, kids, cats, and other loved ones. The process is quite simple: electronic images on your desktop PC (whether scanned, transferred from a digital camera, or downloaded from the Web) are converted to the right format, then installed when you HotSync. Then you load up your viewer and, well, view 'em.

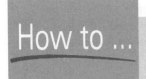

## How to ... Find HiRes+ Applications

Nowhere is the ability to fill the entire 320×480-pixel screen on NR-, NX-, and other Clié models more important than when working with multimedia applications like digital image and video viewers. Trust us: there's nothing in all the world quite like turning your Clié sideways and watching a widescreen movie. But how can you find programs designed with the Clié's HiRes+ mode in mind? Surf over to **www.clieuk.co.uk/cphires.shtml** for a comprehensive list of programs that fill the whole screen.

## Choosing Photo-Viewing Software

Many programs enable you to view images on your Clié, some of them quite similar in form and function. Here are some of the most popular programs:

- **AcidImage**  An excellent photo-viewer for the Clié, it supports HiRes+ 480×320-pixel images—so you can literally fill the screen with your favorite photos. AcidImage also reads plain-old JPG images off the Memory Stick, so you don't have to use a cumbersome desktop conversion program first. Just drag and drop JPG images from the PC onto your Clié.

- **HandStory Suite**  This multifaceted program displays e-book doc files, web clips, memos, and digital images. The desktop transfer process is very elegant; just right-click an image on the desktop and choose Save To Palm from the menu. It, too, supports full-screen HiRes+ images.

- **SplashPhoto**  A more "traditional" photo album program for the Clié, it has a desktop converter that lets you crop and edit images to an appropriate size for the Clié screen and also change them to a special file format for the PDA. It reads pure JPG images as well.

**16**

■ **Photogather**    Similar to SplashPhoto, Photogather supports HiRes+ mode and JPG images, and has a desktop converter to boot. Beware, though: Photogather sends full-resolution images to the Clié instead of shrinking them to fit on the screen—and that can eat up Memory Stick space very quickly.

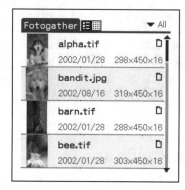

## Mapmaker, Mapmaker, Make Me a Map

Wouldn't it be cool if you could have street-level maps handy when you visit unfamiliar cities? You can, and they won't cost you a dime. Point your web browser to Yahoo! Maps or one of the many other online cartography sources, generate the map you need, then save it to your hard drive. Now, run it through your image viewer's conversion software and load it on to your Clié device. If you want something a little more sophisticated (and precise), check out Solus Pro from Delorme (**www.delorme.com**). It's designed specifically to display maps on your handheld.

## Where to Find It

| Web Site | Address | What's There |
| --- | --- | --- |
| Firepad | www.firepad.com | FireViewer |
| PalmGear.com | www.palmgear.com | Virtually all the applications found in this chapter |
| SplashData | www.splashdata.com | SplashPhoto |

# Part III

# The CLIÉ Multimedia Experience

# Chapter 17

# Painting and Drawing on Your CLIÉ

## How to...

- Paint images on the Clié
- Use Clié Paint to modify digital images
- Copy images from the PC to your Clié
- Share and collaborate sketches with two Cliés
- Use an outliner to organize your ideas
- Capture Clié screenshots

So there you are: at your monthly sales meeting, listening to some guy drone on and on about how you need to more proactively leverage your core competency to win the golden carrot for your department's sales quotas. Or something like that. You're not really sure what he's talking about, since you've been doodling on the top page of your meeting minutes.

Well cut that out! Instead of drawing on a piece of paper, you can be painting a picture on your Clié. It's high tech, it's in color, and people might even think you're working.

# Painting on the CLIÉ

You're probably wondering why you might want to paint on a handheld computer so small that it fits in your pocket. Well, in the world of computers, the answer is often "because you can." Programmers have never let something as silly as a technical limitation get in the way of doing something, so when PDAs first came out, programmers seemed to scramble to become the first to create a paint program for their favorite handheld PC.

Aside from that admittedly flippant answer, the capability to sketch things on your Clié is a handy feature. You can draw a map showing directions to a luncheon, outline a process, or design a flowchart. You can also just doodle—use the Clié as a high-tech Etch-a-Sketch for those boring times when you're waiting for the train or pretending to take notes in a meeting. Perhaps most importantly, you can draw on top of pictures you've stored on your Clié, giving you the ability to annotate images and add captions.

Painting on your Clié is fun and productive, but you need to remember these limitations:

- While some Cliés have a resolution of 160×160 pixels, your Clié may have a resolution of 320×320 or even 320×480. The more pixels you have, the better, but most paint programs can't utilize the full 320×480-pixel screen. Moreover, even the highest resolution devices don't give you a lot of room in which to draw. After your images are transferred to a PC, you'll find that they're still quite small. So, drawing something on the Clié you later plan to export to say, a PowerPoint presentation, generally isn't a practical plan.

- Few paint programs support printing directly from the Clié and not all even let you transfer completed art back to the PC. That means, in some cases, what you draw on the screen pretty much stays on the screen. If you *can* print your work of art, it'll print just as rough and jagged on paper as it looked onscreen.

## Replacement for a Laptop?

**Dave:** PDAs like the Clié are handy little gadgets, but they were never intended to be full-fledged substitutes for laptop and desktop computers. Nonetheless, that's just the way I use mine; I have an office suite and add-on keyboard for word processing, Margi's Presenter-to-Go for showing PowerPoint slideshows, a few games for entertainment, and a Memory Stick full of MP3s for music. In fact, with the Clié's digital camera, paint software, e-books, and video playback capabilities, my PDA does the work of two or three portable devices. I haven't carried a laptop on a trip in well over a year, and I have never once wished I had one with me.

**Rick:** Amen, brother. I like to travel as light as possible, and even a five-pound notebook is more weight than I prefer. With the Clié and a few lightweight accoutrements, like Think Outside's Stowaway keyboard and the aforementioned Presenter To Go, I can go on a business trip and still conduct business. When the day comes that I can watch a full-length movie on my Clié (and that day isn't far off), I'll be in schlep-free heaven.

## Doodling with CLIÉ Paint

The good news is that Sony includes a paint program with most Cliés, so you can doodle with your PDA right out of the box. Clié Paint gives you a small assortment of painting tools and a choice of what image size you'd like to work with. Using Clié Paint, you can create original art from a totally blank canvas, or you can load digital images created with your Clié camera and paint or annotate right on top of them. In other words, you can take a picture of Dave, then scribble in a pair of horns and a devil beard—one of Rick's favorite activities.

### Creating a New Image in CLIÉ Paint

To get started, tap the Clié Paint icon in your PDA's application screen (by default, it's usually in the CLIE category). Your first choice is what resolution you'd like to work with. Depending upon which model you have, your options may vary, but the screen will look something like this:

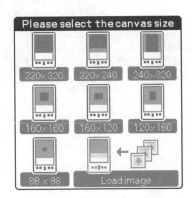

**17**

Not all versions of Clié Paint have all these options, and not all put an option to load a digital image right on this start screen. You can load an image and paint on top of that using one of these two methods:

- If you see an option to Load Image on the Clié Paint start screen, tap it and you'll be taken to the Clié's PG Pocket application, which is a program that displays all of the digital images stored on your Clié. Actually, it displays the digital images taken by your Clié camera. Find the image you want to edit and tap it. Finally, tap the edit icon in the toolbar (it has a pencil in it) and you'll be returned to Clié Paint, ready to work on the photo.

- If you don't have an option to load a photo right from the start, then tap any of the image formats to start Clié Paint. The screen size doesn't matter, because it will have no effect on the image you're about to edit. Then tap the File button (it's the one that looks like a page on the very left side of the screen). Tap the Load Image button and choose a photo from the PG Pocket application. Finally, tap the edit icon in the toolbar (it has a pencil in it) and you'll be returned to Clié Paint, ready to work on the photo.

If you want to work with a blank screen instead of a digital image, just select the starting image size and you're immediately taken to the Clié Paint screen. The paint interface is very simple. When you first start the program, you'll see this toolbar:

The toolbar has three modes, each with additional tools. To switch between the three toolbars, just tap the right edge of the toolbar. You can see which toolbar is currently active by noting which of the three squares is lit with a red block.

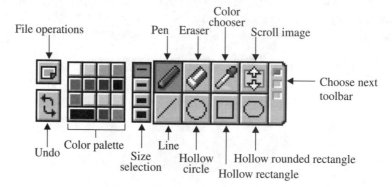

The other toolbars look like this:

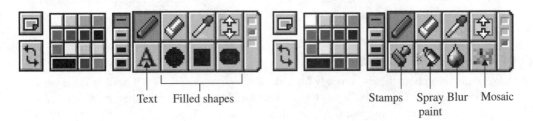

Text   Filled shapes                      Stamps   Spray   Blur   Mosaic
                                                    paint

Note that the middle of every toolbar allows you to change the size of whatever you're painting on the screen. You have a choice of four sizes for painting, text, stickers, and the range of effects like blue and mosaic.

The program also gives you control over the color with a palette control. To switch to the color palette, tap the active color bar, which is the rectangle in the lower-left corner of the color box. When you do, you'll get to pick your active painting color from a hexagon like this one:

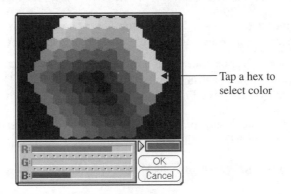

Tap a hex to
select color

Clié Paint lets you do some fun and interesting things to your digital images. You can add text and apply "stickers" to your photos, as well as save them to your Clié for use in e-mail messages and other applications.

17

When you're done with your picture, save it by tapping the File button in the upper-left corner of the toolbar and choose to overwrite the existing image (this will destroy the unaltered image) or save it as a new image. You can transfer the completed image to your PC using the steps outlined in Chapter 16.

### Converting a Desktop Picture

Want to doodle on a photo that is currently on your desktop computer? You'll need to get it onto your Clié first. Not a problem: you'll just have to use the PictureGear application in Windows. PictureGear probably came with your Clié's installation disk or with your Clié camera's installation disc. Either way, here's what you need to do:

1. Start by converting the image to a pixel size that Clié Paint can work with. Clié Paint won't be able to handle a typical 3-megapixel image from your digital camera, for instance; it only understands images that come in Clié-standard formats like 160×160, 320×320, and 320×240. So, open your picture in a program that lets you crop the image to a specific pixel size and save a copy in this new format. Dave really likes a program called A Smaller Image (from **www.trivista.com**) for this sort of job. (See Figure 17-1.)

2. After the image is in a Clié-friendly form, turn on your Clié, place it in its HotSync cradle, and tap the MS Import program—we're going to copy the picture to the Clié's Memory Stick.

3. Start PictureGear on your desktop PC and navigate to the image in question. Once you find it, select the image and choose File | Output Services | Output Clie Handheld Format To Memory Stick. (See Figure 17-2.)

4. In the resulting dialog box, choose the drive letter that corresponds to your Clié and click OK. Moments later, the file will be on your Clié's Memory Stick.

Now you can open the image in Clié Paint and fiddle with it to your heart's content!

## Other Painting Programs

If you have a hankering to paint, you'll be happy to know that Clié Paint isn't your only option. There's a plethora of painting tools for the Clié—so many, in fact, we decided to narrow the crop for you to only a pair of programs you should evaluate.

■ **TealPaint**    Perhaps the most full-featured paint program for the Clié, TealPaint seems to do it all. The program has a complete set of painting tools, including lines, shapes, fill tools, an eraser, and a variety of brushes. The program starts you in this screen, which displays thumbnail images of your pictures and lets you view, edit, or animate them. Using TealPaint, you can copy-and-paste selections of your image, not just within the same picture, but in any picture in your database. TealPaint is also an animation tool. We discuss animation programs later in this chapter, but it's worth pointing out that you can use TealPaint to create animations by playing all the images in a particular database in sequence. To make a simple bouncing ball, for instance, draw a series of images in which the ball moves a bit in each successive image. Then tap the Anim button and tap the first picture in your series.

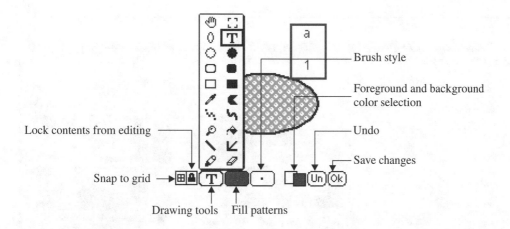

Brush style

Foreground and background color selection

Lock contents from editing

Undo

Save changes

Snap to grid

Drawing tools    Fill patterns

Set the exact size to import into the Clié

17

FIGURE 17-1    Dave swears by A Smaller Image for converting images to the Clié's shape and size.

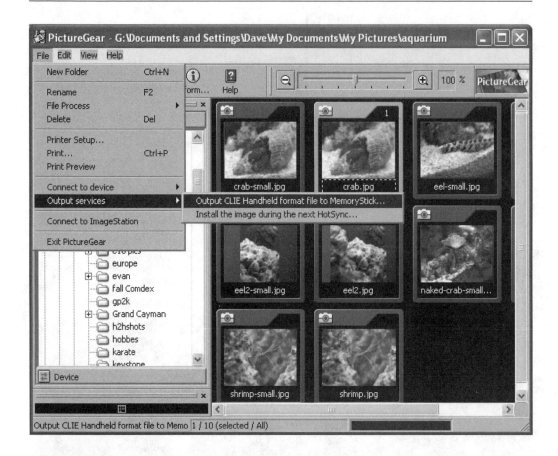

■ **Diddle**   Diddle is a free, neat little drawing program that enables you to sketch with a minimum of clutter to get in the way of your drawing. The interface is composed of a set of graphical menus at the top of the screen—you can choose from among various drawing styles, line thickness, and text. For the most part, the program is easy to explore on your own—just start drawing.

# Collaborating on a Sketch

Drawing on a Clié is usually a solo affair, but what if you're in a meeting trying to lay out office furniture with your business partner? What then, huh? Okay, there may be some better examples, but just work with us for a moment.

Okay, we have a better example! Suppose you're in a long, boring meeting. If you have the right drawing software, you can doodle on your Clié and have it immediately show up on a partner's PDA, who can then add to your drawing and beam it back to you. All the while, your boss is none the wiser. Anyway, if your buddy, business partner, or intern owns a Clié, the two of you can sketch your ideas on your PDAs. The results can appear simultaneously in both devices more or less in real time. That's totally cool, if you ask us.

Most collaborative sketch programs do their magic via the Clié's IR port. Here are some popular applications you can try:

■ **Beamer**   This simple program has just a few buttons but it's free. You can write short notes in a screen that resembles the Note Pad or draw free-form images in a blank sketchpad. When you're ready, tap the beam button (it looks like a tilde sign) to beam it to another nearby Palm-powered PDA. The recipient can add it to their drawing and then beam it back.

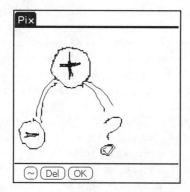

■ **Zapster**   Very similar to Beamer, this program has a slightly more elegant interface. On the downside, it's shareware and costs $10. Like Beamer, you use it to draw and then beam your work to another Clié, where it can be edited and returned.

# Capturing Screenshots of the CLIÉ Display

Perhaps you've thumbed through this book, some Clié web sites, or a magazine like *Handheld Computing* and wondered what it would be like to have lunch with Dave and Rick. (Answer: like keeping a pair of six-year-olds entertained in line at McDonald's.) You might also have wondered how everyone seems to be able to capture screenshots of the Clié display and publish them in ordinary desktop software. As it turns out, capturing Clié screens isn't that hard to do because several tools are available to automate (at least partially) the process for you.

The easiest way to capture a screen from your Clié—and our favorite, by far—is by using ScreenShot Hack, a Palm OS extension that works with X-Master or HackMaster (see Chapter 13). ScreenShot Hack is a great general-purpose tool because you needn't do anything special

## Experimenting with Fractals

If you're somewhat new to computing, you may have missed the fractal craze of the '80s. That was when everyone and her cousin seemed to be writing a graphics program for the PC, Amiga, Atari, and TI/99 that generated fractal images.

What's a fractal, you ask? A *fractal* is a class of mathematics invented in the 1970s by a mathematician named Benoit Mandelbrot. This is more interesting than it might sound—it's concerned with reproducing infinitely repeating structures, both mathematically and visually. Consider a mountain, for instance—you can zoom in and in on it and, no matter how far you zoom, the structure remains essentially the same, all the way down to the rocks that make up the mountain. Another example: think of a fiord. On the surface, calculating the total perimeter of the shoreline seems easy but, as you enlarge the fiord, you find there's a virtually infinite amount of structure to the shore, as it weaves back and forth in tiny jagged edges. A fiord is an infinitely repeating structure.

All of this has practical applications, though, because fractal equations do a darned good job of drawing computer-rendered natural objects like trees, mountains, snowflakes, and flowers. When done well, the perceived reality can be stunning.

All this is great, but what about the Clié? Well, you can use your Clié to draw fractal sets that are beautiful in their own right, and you can experiment with them by zooming in and letting the Clié render the new scene. No matter where you zoom, you get an interesting picture and you can always zoom in further.

Luckily, a few fractal programs are available for the Clié. You won't get stunning, full-color results like you can on a Mac or PC, but you can have fun, nonetheless. Try Fractal Maker Color, or P.Fract, both available at **www.palmgear.com**.

One word of warning: The Clié's processor is no supercomputer. As a result, the time it takes your Clié to draw a fractal onscreen may well remind you of drawing fractals on 486's and Amigas in the '80s. It can take quite some time to render each image.

to activate it. There are no countdowns until the screen is captured (unless you specifically set a capture delay), and no funky menu selections. Just display the screen you want to capture and draw the screen capture gesture in the Graffiti area.

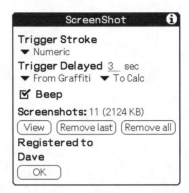

Most importantly, the program converts the images to a usable file format for you—many other screenshot utilities don't. You have two choices regarding how to get images to the PC:

- **The ScreenShot Conduit**   This is a separate program you need to download and install. The conduit grabs the captured screens from the Clié and puts them in BMP or GIF format in a folder of your choice.

- **The ScreenShot Converter**   If you don't want to use the conduit, the images are transferred to the PC anyway (as long as you set the System conduit to Handheld Overwrites Desktop). Then you need to use the ScreenShot Converter utility (again, a separate program you need to download and install) to transform the images into Windows bitmap files.

You can use either method, though we prefer the conduit—it's a bit more automated. Once you've got the images on your PC, you can convert them to any format you like. In this book, for instance, Dave uses Jasc's Image Robot to convert all the BMP screenshots automatically into TIF format, Osborne's file format of choice. Because the whole process is automated, no one has to sit around saving files over and over again to get them into the right format.

## Where to Find It

| Web Site | Address | What's There |
|---|---|---|
| PalmGear.com | www.palmgear.com | Virtually all the applications found in this chapter |
| TealPoint Software | www.tealpoint.com | TealPaint and other Teal products |
| TriVista | www.trivista.com | A Smaller Image |

**17**

# Chapter 18

# Music
# and CLIÉ Audio

## How to...

- Play MP3s on your Clié
- Transfer MP3 files from your desktop
- Manage MP3s using a Clié
- Check free space on a Memory Stick
- Use the Clié to make music
- Tune a guitar with a Clié
- Determine if your Clié has standard or enhanced audio
- Expand your Clié's alarm collection
- Convert WAV files to Clié alarm sounds

There was a time when a computer that could reproduce lifelike sound or make quality video was dismissed as a game machine. People Who Knew Things would sternly deride a computer with even a hint of multimedia prowess as something that serious people shouldn't waste their time or money on. After all, only kids play games.

These days, we wouldn't even know where to begin with an assessment like that. Games, for instance, are for everybody—even the CEO of OmniCorp probably passes time on a long plane flight with a quick little game of *Bejeweled*. More importantly, even multimedia savvy computers are great for business applications. Take the Clié, for instance. You probably use it to track your schedule and contacts, do some occasional word processing, and maybe even dabble in databases. But some Clié models come with excellent audio and video, making them ideal for stuff like music, watching movies, and playing games. In this chapter, we'll look at the audio capabilities of Clié. Not only can you listen to tunes, but you can customize your alarms and brush up on a musical instrument. Read on and see.

# Listening to MP3s on Your CLIÉ

Some Clié models come with a built-in MP3 player. Others are compatible with an MP3 add-on that lets you listen to music while you're on the go. If your Clié doesn't come with MP3 capabilities, feel free to skip this section. We don't mind, and we'll catch up with you later.

By and large, the MP3 player is pretty self-explanatory; to use it, just copy tunes to your Clié's Memory Stick and tap the AudioPlayer application on your Clié.

NOTE     *Don't try to load MP3s via the normal Install Tool, which transfers them when you HotSync. It will take a very, very long time to copy music this way. The direct connection is much faster.*

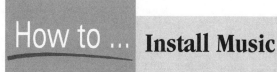 **Install Music**

To get your songs on to your Memory Stick, you can use a Memory Stick reader that connects to your PC's USB port, or just put the Clié in the HotSync port and connect with the AudioPlayer program directly. Here's how to do that:

**1.** Start the AudioPlayer and choose Options | Transfer from the menu. Wait until you see a message on the Clié that says "Status: Transfer" with a warning not to remove the Memory Stick while a data transfer is in progress.

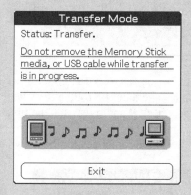

**2.** On your PC, double-click My Computer and find the removable drive that corresponds to your Clié. Open it, and double-click the folder marked Palm. Then double-click Programs, and open MSAudio. This is where you'll copy your music.

**3.** Open the folder on your PC with your MP3 files and drag and drop them onto the MSAudio folder. When the files have copied, you can disconnect your Clié from the desktop computer.

TIP    *Instead of venturing into AudioPlayer, you can simply run the MS Import utility on your Clié. It establishes a direct connection to your PC, thus allowing you to proceed directly to Step 2.*

18

## Playing Music with AudioPlayer

Once you have a small music collection on your Memory Stick, you're ready to listen to music. Tap the AudioPlayer icon on your Clié and you should see a list of tunes, like this:

In addition to the onscreen controls, you can also use the scroll wheel on the side of the Clié to operate the music player. You can change tunes by rolling the wheel up or down, and you can pause and play music by pressing the wheel. Want to reassign the functions of the Jog Dial? Tap the picture of the jog wheel in the upper-left corner and you'll see the Jog Function Select screen, where you can choose from among five different modes for the jog wheel.

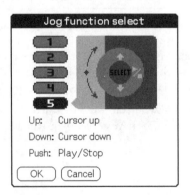

Want to listen to music while you do other work on your PDA? You *can* play music while you type into a Clié word processor, but first you have to enable "background play." Background play lets the Clié multitask, so it plays music while it's also running another program.

To enable background play, choose Options | Preferences from the menu and tap the option for Enable Background Play. When checked, you can change programs and the music will continue to play. When unchecked, the music player will stop as soon as you try to switch applications.

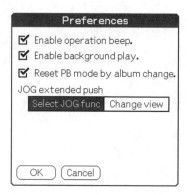

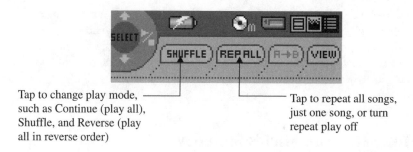

*Not all Clié models allow background play—if you have an MP3 add-on that connects via the PDA's HotSync port, you may not have the ability to play music in the background while doing other things.*

As you've no doubt noticed, even a Clié with enhanced audio is not cut out for playing music through that tiny speaker. Instead, for best results, you should use a headset, like the earbuds that came with your Clié. Remember, though, you don't have to use Sony's; you can substitute your own.

*The MP3 player eats a lot of the Clié's precious battery life. To conserve battery power while listening to music—especially if you're not doing anything else with the Clié—you might want to use the Clié's Hold switch. When you press the Hold button on the side of the Clié, you lock the Clié's controls so you can't accidentally interrupt the music. At the same time, the screen goes off. You need to deactivate Hold to turn the Clié on again.*

## Play Modes

You can play your music just by tapping the Play button. But like any good music player, you have options, as shown next:

Tap to change play mode, such as Continue (play all), Shuffle, and Reverse (play all in reverse order)

Tap to repeat all songs, just one song, or turn repeat play off

Don't want to listen to all the songs in your Memory Stick? You can also create a custom playlist. To do that, choose Tool | Pickup... from the menu and select just the songs you want to play.

18

The AudioPlayer also has one other cool—but slightly unusual—feature. You can create a musical loop that plays just a specific part of a song. To play a loop, start your song and, when you reach the point that you want your loop to start, tap the Loop button. You should see the *A* and the arrow illuminate.

When you reach the end of the loop, tap the Loop button again. The *B* will also be illuminated now, and the selected portion of music will play forever until you tap the Loop button a third time to cancel the loop play.

## Your CLIÉ as an MP3 Remote

Here's a novel way to use your Clié—as a remote control for the popular WinAmp music player for Windows. If you're adventurous, check out MP3Remote, available from PalmGear.com. This program uses the Clié's IR port to command WinAmp, turning your Clié into an MP3 remote control. On the downside, it requires you to use WinAmp on a computer (most likely a laptop) that has an infrared port.

## Checking Your Memory Stick's Memory

How much free space is left on your Memory Stick? The easiest way to check is to tap the icon of the Memory Stick atop the AudioPlayer screen. You can get the same information by choosing Tools | About Memory Stick from the AudioPlayer's menu. Either way, this is a handy trick to remember even if you want to know about free space for matters unrelated to music. Wondering if that video or e-book will fit? Tap the AudioPlayer application and check the Memory Stick status.

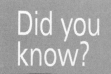

## AudioPlayer Alternatives

While Sony's AudioPlayer is a good, simple, and free music player (well, free in the sense that it comes with your Clié), there are alternatives.

- **eNeRgy** A small, functional, freeware MP3 player. Downloadable from PalmGear.com.

- **AJVMP3** A pretty-looking HiRes+ MP3 player, ideal for devices like the NR- and NX-series. Find it at **http://ajvmp3.paradise.net.nz**.

- **AudioControlcDA** Play your MP3s through a small pop-up window on the Clié. Available for free at **http://isweb41.infoseek.co.jp/computer/crspalm/#acda**.

TIP *Remember that you can carry multiple "albums" of music just by bringing more than one Memory Stick. You'll get about two hours of music per 128MB Memory Stick (assuming your MP3s are encoded at about 128 Kbps), so you can have several hours of music on just a few sticks.*

# Managing MP3s

If you've been around the PDA block a few times, you no doubt know that a million database programs exist that track everything from your stocks to your favorite books on your Palm-powered PDA. MP3s are no different. There are at least half a dozen applications out there that promise to make your life a nirvanaesque dream through MP3 micro-management. And lo and behold, a few of them are pretty good. Here are our favorites:

- **Playster** Now, this program is pretty darn cool. Playster searches your hard disk for MP3s and synchronizes the track data—like title, artist, genre, year, and comments—with

18

a database on your Clié. If you're, um, "extremely diligent" (yeah, that's the expression we were trying to think of) about entering all the ID3 tag data for all your music tracks (you know, stuff like artist, track, album title, and so on), you can do it at your leisure on your Clié, and the changes get HotSync'd back to the PC. You can even build custom play lists stored on your PC as M3U files for your favorite MP3 player to play for you. Because Dave is an, um, "extremely diligent" person, he loves this application.

■ **Nappy**   If you visit online music sites on a frequent basis, you might want to try Nappy, a program you can use to take note of songs you'll download later when connected to the Internet at home. The name comes from the long-defunct Napster, but it's a good tracking program nonetheless.

# Making Music on the CLIÉ

When you tire of simply listening to music and instead want to be in the band, it's time for some music software. And believe it or not, you can indeed use the Clié for a large number of music applications. It has a built-in speaker for creating (admittedly, very basic) sounds, and the display is perfectly suited for musical notation in a small space. If you're a musician, be sure to check out some of these applications.

## Metronome and Drumming Software

It doesn't take a rocket scientist to figure out the Clié's sound capabilities aren't exactly symphonic in nature. So, one obvious application for your Clié is to keep time, either as a drum machine or a metronome. In fact, this would have come in handy a long time ago—Dave used to carry a guitar around wherever he went, and having a metronome or mini-drum machine in a box as small as the Clié would have been really cool.

■ **Meep**   This is your standard metronome. Meep has a slider for choosing any tempo from 40 to 280 beats per minute, and you can select up to 8 beats per measure, as well. You can also work from onscreen counts or add an audible beep to each beat.

■ **Responsive Metronome** Another simple metronome tool, Responsive Metronome enables you to choose any tempo from 35 to 300 beats per minute, and both see (via a pulsing quarter note) and hear the beat. This program is quite simple and, in fact, there's no on/off switch for the beat—you have to disable both the audio and video filters to shut it off.

■ **Pocket Beat** This application simulates a drum kit right on your Clié. It can remember two distinct tempos and you can switch between them easily by using onscreen controls or the Scroll button. Pocket Beat can also play straight or shuffle beats, and it can vary between 40 and 196 beats per minute. The best part, though, is you can tap out your own meter on the Clié screen—Pocket Beat memorizes the tempo and plays it accordingly.

Here you can see images from Meep, Responsive Metronome, and PocketBeat:

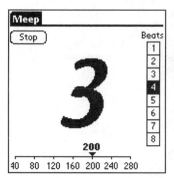

## Nice, but Impractical?

**Dave**: I love the idea of integrating an MP3 player into a PDA. The thought of listening to music on my NR70V as I read an e-book gives me little chills of excitement. But in the real world, it's more trouble than it's worth. Sony's Memory Sticks are just too limited and expensive to be practical. It costs $75 to get a 128MB stick, good for perhaps two hours of music. For $250, I can buy an MP3 player with a 20GB hard disk, capable of storing hundreds of hours of music. For that reason, my Clié's MP3 player goes unused while I carry my iPod along on lengthy trips.

**Rick**: Where are you shopping? I bought a new 128MB stick on eBay for $50, and prices will undoubtedly go even lower once 256MB sticks hit the streets. And unlike you, I don't need to bring three weeks' worth of music when I travel—a few dozen songs is enough. Are you actually criticizing the NR70V for having MP3 capabilities just because Memory Stick capacities aren't to your liking? Go back to Russia! Honestly, though, I do want a 1GB stick (priced at $50, please), which will give me room for books, music, and a couple episodes of *The West Wing*.

18

## Portable Music Lessons

Budding musicians can carry around the following applications with them to bone up on notes, keyboard positions, and fingering:

- **MusicTeacher**    This program can be used as an aid to learning to sing *prima vista*—that is, by reading sheet music by sight. Several tunes are stored in the MusicTeacher database, and you can also enter your own using the onscreen keyboard.

> **NOTE** *This program is interesting because it's written in Java and uses a Java interpreter to run on the Clié. Because it's a Java application, the MusicTeacher program can also be found on the Web and runs from within a web browser window. You can find it at **mathsrv.ku-eichstaett.de/MGF/homes/grothmann/java/waba**.*

- **GTrainer**    If you're learning to play guitar and don't want to be forever tied to "tab" sheet music, try GTrainer. This application displays a note onscreen and you need to tap the correct place on the guitar fretboard. It isn't enough just to choose the right note—you have to tap the correct octave, as well.

- **McChords**    If you're learning piano, McChords is an essential portable tool for working through chord fingerings. It shows you which keys to press to form the majority of chords you need to master basic piano playing.

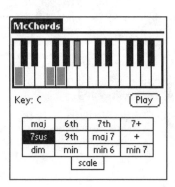

■ **PChord**   This program, seen next, is indispensable for anyone trying to get the hang of the guitar. In fact, Fretboard also supports mandolin, banjo, violin, and other stringed instruments. Choose a chord and Fretboard displays a variety of ways to finger it. Fretboard includes every chord we could think of, including obscure  chords (minor 9th and stacked fourths) you might play only once in a great while. As such, it's a good memory jogger even for experienced players. Similar programs to try include *Guitar Power* and *FretTrainer* and *CDB FretBoard Trainer*.

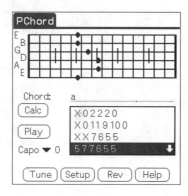

## Tools for Musicians

Tuning—bleh. I hate tuning my guitar. If only there were some automated way to...

Well, of course there is. Every guitarist on earth probably owns a $30 electronic tuner, but did you know you can use your Clié for tuning as well? We've found a bunch of tuners for the Clié—one good example being a program called Guitar Tuner Lt. Dave has used it himself on several occasions. It comes with standard and alternative tunings. Tap the appropriate onscreen string and the tone plays for several seconds. Or, tap the Auto button to hear each string's tone in turn.

## Music Annotation and Recording

You may have experimented with (or frequently use) applications on the Mac or PC that enable you to compose and play music. Those programs generally let you drag notes on to musical staffs or play an onscreen keyboard to construct musical compositions. Well, you can do the same thing on the Clié—the screen is just a bit smaller, and you don't have multiple voices to hear your multitimbral creations. Here are a few applications you can try:

■ **TS Noter**   This unusually named program is an online favorite because it's so good at helping you create music. TS Noter features a staff and a set of tools for placing notes and rests. When you create your song, you can save it, play it, or even export it as an alarm for the Clié's Date Book. A desktop companion program lets you play the music you create on your Clié from a PC using a MIDI instrument.

**18**

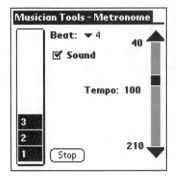
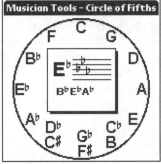
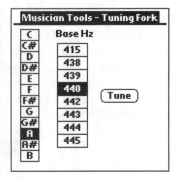

■ **miniPiano**   This program enables you to play an onscreen keyboard while the notes you strike get added on a staff. You can then play back your creation. miniPiano has a Free Play mode in which the keys are duration sensitive—the longer you hold the stylus on the key, the longer it plays.

■ **Palm Piano**   This simple program records the notes you tap out on a four-octave keyboard and it can play back the results. Palm Piano has some simple editing tools built in, but it doesn't have rests and there's no way to select note lengths—they all play back at the same timing.

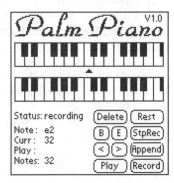

- **PocketSynth**   Like Palm Piano, this program enables you to create music by tapping on an onscreen keyboard. PocketSynth enables you to select note lengths and rests, though, which gives you more composing flexibility. Unfortunately, you must select the length of the note, and then tap it on the keyboard, which makes the composition process less than entirely fluid.

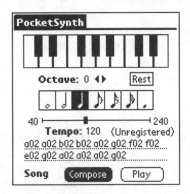

# Adding Sounds to the CLIÉ's Alarms

After all that fancy music stuff, you might think the Clié's alarms are kind of mundane. But think about it: wouldn't you like to be warned about upcoming appointments by the theme to *Superman* or some home-brewed song?

If you have a Clié model with Sony's "enhanced audio," there are two ways to enhance the Clié's built-in alarm library. If you have the ordinary Palm OS audio, you have just one option. How can you tell which you have? For starters, the enhanced audio is an important feature, so it's probably mentioned on the box. Another way to find out: if your Clié has enhanced audio, it'll have a program, probably located in the Clié category, called Audio Utility.

If you have enhanced audio in your Clié, you can either download new material from the Internet or you can convert MIDI and WAV files you've stored on your desktop PC. If you have standard Palm OS audio, there's no way to convert your own stuff—so let's start by looking at getting those prefabbed alarm tunes.

## Getting Prefabbed Alarm Tunes

The few alarm sounds that come with your Clié are all simple tunes that use a chip in your Clié to convert musical instructions (in the MIDI language) into music that plays through your Clié speakers. Since the Clié uses standard MIDI files, there are several add-on musical libraries available. For a few dollars, you can get popular movie tunes, pop songs, folk tunes, and other musical pieces to choose from when setting your alarms. If your Clié has enhanced audio, here are some of the available options:

- **CliéSounds 2.0**   Includes several dozen replacement tunes for your Clié. Available on PalmGear and written by Jeffrey VanderWal. It's free.

18

■ **Clié Sounds Collection 1.3**  Offered on PalmGear by a company called PalmGSM, this
$10 collection of songs costs a little, but it actually features no less than 130 songs from
TV, movies, and popular bands.

If your Clié doesn't have enhanced audio, you actually have a lot more options, just because
developers have had years and years to release old-style audio. Here are some places to look for
Clié models without enhanced audio:

■ **GeekSounds**  A free collection of songs that include many of your classic movie favorites.

■ **Alarms for PalmOS**  Over 300 songs for your Clié, including all of your favorites from
ABBA, sci-fi films, and dance songs. Costs $10.

## Converting Songs

If your Clié has enhanced audio, you can also copy your own individual tunes to the Clié's alarm
library. The Clié comes with a desktop program for Windows called, simply enough, Sound
Converter. Sound Converter accepts music in MIDI and WAV format and converts it to a form
acceptable to the Clié, then puts it in the Install queue for the next HotSync.

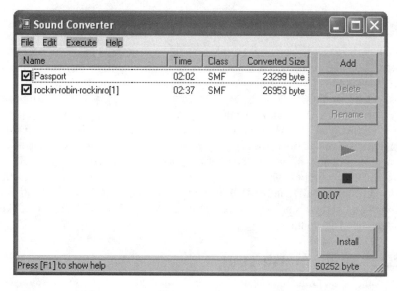

  *You can find Sound Converter on the installation CD-ROM that came with your Clié.*

Any MIDI file will work in Sound Converter, though you have to make sure your WAV files fit the Clié's narrow range of acceptable specifications. You can only import WAV files with these characteristics:

- 8 kHz, 8 Bit, Mono
- 8 kHz, 16 Bit, Mono
- 22 kHz, 8 Bit, Mono
- 22 kHz, 16 Bit, Mono

- 8 kHz, 8 Bit, Stereo
- 8 kHz, 16 Bit, Stereo
- 22 kHz, 8 Bit, Stereo
- 22 kHz, 16 Bit, Stereo

So, suppose you have a 44 KHz WAV file you want transferred to your Clié as an alarm sound? You need to convert it first. The easiest way to do that is with the Windows Sound Recorder, following these steps:

**1.** Start the Windows Sound Recorder. It's usually in the Start menu, in Accessories | Entertainment.

**2.** Choose File | Open from the menu and load your WAV file that needs transformation.

**3.** Choose File | Save As from the menu. Make sure the Save As Type list box is set to WAV, and then click the Change... button.

**4.** In the Attributes menu, choose a compatible format, such as 8.000 kHz, 8 Bit, Mono. Then click OK.

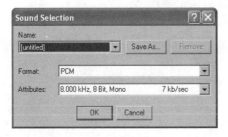

**5.** Save the file with these new attributes.

Now you can add the file to Sound Converter and transfer it to the Clié.

Keep in mind that while MIDI files take up very, very little space on your Clié, a WAV file is comparatively huge. If you like the idea of using a digital song file as an alarm sound, we recommend you stick to just one or, at most, two at a time. These files can only be stored in the Clié's internal memory (not a Memory Stick), so you can find yourself committing a lot of system memory for something silly like the theme to *Knight Rider*.

## Managing Songs on Your CLIÉ

On the other hand, enhanced-audio Cliés come with a very cool little program called Sound Utility. Sound Utility is essentially a library of all the MIDI and WAV alarm sounds on your device. You can play songs, rename them, and delete tunes that have worn out their welcome. So, when you—or your coworkers—tire of listening to Rod Stewart's *Hot Legs* as your 11:00 A.M. meeting alarm, you can delete the file and make room for more tunes.

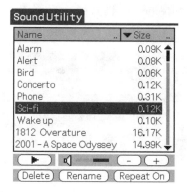

## Where to Find It

| Web Site | Address | What's There |
| --- | --- | --- |
| PalmGear.com | www.palmgear.com | Virtually all the applications found in this chapter |
| Handango | www.handango.com | Virtually all the applications found in this chapter |

# Chapter 19

# The CLIÉ as a Remote Control

## How to...

- Use your Clié as a universal remote
- Work with Clié RMC
- Find other Palm OS remote software
- Decide between Clié RMC, OmniRemote, and ProntoLite
- Turn your Clié into a TV guide

Is there no end to your Clié's capabilities? When you add "universal remote" to the list, it probably seems that way. The infrared (IR) transceiver that's built into your Clié can be used for more than just swapping programs and contact listings. In fact, with the right software, it can double as a universal remote, capable of controlling everything from TVs to stereos to DVD players.

Okay, but what's the right software? Before we tell you, we need to explain a subtle difference in the infrared capabilities of various Clié models. Specifically, many Cliés have roughly the same IR power as other Palm OS-based handhelds—a transceiver with a range of about five feet. Unless you like to sit really close to your TV or stereo, that's obviously not too great. However, some Cliés—most notably the T-, NR-, and NX- series—have enhanced IR ports with roughly triple the range. Now you can plunk down on the couch and get some serious channel-surfing done.

The products we discuss in this chapter will work with any Clié model. But, suffice it to say, unless you have a T415, T615C, T665C, NR70, NX70, NR70V, or NX70V, you may not enjoy them to the fullest. Furthermore, the idea of using your handheld as a remote may seem a little kooky, especially if it doesn't spend a lot of time near your entertainment center. However, there are some occasions in which it can be quite practical—and good for a few practical jokes, too.

### Our Favorite TV Shows

**Rick:** I'll take television over the movies any day. Movies are a crapshoot, and most of them are, well, crap. But just look at some of the intelligent, inventive and entertaining shows TV has given us in recent years: *Alias*, *24*, *Frasier*, *The West Wing*, *Watching Ellie*, *King of the Hill*, *Scrubs*, *Andy Richter Controls the Universe*...the list goes on and on. Even my guilty pleasures—*Boston Public*, *Survivor, Trading Spaces*—have elements of quality to them. Why spend $8.50 on two hours' worth of drivel when I can enjoy the good stuff in the comfort of my own home?

**Dave:** What??? Are you seriously comparing two completely different mediums—TV and cinema—and declaring one a winner? Using that logic, I see no reason to build mass transportation, because vegetables are better. It's interesting that you anecdotally find a few good TV shows and use those as examples, but don't mention any life-altering films that have graced the big screen: *Schindler's List, The Sixth Sense, Gone with the Wind, Life is Beautiful, Memento*... Good grief, I don't have room for them all. But that's okay; we don't need to read books, because I have a fridge full of salad dressing.

**Rick:** As usual, you miss the point entirely. Obviously in the entire history of cinema there have been some great movies. But let's see what's playing as I write this: *Stealing Harvard, The Banger Sisters, Ballistic: Ecks Vs. Sever*, and several dozen other flops. Now let's see what's on TV: every single one of the shows I mentioned, and they're all jewels. I find it interesting that you didn't bother to mention any of your favorite shows. Could it be because you don't want people to learn of your secret love of *The Anna Nicole Show*?

**Dave:** I'm sorry, did I insult your "picture stories?" In truth, and despite your cheerleading, the percentage of good TV to bad is depressingly low. Out of the hundreds of shows on TV each week, there are only a few worth watching—last year, I watched *24* as if my life depended upon it. I also looked forward to *Enterprise, Friends, Dennis Miller*, and *The Daily Show*. This year I've added *Alias* to the lineup, but I actually try to watch less TV, not more. It's a little something I have called "culture."

## Sony's Remote Software: CLIÉ Remote Commander

We didn't hatch the idea of using your Clié as a remote—Sony did. (Actually, turn-your-handheld-into-a-remote software has been around for Palms for quite some time, starting with OmniRemote, which we discuss later in this chapter. But Sony was the first hardware maker to write remote software from scratch and include it with a handheld.) If you have one of the aforementioned models, you can use it as a remote right out of the box, thanks to a bundled application called Clié RMC (also known as Clié Remote Commander). With it you can control up to four different kinds of devices: TVs, VCRs, DVD players, and stereo components. And you don't necessarily need to squint at the screen every time you want to control something—Clié RMC takes full advantage of the Clié's hard buttons and Jog Dial.

You can find complete setup instructions in Sony's Add-on Application Guide, so we won't rehash them here. However, we should point out a few key items before you get started with Clié RMC:

- This is a fairly confusing program to set up, so it's a good idea to read the documentation thoroughly before getting started.

- Clié RMC has a limited database of TVs, VCRs, and so on, and all the remote control codes that go with them. However, if you own a model that's not in the database, you're out of luck—the program cannot "learn" to control unknown devices (as many regular universal remotes can). What's particularly unfortunate is that many of Sony's best products—like DIRECTV with TiVo—aren't supported.

- Clié RMC has four quick-launch buttons—labeled A–D—across the top of the screen. In order to set the parameters for each one (that is, to choose which device it should control), tap the desired button, then tap Menu | Details.

- In the Details screen, one of the available settings is called Mode. Usually your choices here are nothing more descriptive than mode1, mode 2, and so on. Here's an explanation by way of example: Panasonic makes dozens of different VCRs, but many of them use the same sets of control codes. Thus, if you choose a Panasonic VCR, but nothing happens when you tap the Test button, choose a different mode and try the test again. Chances are one of them will work.

- You're not limited to four components—just four *kinds* of components. Thus, if you want to use Clié RMC to control, say, two VCRs and three TVs in your home, you can add them all (provided they're in the database).

**TIP** *If you find yourself using Clié RMC on a regular basis, it may be practical to reassign one of your Clié's hard buttons to launch the program. That way, you won't have to hunt for its icon every time you plop down on the couch. Refer to the section entitled "Buttons" in Chapter 2 for information on reassigning buttons, or just choose Prefs | Buttons and jump right in. It's not complicated.*

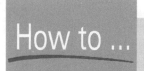 **Play a Great Practical Joke**

One of the really fun things about Clié RMC is how easy it is to choose a device to control. Just tap Select, then New, and then fill in the appropriate details (Category, Maker, Name, and so on). In about 30 seconds, you can add an entry for, oh, say, a friend's TV set. The next time you're over watching *Alias*, use your Clié to secretly change channels or the volume—then say, "Dude, what's up with your TV?" Of course, *Alias* is too good to mess with, so wait for a commercial—or just play around during a dumb show like *Fear Factor*.

## Other Remote Control Programs

If your Clié didn't come with Clié RMC or you'd like a program that's a little more robust, there are two solid alternatives available: OmniRemote Pro and ProntoLite.

Pacific NeoTek's OmniRemote was the first remote-control program ever created for the Palm OS, and the company has refined it quite a bit over the years. The Pro version supports high-resolution screens, Jog Dials, and an unlimited number of remotes (meaning you can train it to operate virtually any device). Better still, you can design customized button layouts right on the Clié screen, design macros (used to perform a sequence of actions—like turn off the TV, turn on the stereo, and turn on the CD player—with a single button-tap), and set timers (so you can, say, turn the TV into your alarm clock by instructing OmniRemote to turn it on in the morning).

In short, if you're interested in turning your Clié into a full-featured universal remote, OmniRemote is worth a look. It sells for $24.95—a lot less than the price of stand-alone programmable remotes.

You should also check out ProntoLite, which is based on the Philips Pronto remote that's so popular among home-theater enthusiasts. However, where the Pronto sells for about $400,

ProntoLite costs just $19.95. Plus, it has the most attractive, streamlined, and logical interface of any of the remote programs, so it should be easier for novices to manage. ProntoLite can control up to 10 A/V devices, but you're a bit limited in adding devices not directly supported—like, say, a TiVo or Replay recorder. Still, as with OmniRemote, there's a free trial version, so you can put it through its paces before plunking down your cash.

# Turning Your CLIÉ Into a TV Guide

ConnectedTV takes a step further the idea of using your Clié as a remote. Instead of just letting you flip channels and adjust the volume, ConnectedTV—which is both a software and service—downloads TV listings into your Clié when you HotSync, then presents those listings on the screen as an interactive TV guide. Tap the show you want to watch, and your TV automatically switches to that channel.

The software offers a variety of nifty features, including a Favorites page, details about each show, and support for the Clié's Jog Dial and hard buttons (for functions like mute, power, and volume). ConnectedTV also has the distinction of being one of the few subscription-oriented Palm OS programs—it costs $30 per year (a reasonably affordable price tag, in our humble opinions). The only downside is the interface: it's atrocious, meaning you'll expend considerable time and effort getting the software set up properly, then more time learning to navigate it. Hopefully the creators will refine the interface as time goes by, as this is one cool program.

## And If You're Really Serious about Using Your CLIÉ as a Remote…

As we noted at the beginning of this chapter, different Clié models have different IR strength. If you really want to maximize your handheld's infrared capabilities, consider this handy accessory: the TaleStuff IR Blaster. This little module plugs into the bottom of your N- or S-series model and comes with its own IR port—one that has a range of 35–65 feet (depending on the device you're pointing it at). Okay, you're thinking, sounds good, but if the IR Blaster plugs into the *bottom* of my Clié, won't I have to turn it upside down? The answer is yes, you smart reader, you. Fortunately, programs like ConnectedTV and OmniRemote allow you to flip the screen 180 degrees, so you can still use your Clié while it's inverted. The IR Blaster costs $24.95.

## Where to Find It

| Web Site | Address | What's There |
| --- | --- | --- |
| ConnectedTV | www.connected.tv | ConnectedTV |
| Pacific Neo-Tek | www.pacificneotek.com | OmniRemote Pro |
| Philips | www.pronto.philips.com | ProntoLite |
| TaleStuff | www.talestuff.com | IR Blaster |

# Chapter 20 Playing Games

# How to...

- Adjust your Clié's volume for games
- Install new games
- Control games on your Clié
- Get a real joystick for your Clié
- Play interactive fiction games
- Use the Clié as a substitute for dice
- Find great games for your Clié
- Turn your Clié into a Game Boy

Spreadsheets, databases, document readers, and memos are all well and good. If that's all you ever plan to do with your Clié, that's fine—you're just unlikely to ever get invited to one of our parties.

Your Clié is a miniature general-purpose computer, and, as a result, it can do almost anything your desktop PC can do—including play games. Sure, there are limitations. The display is pretty small and the processor isn't nearly as fast, but the fact remains your Clié is a great game machine for passing the time in an airport, on a train, in a meeting (where it looks like you're taking notes), or any other place where you're bored. In this chapter, we discuss what you should know to get the most out of your Clié as a gaming machine, and recommend some of the best games to try.

# Turning Your CLIÉ Into a Game Machine

No, playing games isn't exactly rocket science, but before you get started with them, you should learn a few things that'll come in handy. You should know, for instance, how to control your Clié's volume, install applications, and enable beaming. After all, some games let you play against other handheld users via the IR port.

## Controlling the CLIÉ's Game Volume

At the top of the list is the Clié's sound system. The Clié has a control for how loud to play game sounds. Logic dictates you'll want to set this loud enough to hear what's going on in your game, but this might not always be the case. As much as we like to play games, we don't always want others to know that's what we're doing. Fortunately, it's possible to set the game sound level low or even off completely. This means you'll play your games without sound (which, if you're at work, is probably a wise decision).

To tweak game sounds, do the following:

1. Tap the Prefs icon to open your Preferences application.
2. Switch to the General category by tapping on the category menu at the top-right corner and choosing General.

**3.** Find the Game Sound entry and choose the volume level you're interested in.

*If you play a game that squeaks and squawks even if the sound is off, the game must have its own sound preferences. Check the game's menu for a preferences control to set the sound volume. Indeed, many games have built-in volume controls that eliminate the need to futz around with the settings in Prefs.*

## Enabling Beaming

If you know other Palm OS handheld users, you might want to try your hand at some head-to-head games, which are made possible thanks to the devices' infrared ports. It's fun and addictive, and very nearly sociable. For two games on different handhelds to "find" each other, though, you need to make sure the Beam Receive setting in Prefs is enabled.

**1.** Tap the Prefs icon to open your Preferences application.

**2.** Switch to the General category by tapping the category menu at the top-right corner and choosing General.

**3.** Look for the entry called Beam Receive and make sure it's set to On. (By default, it is.)

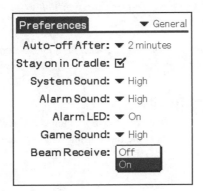

20

## Installing Games

Installing games is a snap. We discussed how to install applications on your Clié in Chapter 4, and working with games is no different. After all, a game is just another kind of Clié application.

If you're new to downloading applications from the Internet, you need to know that most applications come compressed in one of two popular formats:

- **Zip**   This is the standard way of managing files in Windows. To install a Zipped file, you need a program capable of unzipping it first. Typically, this means using an application like WinZip 7.0. (Windows XP can automatically extract the contents of Zip files.)

- **Sit**   Macintosh files are compressed in the SIT format, which can be uncompressed with a program like Aladdin Stuffit Expander 5.0.

Once expanded, you'll probably have a folder with several files in it. Installation instructions typically come in one or more file formats:

- Plain text files—usually called something clever like readme.txt or install.txt.

- Web pages. Double-click them to see the directions in your web browser.

- Adobe Acrobat files, which end with the PDF file extension. You need Adobe Acrobat to read these files, though it's probably already installed on your computer. If not, visit **www.adobe.com** to get this popular document reader.

- Finally, there should be one or more files with PRC and PDB extensions. These are the actual game files that need to be installed on your Clié. Open the Install tool and use the Add button to set these files for installation at the next HotSync.

*If you use WinZip 7.0, a faster way to install applications in the Install tool is simply to drag the PRC and PDB files from the WinZip window into the Install Tool dialog box (they'll dynamically expand as you drag them, meaning you needn't unzip the files into a folder on your hard disk at all). Or, just try double-clicking the PRC and/or PDB files from within WinZip.*

*Need to pause a game? Just turn off your Clié or switch to another application. The game remains frozen until you turn it back on.*

*If you reset your Clié while a game is paused, the game session you were playing will be lost and you'll need to start over.*

## Game Controller Peripherals

As you'll see throughout this chapter, lots and lots of cool games are available for the Clié—more to get the high score. But they all have the same basic limitation—you need to use a stylus or the buttons to control the action.

# How to ... Control the Games

Now you're all set to start playing some Clié games, but where's the joystick? There isn't one, silly. Many games use the Clié's buttons to control the action. While the game is running, the Date Book, Address Book, Memo Pad, and To Do List buttons are typically diverted to game controls and won't switch you to the usual applications. To find out which buttons do what in a given game, you can experiment (our favorite way) or check the game documentation. In most games, you can find basic instructions by checking the game's built-in Help screens (tap Menu to find them).

Depending on which Clié model you own, there may be a better way. Add-on game controllers let you get a more authentic arcade experience, complete with joystick or gamepad, instead of mashing the Clié's buttons. Here are two options:

■ **Sony Game Controller**   Compatible with most Clié models, Sony's own clip-on accessory uses buttons to recreate the typical d-pad-style controller found on console game systems. It's probably the best bet for serious game fans, as it's designed by the same company that made your Clié and sells for the reasonable price of $40.

■ **SimpleJet PDA Game Pad**   Designed for the Clié N-series, this hard-to-find clip-on makes your handheld look a lot like Nintendo's Game Boy, complete with a traditional four-way d-pad controller and two action buttons.

## Gone But Not Forgotten

**Rick:** *Frogger*, *Galaxian*, *Pac-Man*—these were household names back in my youth, and they're just a few of the arcade classics that have been resurrected for Palm OS handhelds. Of course, a Clié's buttons don't compare too favorably with traditional coin-op controls, which is why I'm happy to have Sony's Game Controller accessory. With it, longtime favorites like *Spy Hunter*, *Joust*, and *Sinistar* are much more enjoyable. Now I just need the programmers to update these games to support the enhanced audio hardware found in some Clié models. I'm not holding my breath—but a man can dream, can't he?

**Dave:** I love the old arcade classics as much as the next geek, but it's time to move on, dude! It's the twenty-first Century! I've put childish games like those well behind me and today, I play mainly just the mature, modern classics—like *Bejeweled*.

# Installing the Bundled Games

Most Clié models come with a handful of games, though you have to install them yourself. Usually this means inserting the Clié Installation CD-ROM, then choosing Install Third-Party Software from the options that appear. (If no such options pop up when you insert the CD-ROM, you can access the games manually. Run the Install Tool application, then navigate to the 3rd party folder on the CD-ROM. Therein you'll find subfolders for the bundled games.) Most Clié models include: *Bejeweled*, a highly addictive puzzle game; *AcidSolitaire*, an attractive solitaire card game; and *Zap!2016*, a fast-paced arcade-style shooter.

# Two-Player Infrared Games

As we already mentioned, two-player games are a cool way to pass the time when you're traveling with another handheld-equipped person. IS/Complete offers perhaps the largest collection of infrared-enabled games, including Palm OS versions of *Battleship*, checkers, chess, and even

*Hangman*. They all work more or less the same way: you make a move, then tap a button. Your move is then beamed to your opponent's handheld, where the board is updated to reflect the new data. Then you perform the same process in the other direction.

The games and graphics are nothing spectacular, but they're still kind of cool. And you don't need to pre-arrange a gaming session with another player. That is, if you've got one of the IR games and your buddy doesn't, no problem—just beam it to him. Of course, there may be a few limitations, depending on whether the game in question is commercial or freeware. If it's commercial, then the beamed copy will often work only on the one from which it was beamed. Or, it might stop working after a short period of time, like two weeks (this is to encourage "player 2" to buy his own copy).

What other kinds of IR games can you find online? There's *Rapid Racer*, an early-arcade-style racing game; *Codefinder*, a *Mastermind*-like 2-player puzzle; and even *3D Bingo*. Perhaps the best examples of infrared gaming, though, are *IR Pong* and *IR Battleship*. These games, like the one pictured next, are definitely worth keeping on your Clié for head-to-head gaming opportunities.

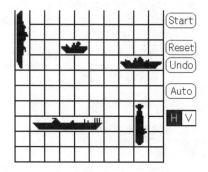

Of course, those games are pretty basic. If you really want to have some IR fun, check out Handmark's *Scrabble* and Astraware's *Biplane Ace*.

 *These and other games are available from **www.handango.com** and/or **www.palmgear.com**.*

# Playing Text Adventures

Remember *Zork*? How about Douglas Adams' *Hitchhiker's Guide to the Galaxy* text adventure? What about *Trinity*? These games were popular decades ago, at the dawn of the modern computer age. Text adventures put you in a text-based world, with flowing narratives and extensive descriptions of your surroundings. When it was time to make your hero do something, you typed instructions into your PC. The computer then moved you along through the story based on your decisions. These games were often fiendishly clever, composed largely of logic puzzles and intellectual challenges.

So why are we telling you all this? Text adventures are long-lost icons for the museum, right?

Not quite. Text adventures have made something of a comeback in the last few years, largely because handheld PCs like the Clié are an ideal platform for playing them. And although their name has changed with the times—they're now usually called *interactive fiction* instead of text adventures—they're still a lot of fun to play. No serious gamer would consider his Clié complete without one or two interactive-fiction games installed for a rainy day at the airport (see Figure 20-1).

## Unlocking Interactive Fiction Files

You can find hundreds of interactive fiction titles on the Internet. But these files aren't playable all by themselves. They usually come encoded in a format called *Z-Code*. Like a spreadsheet or document file, a Z-Code file is useless without the appropriate reader application. In this case,

### The Best Way to Find Color Games

If you have a Clié with a color display, you have the potential for some wonderful gaming experiences. Color games look every bit as good—and, often, quite a bit better—than what you see on your kids' Game Boy. Our favorite hunting ground for games, **PalmGear.com**, makes it easy to tell whether a game (or any application, for that matter) supports color: just look for the colorful paintbrush icon. On the PalmGear.com home page, the new software list identifies color applications this way:

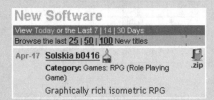

If you're looking at the detailed application description, the color icon is always shown next to the product's name, like this:

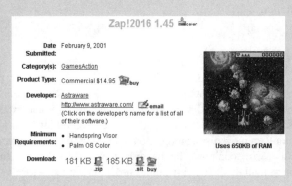

Finally, the easiest way to find color applications at PalmGear.com is to search the archives. Choose Software | Search The Archives from the Navigation menu on the left side of the PalmGear.com screen. On the Software Archives page, enter a software category to search for. Be sure to click the Search For Color Applications check box, as you can see in the following. Your search results will only include color applications.

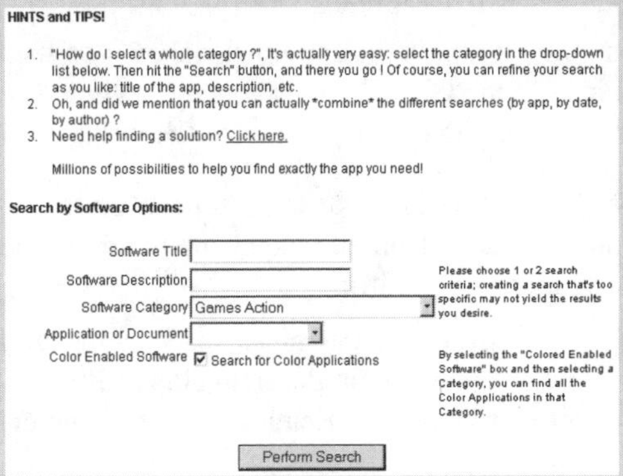

you need a program called Pilot-Frotz (or Frotz, for short). Install Frotz, and you can play any interactive fiction games you find and transfer to your Clié.

Frotz essentially gives you the same experience as when you played these text adventures years ago. It displays the game's text on the screen and provides you with a text prompt in which to enter your next move. When you start the game, you see the Frotz list view, along with any games you have currently installed. To play a game, tap its name, and then tap the Play button.

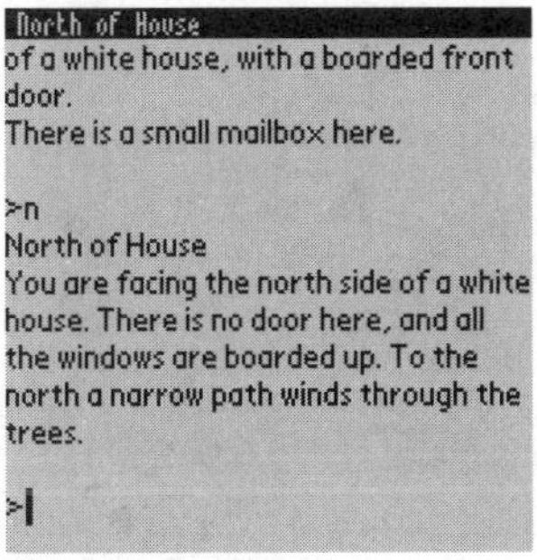

**FIGURE 20-1**   Interactive fiction combines good old-fashioned storytelling with a bit of brain-teasing puzzle-solving.

From there, you're taken to the game view, where you actually play the game. Unlike those early text adventures, Frotz gives you a few graphical tools that make these games easier to play. Here's how to use Frotz:

- If the game displays a long text description, you might see the word "MORE" to indicate more text occurs after this pause. Tap the screen to continue.

- To enter your text command, write it in the Graffiti area.

- You can display a list of common verbs and nouns (shown on the left in Figure 20-2) by tapping the right half of the Clié screen in any spot where no text exists. Instead of writing Look, for instance, tap the menu and tap the word "Look."

- You can tap any word in the story and that word appears on the text prompt line. Thus, you can assemble your command from the menu and words already onscreen, instead of writing it all from scratch with Graffiti.

- If you want your character to move, tap any blank space on the left half of the Clié screen. You'll see a map window, like the one on the right side of Figure 20-2. Tap the desired compass direction. Other icons help you Enter, Exit, and go up or down stairs.

> **TIP** *You can add custom words and phrases to the word list. Enter the desired word or phrase at the text prompt and select it with your stylus. Then choose List | Add from the menu. To see custom words, open the list menu and then tap on the first entry, USER LIST.*

Your position is automatically saved when you leave the game to do something else with your Clié. If you want to switch to another title, choose File | Force Quit to go back to the List view to choose another game. If you do that, though, your position in the current game is lost.

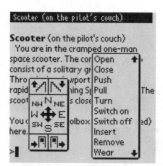

**FIGURE 20-2**　Frotz helps you play interactive fiction titles by displaying common commands and mapping tools.

### Finding Interactive Fiction Titles

Interactive fiction is scattered around the Web. Try both of these sites:

- **www.refalo.com/palm/interactive.htm**
- **www.csd.uwo.ca/~pete/Infocom/**

If you're really diligent, you may be able to find some of the classic Infocom adventures (like *Zork* and *Planetfall*). Check eBay to see if anyone is selling them used, or do a Google search for Infocom. There may even be a site or two where you can pay for the adventures and download them directly, without having to purchase an actual CD. Look for bundles like Lost Treasures of Infocom and Masterpieces of Infocom, which include multiple games.

# Using the CLIÉ as a Pair of Dice

If you like to play board games in the real world, you might be interested in using your Clié as a virtual pair of dice. After all, the Clié is harder to lose (we always misplace the dice that go with our board games). Several applications are available, but many of them have the disadvantage of requiring run-time modules of programming languages like Forth or C. We don't care for that approach, because it's just extra stuff you have to install.

Some dice simulators you might want to try include *Gamers Die Roller*, *DicePro*, and *Roll Em*, all of which are available from **PalmGear.com**.

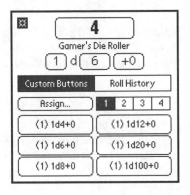

# The Universe of CLIÉ Games

Games account for a pretty healthy chunk of all software sold for handheld PCs, so it should come as no surprise that you can find hundreds upon hundreds of titles spanning every genre. Card games, action games, puzzle games—you name it, it's out there. Of course, we can't list all of them without doubling the size of the book. It's big enough already, don't you think?

## Getting Started with Text Adventures

So, you want to try your hand at interactive fiction, but that text prompt is a little too intimidating? Fear not, because entering commands in a text adventure isn't too hard. You can enter just a verb—like **Look**—or a complete sentence, like **Pick up the compass**. Each game has something called a *parser* that's designed to decrypt your input. Here's a primer to get you started:

### Directions

Compass points are frequently used: **north**, **south**, **east**, **west**, or any combination, like **northeast** or **southwest**. You can also use one- and two-letter abbreviations, like *n* and *se*. Also: **up**, **down**, **in**, **out**, **enter**, and **exit**.

### Looking Around

The old, reliable command is simply **Look**. You can combine Look with anything that makes sense: **look up**, **look down**, or **look inside**.

### Action Verbs

Anything: **Push**, **pull**, **open**, **close**, **take**, **pick up**, **pump**, **give**, **swim**, **turn**, **screw**, **burn**. When you deal with more than one object, you can use the word **All**, as in **Take All the coins**.

### Make Sentences

You have to combine nouns and verbs into complete sentences to accomplish much in these games. Manipulating objects is the name of the game and the way to solve the puzzles, as in **Take the money**, **Pick up the compass**, **Read the book**, or **Close the gate with the red key**.

As with other kinds of Clié software, games are easy to try before you buy. Most have a trial period, usually from two weeks to a month, after which the game becomes disabled unless you register it (that is, you have to pay for a code to unlock it permanently). Games usually cost between $10–20, though a few will set you back $30. There's also a treasure trove of great freebies like these (all of them available at **www.freewarepalm.com**):

- *Mulg II*    Use your stylus to guide a marble through a maze within a fixed amount of time. Devilishly addictive.
- *PilOth*    A clone of the classic game, *Othello*.
- *Sea War*    A nice implementation of the beloved game *Battleship*. There's even a high-resolution version especially for the Clié.
- *Solitaire Poker*    One of many variations on *Solitaire*, this one involving Poker hands.

- ■ ***Touch Tetris***   If you like *Tetris*, you'll love this unique variation in which you maneuver multiple sets of falling blocks. Very cool.
- ■ ***Vexed* 2.0**   One of the most addictive puzzle games ever, and a Palm OS freeware classic. The 2.0 version includes seven puzzle packs with over 400 levels.

In the following sections, we clue you in on the various kinds of games you can get for your Clié and tell you about some of our favorites.

## Card and Board Games

Games based on paper and cardboard—board games, card games, games of chance—transition well to the Clié because they're games you can relax with, take your time with, and return to after the dentist calls your name. Poker, Hearts, Blackjack, *Yahtzee*, *Scrabble*, *Monopoly*, chess, checkers—there are versions of just about every classic card and board game you can think of.

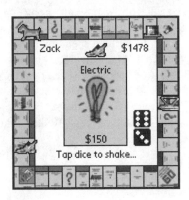

NOTE   *Where to find these and other games? We've already told you countless times about Handango and PalmGear.com, so we won't do that again. Instead, try Palm Gaming World (**www.palmgamingworld.com**), a site devoted entirely to—you guessed it—games for the Palm OS.*

## Puzzle Games

We love puzzles. Many puzzle games for the Clié come from the PC and other traditional gaming sources. You'll probably recognize *Tetris*, for instance, the classic game of falling blocks. But you'll also find far more advanced puzzle games, which represent some of our all-time favorites for the Clié. We're talking about titles like *Abysma*, *Bejeweled*, *Bounce Out*, *Collapse*, *Glom*, *NetWalk*, and *Vexed*. The latter is freeware, making it a definite must-have for your handheld. Many of the others come from Astraware, makers of some of the absolute best puzzle games.

## Game Packs

Occasionally, you may find game compilation discs in the store or online. They promise to deliver hundreds of unbeatable Palm OS games for just 10 or 20 bucks. Should you invest in one of these packages?

Our opinion: probably not. The collection may sound promising, but anyone with a halfway decent Internet connection can get all of the games they like from a site like **PalmGear.com** or **palmgamingworld.com** just as easily, without spending a dime. Remember: Clié games are tiny compared to games for the PC, and they download in seconds.

Also, keep in mind that you won't get the full, registered version of shareware games even though the disc itself cost you cash. Instead, these discs are sort of like samplers for folks who want a guided tour of someone else's idea of the "best" games for the Clié. If you like a game you find on the disc, you'll still have to pay to keep playing it, just as if you downloaded it from the Internet.

## Arcade-Style Games

Did you pump an untold number of quarters into arcade machines in the '80s? Rick and Dave sure did. Games like *Tank Pilot*, *Pac Man*, *Galax*, *Zap!2016*, and *Graviton* will test your dexterity and remind you of the good-old days, when arcade games were high-tech.

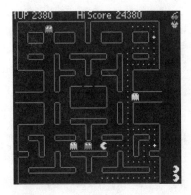

## Strategy and Role-Playing Games

For those folks who want a compromise between the frenetic pace of arcade games and the cerebral thrill of interactive fiction, there's role playing and action-strategy. These games let you don some armor and go fight for gold, glory, or the king's honor. One of the most popular games in this genre is *Kyle's Quest*, a title for which you can download dozens of add-on adventures. If that doesn't excite you, check out *Galactic Realms*, a space-based strategy and domination game. If you're nostalgic for Dungeons and Dragons, there's *Dragon Bane*, a classic dungeon, puzzle, and combat title (see Figure 20-3), similar to the classic PC game *Bard's Tale*.

## Sports Games

Anyone for tennis? How about racing? Maybe even a little Quidditch? Sports games (even fictional ones based on an amazing book) aren't always ideal for a screen as small as the Clié's, but that hasn't stopped developers from making some admirable efforts. Golf, basketball, football, and even bowling are among the other sports represented as Clié games. Whatever your athletic passion—even if it's darts—you're sure to find a game to match.

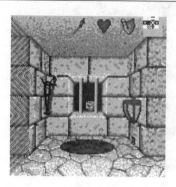

**FIGURE 20-3**   If you're into role-playing games, check out *Dragon Bane*.

# Turning Your CLIÉ Into a Game Boy

It's already about the same size as a Game Boy, right? Well, thanks to a pair of emulation programs (Liberty and Phoinix), it's now possible to play Game Boy games on your Clié. To prove we're not pulling your leg, here's a screen shot:

Here's how it works: you install one of the emulators on your Clié, then download and install Game Boy ROM files. A ROM file is a duplicate of the game program, which someone copied from a Game Boy cartridge and converted to a format for the PC. Before installing it on your Clié, you must first use the conversion program supplied with the emulator.

If you already own a slew of Game Boy titles, this might be something you want to check out. For everyone else, there are a few caveats:

■ First and foremost, it's illegal to download and install Game Boy games you don't already own copies of. The Game Boy ROMs (the game code, essentially) are copyrighted, so making (or downloading) illegal copies is against the law. So, if you don't own a Game Boy game, you shouldn't download a copy of it.

■ A Game Boy emulator is among the most crash-prone Palm OS software, as it pushes the limits of the hardware and the OS. While it's generally pretty safe, it could crash your Clié and even lead to a loss of data.

■ The sad truth is that old black-and-white Game Boy games aren't that good. It's fun to try them out as a novelty, but most Clié games are much, much better.

Where can you find the ROM files for use with the emulators? Try these sites:

■ **www.pdroms.de**

■ **www.gambitstudios.com/freesoftware.asp**

## Lemmings and SimCity

Two classics from the early days of gaming have been resurrected for your Clié. *Lemmings* will be instantly familiar to anyone who owned an Amiga—it's an amusing little game in which you have to guide dozens of the little creatures to safety. As for *SimCity*, it's the same as the original 1980s city-builder. You build a town from scratch, complete with roads, buildings, utilities, and recreation facilities.

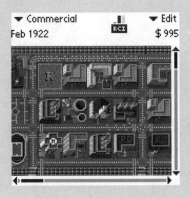

20

## Where to Find It

| Web Site | Address | What's There |
| --- | --- | --- |
| WinZip | www.winzip.com | WinZip file compression tool for Windows |
| Aladdin Systems | www.aladdinsys.com | Stuffit Expander file compression tool for the Mac |
| PalmGear.com | www.palmgear.com | Games for the Clié (get Frotz here) |
| Palm Gaming World | www.palmgamingworld.com | One-stop surfing for all sorts of games for the Clié |
| Gambit Studios | www.gambitstudios.com | Liberty Game Boy emulator |
| Phoinix | http://phoinix.sourceforge.net/ | Phoinix Game Boy emulator |

# Chapter 21 Reading E-Books

## How to...

- Find electronic books
- Understand the differences between Doc files and e-books
- Choose a book viewer
- Work with Mobipocket
- Read e-books on your Clié
- Find free e-books
- Find commercial e-books
- Create your own e-books

You know the future has arrived when a device the size of a Pop-Tart can hold an entire Stephen King novel. Indeed, many users find electronic books (a.k.a. e-books) to be a major Clié perk. You can pay nothing at all and read hundreds of literary classics, or pay discounted prices for mainstream titles. In this chapter, you learn everything you need to know about turning your Clié into a world-class library.

# A Brief History of E-Books

Before Cliés came along, a huge collection of electronic books—mostly public-domain classic literature, like Voltaire's *Candide* and Sir Arthur Conan Doyle's *Sherlock Holmes* stories—existed on the Internet. Because these works had already been converted to computer-readable text, why not copy them to Cliés for reading anytime, anywhere?

In theory, you could simply paste the text into a memo. But there's a snag: memos are limited to about 500 words, so even short stories are out of the question. Hence the emergence of one of the very first third-party Palm OS applications: *Doc*, a simple text viewer that had no length limitation other than the amount of RAM in the handheld itself. Doc rapidly became the de facto standard, not only for e-books, but also for documents created in desktop word processors and converted for handhelds.

NOTE     *In this chapter, we mostly discuss the e-book aspect of Doc files. If you want to learn more about creating and editing text files in a Clié word processor, see Chapter 12.*

We've mentioned this before, but it bears repeating here: The Palm OS Doc format is not the same as—nor compatible with—the Microsoft Word Doc format. Thus, you can't simply HotSync your favorite Word files to your Clié and view them there. (Actually, you can, but you need a program like Documents To Go for that. See Chapter 12 for more information.) Yes, this can be a confusing area. We really wish the creators of Palm Doc hadn't chosen that particular name.

21

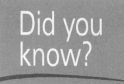

# Format Wars

In recent years, several document formats have arisen to challenge the Doc standard—kind of like AmiPro vs. Word vs. WordPerfect in the heyday of word processing. The cleverly named *TomeRaider,* for instance, uses its own, proprietary format. Why work with a format other than Doc, which is almost universally accepted? Cross-platform compatibility, for one thing. The TomeRaider program is also available for Pocket PC handhelds, EPOC-based handhelds (like the Psion Series 5), and Windows. Thus, a single text file can be viewed on a variety of devices and PCs, without having to be converted. The Doc format, in comparison, works only on Palm OS devices, and must be converted back and forth between handheld and PC.

## Choosing a Doc Viewer

Many people make this mistake: they download a bunch of nifty e-books from MemoWare (or wherever), load them on to their Cliés, then spend lots of time trying to figure out why they can't find the books. (When you install software, there's usually an icon for it.) The reason, of course, is they don't have a Doc viewer installed. Without one, there's no way to view Doc files.

Fortunately, there are plenty of Doc viewers out there—all free or quite inexpensive. The best place to start is with Palm's own program, Palm Reader, available at **www.palmdigitalmedia.com**. Here's a rundown of some other choices:

| Doc Viewer | Noteworthy Features |
| --- | --- |
| CspotRun | Free; supports auto-scrolling |
| DeepReader | Lots of great features, including automatic scrolling, anti-aliased fonts, and support for HiRes+ |
| Isilo | Supports HTML and .txt files as well as Doc files |
| FastWriter, Quickword, WordSmith | These programs, discussed in Chapter 12, can all double as word processors |
| TealDoc | Supports images and links between documents; advanced search options |

*All of these programs are available from PalmGear.com.*

Here's a screenshot of Deep Reader (running in HiRes+ mode, meaning it's taking advantage of the NR/NX's full screen) alongside one of Palm Reader (going a step further in HiRes+ by rotating the text 90 degrees):

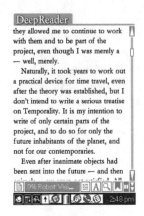

*If you have an NR- or NX- series Clié, make sure to choose a Doc reader that supports HiRes+, that is, one that will collapse the Graffiti area and display your books using the full length of the screen. Palm Reader is one that does, and it also allows you to rotate the text a full 90 degrees. Thus, you get a "wider" viewing area that's more akin to reading a real book. This is, without a doubt, our preferred method for reading books on a Clié.*

## All About Mobipocket

Depending on when you purchased your Clié, you may already have an e-book reader: Mobipocket. (As of press time, it was bundled with the SL10, SJ20, and SJ30.) This is an interesting product in that it not only lets you view standard Doc files, it also downloads news feeds from the Internet (not unlike AvantGo, which we discussed in Chapter 11) and lets you convert HTML and text files stored on your PC for viewing on your Clié. A Windows utility handles the latter two features, and looks like that shown in Figure 21-1.

As for the Mobipocket Reader, this is how it appears:

21

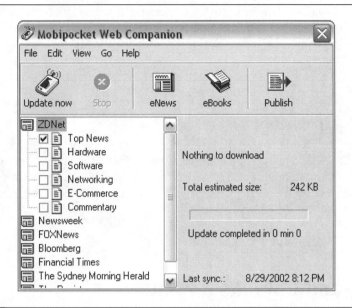

FIGURE 21-1   Mobipocket Web Companion manages the e-books and other materials you want to load on your Clié.

At the Mobipocket web site, you can purchase and download hundreds of commercial e-books, including L. Ron Hubbard's sci-fi classic *Battlefield Earth*, dictionaries and encyclopedias, and even a couple dozen medical texts. For $19.95, you can buy the Mobipocket Office Companion for Microsoft Office, which enables you to export Word, Excel, and PowerPoint documents to your Clié. All told, Mobipocket is a fairly comprehensive e-book solution. Even if it didn't come with your model, you can download it free from the company's web site.

NOTE   *At press time, Mobipocket Reader seemed to have a problem with the Clié's Jog Dial, which is used to scroll up and down within documents. Scrolling down worked just fine, but turning the dial up produced some wacky results. Hopefully this will be fixed by the time you read this.*

## Making Room for the Books

Before we delve into the details of finding, buying, and viewing e-books, you should know that e-books can be extremely large files. Jules Verne's *The Mysterious Island,* for instance, takes a whopping 622K, while the infamous biography *Monica's Story* nabs 500K. Fortunately, not all titles are quite so gargantuan. Most short stories are under 50K, and even Stephen King's novel, *The Girl Who Loved Tom Gordon,* is a reasonable 226K.

The good news is that most of the popular Doc readers (including Palm Reader, WordSmith, and TealDoc) support Memory Sticks, meaning you can store your e-books on a stick and not sacrifice any main memory (see Chapter 22). Indeed, with just a 16MB module, you could carry a rather significant library of titles.

## An E-Book Love Affair

A few years ago, Rick found himself on a train with nothing to do for several hours. Then he remembered he'd loaded an e-book onto his handheld just before leaving. He started reading, found the novel totally engrossing, and passed the time as happy as a clam. From that day forward, he vowed never to travel anywhere without an e-book. And when people ask him to explain what that little gadget is he's holding, he says it's a handheld PC—and a portable library.

# Free E-Books and E-Books for Sale

There are dozens of online sources for e-books, both free and commercial. The former are works considered public domain: either their copyrights have expired (as in the case of classic literature), or they've been written and released by authors not seeking compensation. There are literally thousands of titles available in the public domain, many of them already converted to the Doc format.

## Our Favorite E-Books

**Rick:** I've become something of an e-book zealot, recommending MemoWare and Palm Digital Media to friends, family, and any strangers who will sit still for five seconds. Among the great titles I've read on my Palm are *Angela's Ashes, Battlefield Earth, The Corrections,* and *Kick the Can.* I also enjoyed rereading *The Most Dangerous Game,* a story I remembered fondly from high school. I got that one free from MemoWare. My only hope is that Dave will one day read something that doesn't involve robots, hobbits, or robot hobbits.

**Dave**: I have to commend Rick on the progress he's made. When I met him a scant six years ago, he hadn't yet learned to master the written word. Since then, I've seen him get his equivalency diploma, start on "chapter books," and even sign his name in ink instead of crayon. Bravo, Rick! Well done! As for me, I find the best for the buck is the magazine *Fantasy & Science Fiction*—Palm Digital Media has a good assortment of them going back to 1997. I'm rarely disappointed by any of those tales, and there's a month's worth of bedtime reading in each collection.

Commercial titles aren't unlike what you'd buy in a bookstore: they've simply been converted to an electronic format and authorized for sale online. Notice we didn't mention Doc: most commercial e-books are created using a proprietary format, meaning a special viewer is required. This is primarily to prevent unauthorized distribution—unlike actual books, commercial e-books aren't meant to be loaned out or given to others. When you buy one, you're effectively buying a license to read it on your Clié and only your Clié.

## Finding Free Stuff

If one site is synonymous with Doc files, it's MemoWare (**www.memoware.com**). Here you can find thousands of texts divided into categories such as business, history, travel, biography, sci-fi, and Shakespeare. Whether you're looking for a collection of Mexican recipes, a Zane Grey western, a sappy love poem, or a classic work by Dickens, this is the place to start.

MemoWare offers a convenient search engine, so you can type in a title or keyword to quickly find what you're looking for. It also has links to other e-book sites, although none are as comprehensive. Finally, MemoWare provides numerous links to software programs (most for Windows, a few for Mac) that turn computer documents into Doc files. More on that later in the chapter.

## Finding Commercial Stuff

The thing about public domain e-books is that most of them are, well, old. Somerset Maugham and Jack London are all well and good for catching up on the classics you promised yourself you'd read one day, but sometimes you just want a little Stephen King, or Mary Higgins Clark, or Captain Kirk. Fortunately, you can have them all on your Clié, provided you're willing to pay for them.

The top place to go for contemporary, mainstream fiction and nonfiction is, without a doubt, Palm's own online bookstore, Palm Digital Media (at **www.palmdigitalmedia.com**). The site offers thousands of books from prominent authors like Stephen Ambrose, Elmore Leonard, and Anna Quindlen.

### How to View Palm Digital Media Books

When you purchase a book from Palm Digital Media, you supply your name and credit card number, then receive a Zip file to download. (If you need a utility to expand Zip files, we suggest downloading WinZip from **www.winzip.com**.) This file contains the e-book itself (in an encrypted .pdb format), along with the Palm Reader program. If you don't already have the Palm Reader installed on your PDA, be sure to install it before trying to read your new book.

 *When buying subsequent books, you need to install only the books themselves. You needn't install Palm Reader again.*

You also receive, via e-mail, a code number that's used to "unlock" the e-book. You need to enter this number on your Clié the first time you open your e-book.

 *The code number is usually the credit card number you used to purchase the book. If you don't mind divulging it, you can indeed share the book with another handheld user. Just e-mail the file for them to install, then give them the number so they can unlock the book. This is pretty smart copyright protection, if you ask us, as it allows for sharing among family members and close friends, but prevents you from giving books to strangers.*

One more note about Palm Reader: you must use it to view books purchased from Palm Digital Media; no other e-book reader will let you read them. However, Palm Reader will let you view standard Doc files, such as those obtained at MemoWare and Fictionwise. Thus, it's a pretty good all-purpose program.

## Other Sources for Contemporary E-Books

Palm Digital Media may be the largest source for commercial e-books, but a couple other web sites are gaining popularity.

■ **Fictionwise**   Here you'll find a growing collection of fiction and non-fiction stories and novels, all of them discounted. In fact, you can buy short stories for as little as a buck—sometimes even less. One nice thing about Fictionwise is that the books are provided in the standard Doc format, so you can use your favorite Doc viewing program. (The company also recently added Palm Digital Media format books to its library, so you can read those with Palm Reader as well.) Furthermore, the site includes reader-supplied ratings for each book and story, so you can make more informed decisions on what to buy. Fictionwise also keeps a decent collection of free short stories for you to try out, so we highly recommend a visit.

■ **Mobipocket**   This is not only an e-book content provider, but also a document viewer—one that may have come bundled with your Clié (along with a couple sample e-books). See "All About Mobipocket" earlier in this chapter for more details.

# Making Your Own E-Books

Become a published author! Well, not published in the "Stephen King" sense. More in the "kooky old uncle who staples warnings to telephone poles about how mailboxes are alien mind control devices" sense. Nonetheless, if you have your own documents, short stories, novellas, or doctoral theses you'd like to convert to the Doc format, you've got a lot of options. Among them:

■ Alexis Lorca's *pDocs* makes it a snap to transfer Microsoft Word documents to your Clié. It converts them to the Doc format, then adds them to the Install Tool so they'll be loaded the next time you HotSync. It can also pull Doc files from your Clié into Word.

■ *Palm eBook Studio* is a $30 program (available from Palm Digital Media) that lets you easily convert text and images to a format that's compatible with both Palm OS and Pocket PC handhelds.

■ *MakeDoc* (for Windows users) and *MakeDocDD* (an equivalent program for Mac users) are free, no-frills converters. They turn text and HTML files into Doc files, making them readable using any Doc reader. (For the record, Mobipocket's Web Companion utility does the same thing.)

## Reading in Bed Without Disturbing Your Spouse

Since the dawn of time, one seemingly insurmountable problem has plagued the human race: how to read in bed without disturbing one's spouse. Torches didn't work: they tended to set the bed on fire. Battery-operated book lights didn't work: they made books too heavy, leading to carpel reader syndrome. But finally there's an answer: the Clié handheld. Just load up a novel and turn on the backlight. You'll have no trouble seeing the screen in the dark, and your spouse will barely know it's on. PDA or marriage-saver? You be the judge.

## Where to Find It

| Web Site | Address | What's There |
| --- | --- | --- |
| Palm Digital Media | www.palmdigitalmedia.com | Huge library of commercial fiction and non-fiction |
| Mobipocket | www.mobipocket.com | The Mobipocket Reader and accompanying software, plus e-books for sale |
| Fictionwise | www.fictionwise.com | A growing collection of short stories and novels |
| MemoWare | www.memoware.com | Public domain literature formatted for the Clié |
| Alexis Lorca | www.thinkchile.com/alorca | pDocs |

# Chapter 22

## Making the Most of Memory Sticks

## How to…

- Work with Memory Stick media
- Find the best prices
- Lock a Memory Stick
- Manage files on a Memory Stick
- Automatically run programs from a Memory Stick
- Access a Memory Stick from your PC
- Transfer files to and from Memory Sticks

By now you know the twenty-first century spin on the old adage: you can never be too rich, too thin, or have too much memory. Sure, it's grammatically iffy—but it is accurate. What with RAM-devouring e-books, games, photos, productivity software, and even MP3 files, 8MB and 16MB just don't go as far as they used to. Fortunately, all Clié handhelds offer simple, inexpensive, potentially limitless memory expansion.

And not just memory expansion. Though most Memory Sticks are exactly that—memory—you can also find a Bluetooth networking card (which, at press time, is being sold only in Japan and Europe, but may be available elsewhere by now) and a digital camera mounted right on a stick. In the future, don't be surprised to see other Memory Stick-based expansion hardware, such as GPS receivers (already available in Japan) and wireless network adapters.

Nevertheless, in this chapter we focus primarily on the memory aspects of Memory Sticks: how to copy files to them, access programs from them, keep them organized, and more.

# It's in the Cards

Just what is a Memory Stick? True to its name, it's a small card—about the size of a stick of chewing gum—that contains a fixed amount of "Flash" memory. Flash memory is solid-state storage, meaning everything is electronic instead of mechanical. Think of it as a small hard drive with no moving parts. And, like a hard drive, a Memory Stick (MS for short) is rewriteable, meaning you can copy data to it over and over again.

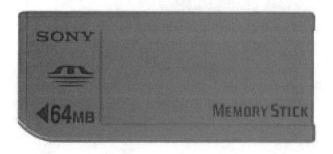

You may be familiar with CompactFlash and Secure Digital cards, which are also used as Flash storage for handheld PCs. Memory Stick is Sony's proprietary format, meaning you won't find the technology used in, say, Palm or Handspring devices. You will, however, find it in other kinds of Sony electronics, most notably digital cameras. We talk more about that later in this chapter.

**NOTE** *As you may have surmised, Memory Stick cards aren't compatible with CompactFlash, Secure Digital, or other kinds of memory media. That's because they're physically different. However, adapters do exist that would allow you to plug a Memory Stick into, say, your notebook computer's PC Card slot—helpful if you want a quick and easy way to transfer photos, MP3 files, or other data.*

## How to ... Lock a Memory Stick

If you're worried about the files or data stored on your Memory Stick, there's an easy way to lock the card so no additional data can be written to it—or deleted from it. On the back of every card there's a tiny sliding switch labeled "Lock." Slide the switch to the right and your MS is secure. Your Clié will still be able to read information and run programs from the card, but there's no danger of anything getting erased or overwritten. This is just like those write-protection tabs on the 3.5-inch floppy disks of yesteryear.

# What Price Memory?

So, what will it cost you to add, say, 8MB or 32MB or 128MB to your handheld? Prices drop all the time, so the information we've gathered here may be inaccurate by the time you read it—but in a good way. We spent some time shopping at Buy.com, where we found the following prices on MS cards:

- 32MB: $22
- 64MB: $36
- 128MB: $60
- 256MB: At press time, this wasn't yet available, but it should be by now. Sony plans to offer 512MB and 1GB cards in 2003.

As you can see, the higher the capacity, the lower the price per megabyte. How much space do you really need? If you plan to work with goodies like MP3 files and digital photos, buy the largest card you can afford. If you just want storage for extra programs, games, e-books, and such, a 32MB card would probably suffice.

**TIP**    *What about 8MB and 16MB cards? We found one of the latter selling for about $19, which doesn't make sense given that the 32MB card costs just $3 more. As for 8MB cards, they're not readily available any more, as the higher capacities have become so inexpensive. The same is likely to happen to the 16MB cards. Our advice: don't bother with anything less than 32MB.*

Keep in mind that you needn't buy media directly from Sony. Lexar Media, I-O Data, and SanDisk also sell the cards, and often for less than Sony. You should also steer clear of Sony's MagicGate-flavor Memory Stick cards. They cost more and offer absolutely zero benefit—unless you're buying and downloading copyrighted music content.

## What Is MagicGate?

As you shop for Memory Stick media, you may encounter some cards that are purple and some that are white. The latter are labeled "MagicGate," which refers to a proprietary copyright-protection technology created—and used—by Sony. Put simply, if you were to buy music online from a service like Pressplay (of which Sony is a part), you couldn't copy the music files to a "plain" Memory Stick as you can with ordinary MP3 files. Because the music is copyrighted, it will play only on a MagicGate Memory Stick that supports copyrighted files. Make sense? Yes, it's confusing to us as well. Bottom line: unless you're one of the 27 people who subscribe to Pressplay, you probably won't need to worry about MagicGate. See Chapter 18 for more information on playing music on your Clié.

# Memory 101

With the introduction of Palm OS 4.0 (almost every Clié model includes version 4.1, the exceptions being the S300 and N710C), Palm also introduced the Virtual File System (VFS)—a way for the operating system to recognize removable memory cards and access the programs and data stored therein. Thus, you could relocate, say, Palm Reader and all your e-books to a card, freeing a fair chunk of your handheld's valuable internal memory.

## More Memory on the Inside

If you're wishing you'd purchased a Clié with more memory on the inside, take heart. It may be possible to increase your model's internal memory—provided you're willing to part with it for a few days. Just send it to STNE (**www.stnecorp.com**) or Tony Rudenko (at **www.palmpilotupgrade.com**). Both can upgrade certain Clié models.

STNE, for instance, will upgrade an N760C to 16MB for $109.95. An N610C can have the same treatment for $99.95. Check the site for the latest prices and more details.

It's important to note that utilizing either service will void your handheld's warranty, but both vendors offer a 90-day warranty of their own.

## Working with Memory Cards

You can get programs and data onto a memory card in two basic ways. First, if you have software that's already loaded in internal memory, you can use the Palm OS Copy tool to copy it to the card. (This works both ways: you can copy items from a card back to internal memory as well.) To access it, tap the Home button to return to the main screen, and then tap Menu | App | Copy. Select the program you want to copy (you have to copy them one at a time), making sure to select the desired Copy To and From destinations. Tap Copy to begin the process.

Alas, because there's no "move" option, the original file remains on your handheld. To claim the extra storage space you were after, you must then delete the software from internal memory.

This is exactly as tedious as it sounds, which is why we strongly recommend a third-party file manager like FilePoint (**www.bachmannsoftware.com**) or McFile (**www.handango.com**). These programs make it much easier to move, copy, beam, and delete files than the Palm OS.

A better way to place applications onto a Memory Stick is by installing them there directly. The Palm OS Install Tool lets you specify the destination for new software at the time you install it, meaning you can HotSync applications right onto a memory card.

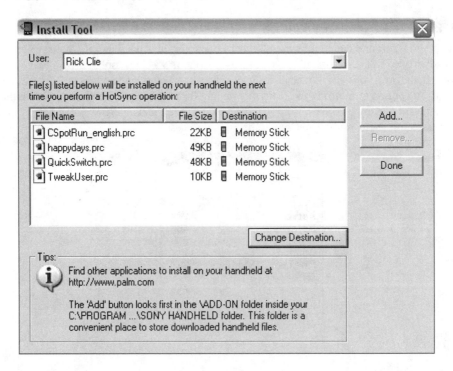

Ah, but what happens to them after that? Novice users often fall into the same trap: they install programs on their memory cards, and then can't understand why they don't see the icons in the Apps screen. The answer lies in a quirk of VFS: all applications stored on a memory card are automatically segregated into a category called Card. Thus, you must look in that category to find your newly installed stuff.

This can be inconvenient, to be sure, especially for users who like to keep their icons orderly. If you wind up with, say, 30 applications on a storage card, you've got an organization problem—you can't subcategorize the Card category. Fortunately, there's a solution in the form of third-party launchers, most of which now support external storage. One of our longtime favorites, LauncherX (formerly LauncherIII), lets you organize your icons however you see fit, regardless of where the actual applications are stored. MegaLauncher and Silver Screen, two more launchers we like, offer VFS support as well. See Chapter 13 for more information on launchers.

## What's on Your Stick?

**Rick:** I finally bit the bullet and ponied up for a 128MB Memory Stick—currently the largest available (though I'm eagerly awaiting a 256MB card). Why do I need all that space? Because I'm rapidly becoming a portable-video nut. Specifically, I like to record TV shows on my PC's hard drive, then transfer them to my Clié for viewing. Thus, you're likely to find an episode of *Sex and the City* or *Sesame Street* (for my daughter) on my Memory Stick. I also keep a 64MB card packed with MP3 tunes. And why not? The media is cheap!

**Dave:** I'm actually holding off on full-bore video until 256MB Memory Stick cards are available (and trust me—I can't wait). In the meantime, I have a 128MB card packed to the gills—mainly with images. My Memory Stick has a boatload of pictures that I can show off in my NR70's full-screen mode using SplashPhoto 3.0. I also have a few songs in MP3 format, a half-dozen e-books, an assortment of "skins" for my virtual Graffiti area, and a couple of short videos to round things out. And yes, my Memory Stick is always so full that I have to delete something just to make room for "one more thing" that I absolutely have to have on the road.

## Access a Memory Stick from Your PC

In the last section, we talked about the intricacies of accessing a Memory Stick via your Clié. But what about accessing one from your PC? Why would you want to? Here's a list of excellent reasons:

- It's much easier to manage the programs and data stored on your MS.
- It's much faster to install large files like MP3s and photos. We mean *much* faster. Suppose you have, say, a dozen MP3 files you want to load onto an MS. You could place them there using the Palm Install Tool, making sure to specify Memory Stick as the destination. But the HotSync process could take upwards of 30 minutes—no joke. If you copy them there via your PC, however, it should take no more than a few minutes.
- It allows you to use an MS as a kind of portable hard drive.

To allow direct access to your Clié's Memory Stick via your PC, Sony provides a pair of utilities: MS Import and MS Export. The former runs on your Clié and comes preinstalled on it. The latter runs on your PC and must be installed by you. Here's how to get started:

1. Insert the Sony Installation CD into your PC. The setup program starts automatically.

2. Click Install Clié Utilities, then Install Memory Stick Export. Follow the instructions.

3. Once the installation is complete, place your Clié into its HotSync cradle (or connect its HotSync cable). Turn it on, then find and tap the MS Import icon.

*Obviously, Step 3 is all you need to perform on subsequent occasions.*

When you perform this last step, your Clié should beep to notify you that a successful connection to your PC has been made. At the same time, you should now be able to fire up Windows Explorer (or double-click My Computer) and find a new drive letter. Yep, your Clié effectively becomes another drive on your system, meaning you can move, copy, delete, and even rename files just like you would on a floppy disk or hard drive. However, in most cases you won't need to, and you probably wouldn't want to (see the next section for details).

CAUTION
*Do not, under any circumstances, remove your Clié from the cradle/cable without first tapping the "Disconnect" button on its screen. This could seriously harm data, cause weather anomalies, or worse.*

## Working with MS Files and Folders

It stands to reason that if your Clié's Memory Stick becomes another drive on your PC, it should be subject to all the same basic principles of file management. That is, you can create folders to organize your files, then move and copy files between those folders. If you're thinking, "Oh, no, not *more* confusing file management to deal with," don't worry—there's very little to deal with unless you're a power user, in which case you probably enjoy working with folders and all that. (Dave's been known to spend many a Saturday night organizing the data on his Memory Sticks. Yes, "power user" sometimes equals "lame.")

Indeed, we have just a few key bits of information to impart, and then we'll let you go on your merry way.

- When you first insert a blank MS into your Clié, the operating system automatically creates a simple folder structure. You don't have to do anything.

- When you use the Palm Install Tool to install programs directly to an MS, they are placed in an automatically created folder called Launcher. (And they're accessible from the Home screen by selecting the Card category—see Chapter 2 for a refresher.)

- Programs that utilize VFS will often create their own subfolders in a Memory Stick's Programs folder, which also gets created automatically when needed.

- Though the contents of an MS may look like that of a floppy disk or hard drive, you shouldn't practice the same kind of file management. That is, don't start creating your own folders and shuffling files around. Your Clié knows where everything is stored, and if you move or rename files or folders, you're sure to cause problems. There is, however, one exception to this rule.

- An MS can double as a kind of portable hard drive—a repository for desktop files you may want to back up or transport. Suppose there's a Word document you want to store on your MS. You can just copy it to the root folder or create a folder called Word Files (or whatever you like). In both cases, you'd do this while "connected" to your Clié using MS Import and MS Export, as discussed earlier.

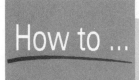 **Copy MP3 Files to a Memory Stick**

If your Clié is capable of playing MP3 files and has the AudioPlayer application installed, the Palm OS will automatically create a Palm\Programs\Msaudio folder on a Memory Stick upon its insertion. This is the folder into which you should drag and drop MP3 files from your PC. As noted earlier, it's much faster to load music using this method than with HotSync Manager.

## Accessing a Memory Stick from Your CLIÉ

Easy as it is to explore an MS via your PC, there are times when it's easier—and more practical—to do so on your Clié proper. For instance, suppose you want to move a file from the internal memory to an MS, or vice versa. That's something you can't even do from a PC. What you need, then, is a file-management program that supports memory cards (or a launcher that has built-in file-management capabilities).

Sony supplies just such a program: MS Gate. This utility enables you to move, copy, rename, and delete files:

Tap the level-up icon to return to the previous folder in the hierarchy.

Tap the little yellow folder icon to access the files and/or subfolders contained within that folder.

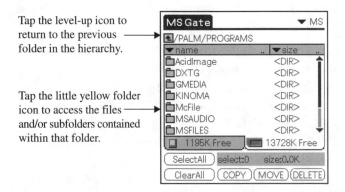

Let's say your Clié is getting a bit short on free space, so you want to move a rather large game to your Memory Stick. Here's the process:

1. Insert the MS if it's not already in.

2. Tap the MS Gate icon.

3. Tap the little arrow in the upper-right corner, then choose Internal. This presents you with a list of all the programs and data files stored in your Clié.

**4.** Scroll down the list until you find the game. If it has any files associated with it (such as a high-score database), you'll see them listed below the main game file.

**5.** Tap the game to highlight it, then tap any associated files that need to be moved with it. MS Gate allows you to select more than one file at a time.

**6.** Tap the MOVE button. This will transfer the selected files to the appropriate folder on your MS.

*Files that have a little "padlock" icon next to them are locked, meaning they cannot be moved, copied, or deleted.*

If you find MS Gate a bit confusing and underpowered, as we do, you may want to consider one of the many available third-party alternatives. Some recommendations:

■ **FileZ**   This file-management utility has just about every feature you could want, but it's extremely confusing, and therefore for advanced users only. Why bother with it? It has the appealing distinction of being a freebie.

■ **McFile**   Like MS Gate on steroids, McFile offers a wealth of file-management features, including beaming and support for HiRes+. It also employs a more traditional method of displaying files and folders, which makes for much easier navigation.

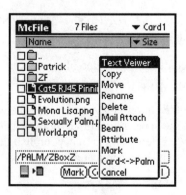

■ **LauncherX**    One of our all-time-favorite launchers (see Chapter 13), LauncherX includes a good measure of file-management capabilities. Which begs the question: why bother with a separate file manager?

■ **YiShow**    Another terrific launcher, YiShow also doubles as a file manager. It has certain Clié-specific features that LauncherX lacks, so you should definitely check it out before deciding between them.

## Automatically Running Programs Stored on a Memory Stick

While fiddling with the various MS-related utilities that came with your Clié, you may have encountered one called MS Autorun. This enables a selected program to start automatically when you insert a Memory Stick. For instance, if you have an MS packed with MP3 music files, you could set AudioPlayer to run immediately when that MS is detected. Likewise, if you've just snapped a bunch of photos with your MS-equipped digital camera, your Clié could run PictureGear Pocket when you pop in that card.

In both those examples, MS Autorun starts a program that's already in your Clié's internal memory. But it can also run a program stored on the Memory Stick itself—like, say, an e-book reader or database application, even if a game, if that's what you prefer—the sky's the limit.

### Setting Up MS Autorun

Let's say you've copied the great game *Bejeweled* to your Memory Stick, and want it to run immediately when you pop that stick into your Clié. Here's how:

1.  Insert the Memory Stick containing the video file.

2.  Start the MS Autorun application.

3.  Tap the left-hand tab near the bottom of the screen, the one with the little picture of the PDA. Or, tap the arrow in the upper-right corner of the screen, and choose Internal from the list that pops up. (Two different ways to accomplish the same end result, which is to specify that we want to pick an application that's already installed.)

**4.** Scroll through the list until you find *Bejeweled*. Tap it, then tap the Set button. After a moment, you see this message:

**5.** Tap the Clié's Home icon to return to the main screen, then remove the Memory Stick. The next time you insert it, *Bejeweled* will run automatically. Neat!

MS Autorun can also load a specific file or database when an MS is inserted. For information on how to do that, consult the Add-on Application Guide that came with your Clié.

NOTE    *MS Autorun will not work with certain file launchers, such as MegaLauncher. That's because these programs have their own ties to Memory Sticks, which tend to override whatever MS Autorun tries to do. We certainly wouldn't give up a launcher just to use this utility, as all it really does is save a few taps of the stylus.*

# Memory 102

While memory cards open the door to carrying much more software than you ever could before, there are a couple hitches. Suppose you have a favorite document reader and a fairly large collection of Doc files that go with it. You decide to move the files to your memory card to free some internal storage space. But the next time you fire up the Doc reader, you discover your Doc files are gone. Why? Because the Doc reader doesn't know to look for them on the memory card. They're still stored there, but the software can't see them. This is true of many older programs (and by "older" we mean those written prior to summer, 2001). The good news is that developers are rapidly updating their wares to support VFS, meaning this problem should disappear before long. (For the record, plenty of Doc readers already support VFS, including Palm Reader, TealDoc, and WordSmith.)

To overcome VFS-related issues like this (and have an easier time overall working with applications and data stored on memory cards), power users should check out utilities like MSMount (**www.palmgear.com**), PiDirect (**www.pitech.com**), and PowerRun (**homepage2.nifty.com/ hackerdudesan/index-3.html**). In a nutshell, these programs trick the operating system into thinking that programs and data stored on a memory card are actually stored in main memory, so everything is accessible all the time.

# Memory Stick Backups

One of the best uses for a Memory Stick is making a backup of your Clié's internal memory. You can perform this invaluable function using Sony's MS Backup utility or one of several more-robust third-party alternatives. See Chapter 13 for more details and MS Backup instructions.

## Where to Find It

| Web Site | Address | What's There |
|---|---|---|
| NoSleep Software | www.nosleep.net | FileZ |
| Handango | www.handango.com | McFile, YiShow |
| Little Mobile Creations | www.launcherx.com | LauncherX |
| Lexar Media | www.lexarmedia.com | Memory Stick media |
| SanDisk | www.sandisk.com | Memory Stick media |

# Chapter 23

# Accessories and Upgrades

## How to...

- Choose a case
- Choose a stylus
- Choose a keyboard
- Protect your screen from dust and scratches
- Add more memory
- Recharge your Clié's battery while on the road
- Turn your Clié into an MP3 player
- Add Game Boy-style controls to your Clié
- Help a lost Clié find its way home

There's more to the Clié than just software. We're talking gadgets, gear, accessories—the stuff that makes your handheld your own and extends its capabilities beyond what mere software can accomplish. Take the Targus USB Charge and Sync Cable, an invaluable travel companion that lets you synchronize—and recharge—your handheld by plugging it into any USB port. Or the Sony Audio Adapter, which lets non-musical Cliés play MP3 files. In this chapter, we look at these and other accessories and upgrades. For starters, let's tackle cases—a subjective category if ever there was one.

**NOTE**     *This is one area where it's important to make sure the accessory you buy is compatible with your particular Clié model. Many of them are different physically or have different ports and connectors, so not every accessory is compatible with every Clié.*

# Pick a Case, Any Case

As a new Clié owner, one of the first things you need to determine is how you plan to convey the device. In your pocket? Briefcase? Purse? Clipped to your belt? Backpack? Dashboard? Your answer will help determine the kind of case you should buy.

There are cases for every Clié model and every occasion, and picking one can be a tough call indeed. Do you opt for practical or stylish? (The two are often mutually exclusive.) Do you look for lots of extras like card slots and pen holders, or try to keep it as slim as possible? Do you shell out big bucks for a titanium shell that can withstand being run over by a car? (This happens quite a bit, believe it or not.)

**NOTE**     *While most Clié models come with screen covers, you may still want something that offers a bit more protection—and that doesn't flop around so much.*

Because there are so many varieties out there, and because everyone's case needs are different, we're going to start by steering you to the case manufacturers themselves, then offer a few general tips and suggestions.

| Company | URL | Cases Offered |
|---------|-----|---------------|
| Arkon Resources | www.arkon.com | Car mounts |
| Case Techworks | www.casetechworks.com | Various |
| E&B Company | www.ebcases.com | Slipper line |
| InnoPocket | www.innopocket.com | Metal cases |
| Piel Frama | www.pielframa.com | Luxury-minded leather cases |
| RhinoSkin | www.rhinoskin.com | Various metal, aluminum, and leather cases |
| Seidio | www.seidio.com | Colorful and contemporary leather cases |
| Sony | www.sonystyle.com | Various |

Here are some things to keep in mind as you shop for a case:

■ **Portability** In the summer, when the tight clothes come out and the jackets get stowed, pockets are hard to come by. That's when something like the E&B Slipper can come in mighty handy.

■ **Screen protection** When your Clié is bouncing around in a pocket, purse, or briefcase, the last thing you want is for some piece of flotsam to gouge or scratch the screen. That's one of the main reasons behind getting a case in the first place. The Seidio U-Clip Napa Leather Case offers Velcro-locking screen protection that looks good and doesn't get in the way of buttons and ports.

■ **Drop protection** Gravity—it strikes without warning (especially if you're a klutz like Rick), and it can fatally wound a Clié in a matter of milliseconds. Likewise, we've heard more than a few stories of people driving over their handhelds. Why they're being left in the driveway in the first place is beyond us, but there's one case that's better suited to handle such punishment than any other: InnoPocket's Metal Deluxe.

■ **Velcro**   Some cases rely on Velcro to keep your Clié device secured. While we look upon this as a necessary evil (who wants a big square of the stuff stuck to the back of their Clié?), we do try to avoid such cases when possible.

# The Stylus Decision

Many Clié users are perfectly happy with the stylus that came in the box—until they get a look at some of the alternatives. Indeed, while those bundled plastic and metal pens do get the job done, they're not as comfortable or versatile as they could be. For instance, wouldn't a thicker or heavier writing implement feel better in your hand? And wouldn't it be nice if it doubled as an ink pen? These are just some of the options available to the discriminating Clié user.

As with cases, we wouldn't presume to pick a stylus for you. That's a matter of personal preference. So, here's a look at some of the stylus makers and their offerings.

| Product | URL | Comments |
|---|---|---|
| Cross DigitalWriter | www.cross.com | Various executive-minded sizes and styles, many with multifunction designs |
| InnoPocket | www.innopocket.com | Metal replacement styluses |
| PDA Panache | www.pdapanache.com | Wide assortment of sizes and styles |
| Pentopia Chameleon | www.pentopia.com | Multifunction replacement styluses |
| Styluscentral.com | www.styluscentral.com | Giant assortment of styluses |
| Ttools | www.ttools.com | Nifty multifunction styluses |

There are basically two kinds of styluses: those that are too large to fit in a Clié's stylus holder, and those that aren't. The former we'd classify as "executive" styluses: they seem right at home in a suit pocket or briefcase. The Cross DigitalWriter falls into this category—it's big, comfy, and has that classy business look.

Replacement styluses, on the other hand, supplant the stock Clié pen. The Pentopia Chameleon, for instance, fits snugly in your Clié's stylus silo and doubles as a ballpoint pen.

23

> **TIP**
>
> *If your Clié should happen to crash, the last thing you want is to have to hunt down a toothpick or paper clip in order to press its Reset button. Thus, look for a stylus that hides a reset pin. Most of them do; it's usually accessible simply by unscrewing one end of the barrel.*

# Keyboards

If you typically enter a lot of data into your Clié device—memos, e-mail messages, business documents, novels—you've probably longed to replace your stylus with a keyboard. After all, most of us can type a lot faster than we can write by hand. Fortunately, there are a multitude of keyboards available for Clié devices, all of them priced under $100.

> **NOTE**
>
> *The NR- and NX- series have built-in thumb keyboards, obviously, but even those aren't ideal if you need to do a lot of writing.*

Okay, but what kind? Handheld keyboards fall into two basic categories: full-size models that allow for touch typing, and palm-size models that give your thumbs a workout. In the sections that come, we give you the skinny on a few of our favorite keyboards from both categories. You're sure to find one—or maybe more than one—that meets your needs.

> **NOTE**
>
> *There's an easy argument to be made in favor of owning two or three keyboards for your handheld PC. You could keep a full-size model on hand for boardroom note-taking, and carry a thumb 'board for when you're out and about. That's what we do—and we're professionals!*

## Full-Size Keyboards

We don't blame you if the notion of carrying around a standard computer keyboard for use with your tiny little handheld PC is making you chuckle. That would be pretty silly, wouldn't it? Still, what better way to do some serious writing than a full-size set of keys? Of the handful of options now available, there's simply no better solution than the Think Outside Stowaway.

As you can see in Figure 23-1, this amazing keyboard folds up to the size of a small diary, and unfolds to produce a set of keys comparable to a notebook PC's. It's a bit pricey at $99 (we've found better prices on eBay, especially for versions compatible with older Clié models), but you won't regret the investment.

> **TIP**
>
> *You can buy the Stowaway direct from Sony, where it sells under the name Compact Keyboard. Why go this route? Amazingly, Sony charges $10 less than Think Outside.*

The Stowaway does have one disadvantage: limited compatibility. That is, you have to buy the version that's designed to work with your particular handheld model, and if you decide to upgrade someday, the keyboard probably won't be compatible with your new handheld. This is a problem that plagues just about all portable keyboards—but there's a solution.

**FIGURE 23-1**    The Stowaway puts a comfy set of keys beneath your fingers, then folds up and fits in a pocket.

It's called the Pocketop Portable Keyboard, and instead of requiring a direct connection to your handheld, it works wirelessly via infrared ports. That means it's compatible with virtually any model (even handhelds that use Microsoft's Pocket PC operating system), so it should be able to "stay with you" for the duration.

The Pocketop's keys are smaller and less comfortable than those of the Stowaway, but it also becomes even more compact when folded. It's a truly ingenious product, one that's well worth investigating.

Same goes for the Belkin G700, which is almost as comfortable as the Stowaway, but can actually be used on your lap (the Stowaway requires a flat surface). It's also less expensive than either of the aforementioned keyboards, with a list price of $79.99.

## Thumb-Style Keyboards

If you've ever seen one of those BlackBerry pagers, you may have noticed that in place of a handwriting-recognition area, they have tiny built-in keyboards. For anyone who's now thinking, "Say, I wish *my* handheld had one of them thar keyboards!", we'd like to remind you that "them thar" is not proper grammar, no matter how many times you hear Dave use it. Fortunately, you can buy a clip-on "thumb 'board" for just about any Clié model, usually for less than $50.

**NOTE** *As we mentioned earlier, the NR- and NX- models are obviously exempt from this equation, as they have fairly decent built-in keyboards already.*

The one we like best is Seiko's aptly named ThumBoard, which connects to the bottom of the handheld, enveloping roughly the bottom third of it (including the buttons and Graffiti area). It includes power, application, and function buttons, plus separate number and arrow keys. Most Palm OS operations are available as secondary-key functions. The only downside? You can't beam anything when the keyboard is attached.

If you own an SL-, SJ-, or T-series Clié, you may want to check out Sony's own Mini Keyboard, which slides onto the front of the handheld and provides a full set of QWERTY keys.

# Protecting Your Screen

Keeping your screen pristine is the first rule of Clié ownership. Why? One word: scratches. A scratch in the Graffiti area can result in inaccurate handwriting recognition, and a scratch on the main screen can impair its visibility. Fortunately, it's relatively simple to forestall such disasters.

What causes scratches? If your Clié device is flopping around unprotected in a purse or briefcase, any loose item—keys, paper clips, a pen or pencil—can create a scratch. That's why we highly recommend a case (see the first section of this chapter). More commonly, however, little specks of grit and other airborne flotsam accumulate on your screen, and when you run your stylus over one of them—scratch city.

 *Dave is a big fan of tapping his screen with his big grubby fingers. They leave behind oil and smudges, which are more likely to trap dust and grit. Rick, who is much daintier, says that if you must use a finger, at least use your fingernail.*

We recommend you buy a lens-cleaning cloth, the kind used to wipe dust from eyeglasses and camera lenses. Every day, just give your screen a little buff and polish to keep it free of dust and grit. Or, consider one of the following products.

## WriteRight

If you want serious screen protection, you'll need something like Fellowes' WriteRight. These plastic overlays cover your screen from top to bottom, thus ensuring that your stylus causes no damage. They also provide a tacky surface that makes for easier handwriting, and they cut down on glare. The only drawback? WriteRights cut down on contrast, too, making the screen a little tougher to read. If you consider that a small price to pay for total screen protection, these plastic sheets are the way to go.

## PDA Screen Protectors

We're not sure this deal will still be around by the time you read this, but it's worth checking out. At a web site called **freescreenprotectors.com**, you can order an entire box of CompanionLink PDA Screen Protectors (which are similar to WriteRights but don't affect contrast) and pay only for shipping. That's right—just enter the coupon code "FREESP" when placing your order, and the sheets are free. Sounds too good to be true, but we placed an order and received our box within about three days. Shipping cost about six bucks. Woo-hoo—free stuff!

# Adding More Memory

Like money, you can never have too much memory. If you run out, you'll have no room for new stuff unless you delete applications or data (that you may still need). Of course, your Clié has a Memory Stick slot, so it's a fairly simple matter to expand your available storage space (see Chapter 22). On the other hand, there's something to be said for having more RAM on the inside. If that sounds interesting, check out these third-party services, which can upgrade your handheld's memory:

| Service | URL | Upgrades Available |
| --- | --- | --- |
| STNE Corp. | www.stnecorp.com | In-house upgrades for many Clié models |
| Tony Rudenko | www.palmpilotupgrade.com | In-house upgrades for many Clié models |

You'll have to part with your handheld for at least a few days. You send it to the company, they perform the upgrade and then send it back to you.

*Any memory upgrade performed on any handheld will automatically void the warranty. That's because it involves removing and replacing memory chips on the main circuit board. Check to see if the service offers a supplemental warranty.*

We should note here that when your handheld is returned to you, its memory will be wiped clean. When you HotSync, your programs and data will be restored—but you might want to consider running a utility like BackupBuddy (see Chapter 13) before sending away your handheld.

While there are some definite caveats to consider, in-house upgrades are usually successful and inexpensive. STNE Corp., for instance, can upgrade a Clié N760C from 8MB to 16MB for $109.95. Prices fluctuate, so it may cost even less by the time you're ready to upgrade!

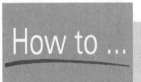

## How to ... **Protect Your Screen with Scotch Tape**

The Graffiti area is where most stylus contact occurs, and therefore it's where scratches are most likely to result. You could cut a WriteRight sheet to fit just the Graffiti area—or you could buy yourself a roll of 3M's Scotch Magic Tape 811. It's almost exactly the right width for most Graffiti areas, and one roll will last you a lifetime. Plus, its slightly rough surface makes for less-slippery handwriting—always a plus. Just cut a piece to cover the input area and replace it every month or so. You'll never see a single scratch.

# Navigating the World with a GPS Receiver

Dave is a huge fan of the Global Positioning System, the network of orbiting satellites used to pinpoint one's exact position on the planet. That's because he tends to get lost in his own driveway. Still, GPS is undeniably valuable if you're driving on unfamiliar roads or trying to find your way to, say, a new client's office. And many Clié devices can take full advantage of GPS, thanks to Delorme's Earthmate.

**NOTE** *At press time, Sony had introduced a GPS module mounted right on a Memory Stick—but it wasn't available in the U.S., and the company wouldn't confirm plans to sell it here. Here's hoping they've changed their minds by now.*

Earthmate is a pocket-sized GPS receiver that uses a special cable to connect to your Clié. XMap is a Palm OS map viewer that lets you download and display street maps created on either Delorme's web site or their Street Atlas U.S.A. software. The result: you can enjoy real-time street-level positioning right on your Clié.

# Recharging Your CLIÉ's Batteries While on the Road

A Clié handheld with a rechargeable battery is a mixed blessing. Sure, you don't have to keep a pocketful of fresh Duracells on hand, but what happens if you're on the road and the Clié runs out of juice? Fortunately, there are several clever solutions to this little travel problem.

One of the most practical is a cable that charges your Clié just by plugging into a desktop or notebook USB port—no AC adapter required. Check out the Belkin USB Sync Charger and Targus USB Charge and Sync Cable. The former is by far the better deal, as it costs $10 less ($19.99) and comes with a cigarette-lighter adapter for use in your car. For easy recharging just about anywhere, the $39.95 Sony Battery Adapter utilizes four AA batteries, making it the perfect traveling companion.

## The Cool Way to Recharge

Another excellent power-supply option is the Instant Power Charger. Instead of charging your batteries from a wall outlet, Instant Power tops off your Clié with a disposable power source. The charger is actually a sort of fuel cell that combines a safe embedded fuel with oxygen drawn from the air. Stored in its aluminum pouch, the charger has a shelf life of about two years. Once you open the pouch, it's good for about three months. That means you can put one in your travel bag and have the peace of mind that you'll have power anytime you need it.

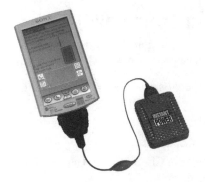

To get started with Instant Power, you need to buy an Instant Power Charger kit that includes a single disposable power cartridge and a connection cable for whatever model handheld you own. There are versions for just about every Clié model, as well as wireless modems, digital cameras, Pocket PCs, and even camcorders. Since the power cartridges are interchangeable, you can charge up your entire mobile arsenal without worrying about carrying three different kinds of batteries or chargers.

You should be able to charge your PDA about three times with a single Instant Power cartridge. After you deplete it, just toss it in the trash, but keep the cable—you need to replace only the interchangeable cartridges.

## Our Favorite Accessories

**Rick:** It's not really an accessory, but I wouldn't be caught dead without my 128MB Memory Stick, which has a permanent home in my Clié and holds a boatload of games, e-books, and MP3 files. But the real star is my Stowaway keyboard, a marvel of modern engineering that lets me write while traveling without having to schlep a notebook. They'll have to pry it out of my cold, dead fingers when I shuffle off this mortal coil.

**Dave:** Using my Sony NR70V is like a refreshing walk through a sun-dappled forest, a cool stream gurgling off to my side and coyotes playfully wrestling over a bone in the distance. It's a sheer delight; a blissful interlude betwixt the hustle-bustle workaday world. Hence, I consider my Clié to be nearly perfect; little could be done to improve it. That said, a Stowaway keyboard is essential for letting me write on the road. I'll love inserting Bluetooth and WiFi Memory Sticks—when Sony gets around to letting me have them. So all that stuff, and whatever I can pry out of Rick's cold, dead fingers.

# Mounting Your CLIÉ in Your Car

Is your car your castle? Your office? Your home away from home? If so, your Clié deserves a place of honor—and a place where you can access it while keeping at least one hand on the wheel.

 **CAUTION** *In all seriousness, you should never, ever try to use your Clié while driving. If you must look something up or write something down, wait until you've stopped at a light. Or, ask a passenger to do it for you.*

Arkon Resources offers a variety of universal car mounts ("universal" meaning they're designed to work with any handheld) that put your Clié device at arm's reach. The kits attach to the windshield, the console, even your car's cup holder.

# Recovering Lost Handhelds

No one ever means to lose anything, but it happens. The only thing worse than losing your PDA would be realizing that whoever found it probably wouldn't know how to go about returning it to you. Sure, an address label pasted to the back might do the trick, but we have a better solution: **stuffbak.com**.

For as little as $1.95, you can buy a specially coded StuffBak label to paste on the back of your handheld. The finder need only call a toll-free number or visit the StuffBak web site to arrange for its return, which requires little effort and includes a reward. You pay a $14.95 transaction fee, plus shipping charges and any cash reward you care to offer. (StuffBak's own reward is a pack of its labels, valued at $20.) If you believe people are generally honest, this is an inexpensive and potentially painless way to help a lost handheld find its way home.

If you like the idea behind StuffBak, be sure to check out Boomerangit, which offers a similar set of products and services.

## Sony's Accessories

As you've already learned in this chapter, Sony makes quite a number of accessories for the Clié: keyboards, cases, battery chargers, and so on. There are a few other Sony-made products we think you should know about:

- **Audio Adapter** Some Cliés have built-in MP3 players, some don't. If yours falls into the latter category, you may want to check out the Audio Adapter. It's a wired remote/headphone jack that plugs into the HotSync port, thereby enabling you to listen to MP3 files (and video clips) stored on Memory Sticks. It also comes with a nice pair of ear-clip headphones. Just one catch: Cliés with built-in MP3 players let you do other things while listening to music, but the Audio Adapter takes over—you can't do anything else until you stop da music.

- **Game Controller** This is one of our all-time favorite accessories. It adds a Game Boy-like set of buttons to your Clié, making certain action games (like *Sinistar*, *Zap!2016*, and *Galax*) much easier to play and a lot more enjoyable. It also comes with a game: the *Tetris* clone *Columns*.

- **Screen Protector** We discussed these a few pages back, but thought you'd like to know that Sony offers its own protective sheets for certain Clié models.

## Where to Find It

| Web Site | Address | What's There |
|---|---|---|
| Fellowes | www.fellowes.com | WriteRight and other accessories |
| Delorme | www.delorme.com | Earthmate |
| Arkon Resources | www.arkon.com | CM220 Universal Car Mount |
| StuffBak.com | www.stuffbak.com | StuffBak labels |
| Boomerangit | www.boomerangit.com | Boomerangit labels |
| Pocketop | www.pocketop.net | Pocketop Portable Keyboard |
| Seiko | www.seiko-austin.com | ThumBoard |
| Think Outside | www.thinkoutside.com | Stowaway Keyboard |
| Sony | www.sonystyle.com | Various Clié accessories |
| Targus | www.targus.com | Charger, Sync Cradle, and other accessories |
| Belkin | www.belkin.com | G700 keyboard, USB Sync Charger, and other accessories |
| Instant Power | www.instant-power.com | Instant Power Charger |

# Appendix A

# Troubleshooting and Problem Solving

## How to…

- Reset your Clié
- Fix a Clié that appears to be dead
- Avoid battery-related problems
- Prevent and fix scratched screens
- Fix a screen that no longer responds properly
- Resolve Hack conflicts
- Deal with a handheld that suddenly won't HotSync
- Troubleshoot HotSync glitches
- Manage two Cliés on one PC
- Manage one Clié on two PCs
- Obtain non-warranty or accident-related repairs
- Find answers to problems on the Web

No computer is perfect. Windows is about as far from the mark as you can get, Macs have problems of their own, and even Cliés suffer the occasional meltdown. Usually it's minor: a Memory Stick that's not recognized, or a wayward Hack that causes the occasional crash. But sometimes something downright scary happens, like a sudden and inexplicable lockup that wipes the Clié's entire memory. In this chapter, we help you troubleshoot some of the most common Clié maladies and, hopefully, prevent the worst of them.

NOTE    *Many common problems are addressed on Sony's web site. We're not going to rehash them here, but we are going to suggest you check there first if you've got a problem we haven't addressed. Chances are good you'll find a solution.*

# Cure CLIÉ Problems with a Reset

Just as rebooting a computer will often resolve a glitch or lockup, resetting your Clié is the solution to many a problem. And it's usually the first thing you need to do if your Clié crashes—or even just acts a little strangely.

## Just What Is a "Crash," Anyway?

When a computer crashes, that generally means it has plowed into a brick wall—software-wise—and can no longer function. Fortunately, whereas a car in the same situation would need weeks of bump-and-paint work, a computer can usually return to normal by being rebooted. In the case of Cliés, a "reset" is the same as a "reboot."

When a Clié crashes, one common error message is "Fatal Exception." Don't be alarmed; this isn't nearly as deadly as it sounds. It simply means the Clié has encountered a glitch that proved fatal to its operation. Very often an onscreen Reset button will appear with this error, a tap of which performs a "soft reset" (as we describe in the next section). Sometimes, however, the crash is so major that even this button doesn't work. (You know because you tap it and nothing happens.) In a case like that, you have to perform a manual reset.

# Different Ways to Reset a CLIÉ

On the back of every Clié, there's a little hole labeled RESET. Hidden inside it is a button that effectively reboots the unit. When that happens, you see the Clié startup screen, followed a few seconds later by the Prefs screen. That's how a successful reset goes. About 98 percent of the time, everything will be as you left it—your data, your applications, everything.

Technically speaking, there are three kinds of resets: soft, warm, and hard. (Mind out of the gutter, please.) The details:

- **Soft**   Only in rare instances do you need to perform anything other than a soft reset, which is akin to pressing CTRL-ALT-DELETE to reboot your computer. You simply press the Reset button, then wait a few seconds while your Clié resets itself. No data is lost.

- **Warm**   This action, performed by holding the scroll-up button while pressing the Reset button, goes an extra step by bypassing any system patches or Hacks you may have installed. Use this only if your Clié fails to respond to a soft reset, meaning it's still locked up or crashing. No data is lost, but the Clié will start with a lot of essential software features disabled, like hi-res support on appropriate Cliés. Use this mode to restart a Clié that won't boot any other way—then delete the offending software and reset it again to enable all the goodies.

- **Hard**   With any luck, you'll never have to do this. A hard reset wipes everything out of your Clié's memory, essentially returning it to factory condition. In the exceedingly rare case that your Clié is seriously hosed (meaning it won't reset or even turn off), this should at least get you back to square one. If it doesn't, your handheld is toast and may need to be replaced (more on repair/replacement options later in this chapter). The good news is this: even after a hard reset, all it takes is a HotSync to restore all your data. Some third-party applications may have to be reinstalled manually, but most will just reappear on your handheld. It's like magic!

## The Toothpick Story

Many years ago, Rick was having lunch with a couple of his buddies when he pulled out his PalmPilot Personal (one of the Clié's PDA ancestors) to jot down a few notes. To his horror, it wouldn't turn on (a problem he later attributed to the extremely cold weather, which can indeed numb a pair of batteries). A press of the Reset button was in order, but Rick didn't have the right tool—namely, a paper clip. So he asked the waitress to bring him a toothpick—the other common item that's small enough to fit into the reset hole. Presto! The PalmPilot sprang back to life.

The moral of the story: be prepared. If your Clié crashes and you need to reset it, the last thing you want is a desperate hunt for a paper clip or toothpick. Fortunately, many styluses have "reset tips" hidden inside them. And now, a tip about tips.

*If your Clié has a metal stylus (most of them do), it may surprise you to learn that it's stowing a reset tip. Where's it hiding? Unscrew the top (or, in some cases, the bottom) from the barrel to find it.*

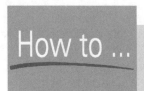 **Perform Warm and Hard Resets**

There's a bit of a trick to doing a warm or hard reset successfully. With your Clié on or off (it doesn't matter), hold down the Scroll-up button (for a warm reset) or the Power button (for a hard reset), then press and release the Reset button on the back of the unit. Now, here's the trick: *wait until the Sony logo appears onscreen* before releasing the Scroll or Power button. If you release both buttons simultaneously, before the logo appears, all you get is a soft reset.

## Fixing a CLIÉ that Appears to Be Dead

So, you fish your Clié out of your pocket, press the Power button, and voilà: nothing happens. Sweating, you press one of the application buttons—again, *nada*. You start to panic. You press the reset button—the screen flashes for a moment, then goes blank. You start making deals with the man upstairs.

Then you remember that your Clié has a built-in MP3 player, and that if you slide the Hold switch on the side of the unit, it disables the screens and buttons in order to prevent an accidental interruption of your music. In short, it makes your Clié appear to be dead. You check, and sure enough, the Hold switch is in the "on" position. You slide it back and your Clié springs to life. Whew!

This has given us more than a few scares, so don't feel badly.

## Fixing a Comatose CLIÉ

Another kind of dead-Clié problem can scare you to death—unless you know how to fix it, that is. Suppose you install a beta version of some new program and it causes your Clié to crash. When you reset it, though, the screen stays blank, the power light stays on, and no amount of fiddling, whimpering, or screaming to the gods will get it to return to life. Dave has had this happen to him, and trust us: it's not a fun experience.

If that happens to you, all is not lost. Leave the Clié out of its cradle for a day. After the battery drains completely, press the Reset button, place it in the cradle, and let it charge again. After a few hours, press the Reset button again and let it restart. You should have your Clié back, though all the data will be lost—a good reason to HotSync and back up your Clié before you install new software.

# Avoiding Battery Problems

Batteries are the lifeblood of any Clié. When they die, they take your data with them, effectively returning your Clié to factory condition. That's why it's vital to keep a close eye on the battery gauge shown at the top of the Applications screen (see Figure A-1), and to take heed when the Clié notifies you that your batteries are low.

Of course, if you HotSync regularly, a wiped Clié isn't the end of the world. Once you've recharged (or replaced) the batteries, a HotSync is all it takes to restore virtually everything. Still, there's no reason to let things reach that point. The following are some tips to help you avoid most battery-related incidents.

■ **Keep 'Em Fresh**   Suppose you head off to Bermuda for a two-week getaway (you lucky vacationer, you), leaving your work—and your Clié—behind. When you return, don't be surprised to find the Clié dead as a doornail. That's because it draws a trace amount of power from the batteries, even when off, to keep the memory alive. If the batteries were fairly low to begin with, the long period of inactivity might just polish them off. The obvious solution is to keep your Clié with you as much as possible. (It's great for games, e-books, and other leisure activities, remember?) Alternately, if you know you're going to be away from it for a while, just leave it in the cradle (if it's a rechargeable model).

■ **Keep a Charger on Hand**   You've been on the road for weeks, your handheld has warned you repeatedly that the battery is low, and there's not a charging cradle in sight. That's

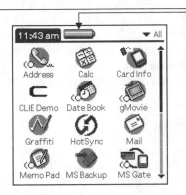

The battery gauge tells you how much juice your Clié has left.

| FIGURE A-1 | All Cliés have this handy—and fairly accurate—battery gauge at the top of the screen. |

the Catch-22 of the rechargeable battery: no Duracells to buy, but no easy way to recharge on the road. That is, unless you have one of the many portable charging accessories now available. See Chapter 23 for more details.

# Fixing Scratched Screens

Scratches happen. They happen most often when your stylus hits a piece of dust or grit. That's why it's important to keep your screen as clean as possible (we recommend a daily wipe with a lint-free, antistatic cloth). Better still, take a few preventative steps:

- **Tape**   A piece of Scotch Magic Tape 811 placed over the Graffiti input area (where most scratches occur) not only makes existing scratches less tangible while you're writing, but also prevents future scratches and provides a tackier writing surface.

- **WriteRight sheets**   As discussed in Chapter 23, Fellowes' WriteRight sheets are plastic overlays that protect the entire screen. They won't remove scratches, but they will prevent them and, like the tape, make them less pronounced. Sony makes a similar screen-protection product, and be sure to check out the sheets at **www.freescreenprotectors.com**.

- **Screen Clean**   Creator Tim Warner says that this bottle of goo—which closely resembles car wax—removes 99 percent of all screen scratches. Basically, you wipe it onto the screen, wait five minutes, then buff it off. Make no mistake: Screen Clean won't fix a really deep scratch, but it does work as advertised on light ones. And it leaves your screen as bright and shiny as the day you unpacked it.

# Fixing a Screen that No Longer Responds Properly

As noted in Chapter 2's discussion of the Digitizer option, it's not uncommon to experience some "drift" in the screen's response to your stylus taps. An example: you have to tap just a bit to the left or right of your desired target for the tap to be recognized. This occurs over time, when the accuracy of the digitizer (the hardware that makes the screen respond to your input) degrades.

Unless the digitizer has gotten so off-kilter that you can no longer operate your Clié, the solution is to hit the Prefs icon, then choose Digitizer from the right-corner menu. Here you can reset the digitizer, effectively making your Clié good as new. If you can't even manage to tap Prefs, you can do a soft reset (as described earlier in this chapter). That gets you to the Prefs screen, where you should at least be able to select the Digitizer option.

# Resolving Hack Conflicts

It bears repeating (see Chapter 13 for the first time we said it) that as marvelous as Hacks are, they can wreak havoc on Cliés. This is especially true if you run more than two or three simultaneously, as these little bits of code can conflict with one another. If you find that your Clié is crashing on a regular basis, you may have to investigate your Hacks. Here's what you should do:

1. Start X-Master, then uncheck the box next to each Hack to disable it.

2. Go back to using your Clié. If you find that the crashes no longer occur, a Hack is the likely culprit. To help pin down which one, go to Step 3.

3. Launch X-Master again, then enable just one Hack. Use your Clié normally, and see if the crashes return. If not, enable a second Hack. Through this process of elimination, you should be able to figure out which one is causing the problem. When you do, stop using it.

**A**

## How to ...  Cure "Mad Digitizer Syndrome"

What happens when the digitizer gets so out of whack that your Clié essentially becomes inoperable? This problem, which some have dubbed "Mad Digitizer Syndrome," can strike even if your handheld is only a year or two old. One very effective way to cure MDS is with a utility called AutoDigi, which automatically recalibrates the digitizer after a reset. You can buy the $15 program at PalmGear.com (**www.PalmGear.com**). If your screen is really giving you trouble, check out OnDigi, a Hack that automatically recalibrates the digitizer each time you turn on your handheld. If neither utility solves the problem, then it's probably a hardware issue that will require service.

# Fixing a CLIÉ that Won't "Wake Up" for Alarms

It's easy to fall out of love with your Clié when an alarm you set fails to go off (meaning the Clié doesn't "wake up" and beep). There are several reasons this can happen, from low batteries to a corrupted alarm database to a conflict with third-party software. The first is easy to resolve by making sure your Clié is adequately charged. For the other two problems, try a soft reset, which very often does the trick.

If you use a third-party program that has anything to do with alarms (such as ToDo Plus or DiddleBug), it's very possible this is causing the snafu. To troubleshoot it, try doing a warm reset (hold the Scroll-up button while pressing the Reset button). This will disable any Hacks or third-party applications that tie into the operating system. Set an alarm in Date Book and see if it works. If so, then another program is very likely to blame. A process of elimination should help you determine which one. In any case, you may have to discontinue using that program if it keeps fouling up your alarms.

If none of these options work, it's possible your Clié is damaged. Contact Sony for service.

# Beaming Problems

Having trouble beaming? Chances are good the problem is caused by one of four factors. First, if your Clié is brand new and won't beam, you're not alone. Both Dave and Rick have noticed that some Cliés don't beam properly right out of the box. Perform a reset. It should work just fine after that.

Second, make sure the two handhelds aren't too close together. People often make the mistake of holding their Cliés right next to each other, which can give the infrared transceivers trouble. Keep the units at least a foot or two apart.

Third, make sure the Beam Receive option is checked in the Prefs | General screen. While you may not have unchecked it yourself, sometimes it just seems to happen.

Still no luck? Try moving to a darker area. Beaming doesn't always work if you're in a brightly lit room or outdoors on a sunny day. If all else fails, perform a soft reset on both Cliés. More often than not, that does the trick.

## The Last Chapter

**Dave:** Well, this is the last chapter… and it's almost complete. It was a blast to write this book, but I have to admit that I'm kind of burnt out on all this tech writing stuff. I think I'll take my half of the advance (a cool half-million or so) and move to Bermuda. There I'll build a cottage on the beach and let my army of trained monkey butlers bring me cool drinks all day long. I'll pass the time staring at the waves as they gently break onto the sandy, white beach, and occasionally dabble at writing a best-selling novel on my Clié with a Stowaway keyboard. My MP3 player will be loaded up with Kristin Hersh music and my cats will be napping in my lap. Yep, that's what I'm going to do….

**Rick:** Always with the monkey butlers. As for me, now that the yoke of another book has been lifted, I'll be returning to the soup kitchen where I volunteer three times a week, though not before I finish the urban-beautification program I spearheaded, along with that fundraiser for Greenpeace. Now I just have to decide which charities will be getting my royalty checks this year—always a tough choice. Honestly, there's no better reward for months of hard work than good old philanthropy. Oh, but, uh, your plan sounds really good too….

# Dealing with a Handheld that No Longer HotSyncs

It worked fine yesterday, but today your handheld just refuses to HotSync. We hear your pain—this drives us up the wall, too. We wish we could blame Windows, because it's just the kind of nonsense we've come to expect from it, but this is usually due to a Clié software, hardware, or cradle problem.

Best bet? Start with a soft reset. Use the end of a paper clip (or unscrew the barrel of your metal stylus to find a hidden tip) to press the Reset button on the back of your handheld. In many cases, this will solve the problem outright, and you can get back to playing *Bejeweled*. If it doesn't, consider reinstalling Palm Desktop. This action won't affect your data, but it will provide a "fresh" version of HotSync Manager—which often solves HotSync problems. If you're not comfortable with that step or it doesn't work, consult Sony's web site for other remedies.

## Solving Memory-Related HotSync Failure

If you try to install a new program or database and your Clié doesn't have enough memory, the HotSync will fail—and fail again every time thereafter. Assuming you can't free up enough space on your handheld to accommodate the new item(s), you have to venture onto your hard drive. Specifically, locate the *c:\Program Files\Sony Handheld\yourusername\Install* folder (the "holding tank" for software waiting to be installed during HotSync), and delete everything in there. Now you should be able to HotSync successfully.

*Deleting programs and data from the Install folder doesn't permanently delete them from your hard drive. When you choose items to be installed on your Clié, copies are placed in the Install folder. The original files remain.*

## Solving the Most Common HotSync Problems

There are a few pesky problems that account for about 90 percent of all the HotSync issues we've ever encountered—and they're all pretty easy to diagnose and solve.

### The CLIÉ Aborts a HotSync Immediately

If you press the HotSync button on the cradle and the Clié immediately insists that "the COM port is in use"—so quickly that it doesn't seem possible for the Clié to have even checked—the solution is to perform a soft reset on your Clié. After it resets, the HotSync should work fine.

## Troublesome USB Ports

All Clié models rely on a USB connection to your PC, which saves you from having to deal with annoying serial ports. But USB isn't entirely foolproof, so keep these things in mind:

■ On a Windows-based PC, USB is guaranteed to work only with Windows 98 or later. If you still have Windows 95, get with the program and upgrade already. It's a must if you expect to reliably use USB devices like the Clié's HotSync cradle/cable.

■ If HotSync sometimes fail to work, you might have too many USB devices connected to a single USB port. Move the cradle to another port. Alternately, you might need a powered USB hub, as there may not be enough juice in the port to supply power to all the devices you have connected, and that may cause the HotSync cradle to cut out.

■ Check the Sony web site for more USB troubleshooting information.

### When HotSyncing, the CLIÉ Displays the HotSync Screen but Nothing Else Happens

This problem is usually caused by HotSync Manager: it's either not running, or one of its dialog boxes is open. If you open the Custom dialog box to change conduit settings, for instance, the HotSync won't run—but you won't get an error message, either. Look on the desktop for an open dialog box, then close it and try the HotSync again. You may have to first tap Cancel on your Clié, then wait a minute or two for it to respond.

### When HotSyncing, this Message Appears: "An application failed to respond to a HotSync"

This one is easy to fix. When you started the HotSync, an Address Book or Date Book entry was probably left open in Palm Desktop. Your Clié can't successfully HotSync with one of those entries open for editing, so you should close the entry and try again.

## Outlook HotSync Problems

As you learned in Chapter 3, most Cliés come with a special conduit for synchronizing with Microsoft Outlook. It's called IntelliSync, and we could fill a separate book with information on using and troubleshooting it. Fortunately, you can get lots of helpful assistance from Puma Technologies, the company that makes it (**www.pumatech.com**).

## Working with Windows 2000

If you're a Windows 2000 user, you'll be glad to know the OS gets along with Clié Desktop just fine. However, at press time there were a few known issues you should consider:

- Windows 2000's "hot undock" feature, usually found on notebook systems, may not work with HotSync Manager running. Solution: shut down HotSync Manager before performing the undock.

■ Infrared HotSyncs won't work. Solution: download the HotSync 3.1.1 update from Palm's web site.

## Working with Windows XP

As with every new version of Windows, XP brought with it a plethora of problems: synchronization and otherwise. Some Clié users reported they couldn't HotSync with the new OS, while others encountered problems with XP's multiple user profiles. If you run into something similar, you may need a patch, a new version of Palm Desktop, or some other solution entirely. Visit Sony's web site for more details.

NOTE      *Palm Desktop doesn't support Windows XP's "switch user" option, which allows multiple users to log onto their PCs at the same time. If you have multiple user profiles set up, each person needs to log out at the end of their session, while the next person logs in.*

# Managing Multiple CLIÉs or PCs

The Palm OS allows you to HotSync the same Clié to more than one PC, or to HotSync several Cliés to the same PC. It's easier than you might think, so feel free to HotSync at home and the office, or to hand out Cliés to every member of the family.

## Two CLIÉs on a Single PC

If you have two Cliés and only one computer, you're not alone. In fact, it's a pretty common scenario: many married couples have their own Cliés and want to HotSync to the household computer.
   Here's what you need to do:

1.  Be absolutely sure that both Cliés have different usernames. Check this by tapping the HotSync icon on each Clié and looking at the name in the upper-right corner. Identically named Cliés, HotSynced to the same PC, will irretrievably trash the data on the PC and both Cliés.

2.  Put the Clié in the HotSync cradle and go. The first time the second Clié is inserted, your PC will ask if you want to create a new account for the other Clié. Click Yes.

CAUTION   *If both Cliés have the same username for some reason, do not attempt to HotSync them to the same PC! In fact, change their names before you HotSync at all to prevent accidentally HotSyncing the Cliés to the wrong PC. There's a freeware utility that allows you to change your HotSync name after you've chosen one: ChangeName, available from PalmGear.com. But that's for making the change right on your handheld; if you want an easier, desktop-based method, just do this: select the Edit Users function in Palm Desktop, choose Rename, then HotSync the Clié.*

TIP *As long as you're using two Cliés in the same family—like a pair of T665Cs—you can use one HotSync cradle for both handhelds. However, you can't always mix and match. An S360, for instance, won't work with an NR70V cradle, and vice versa. However, it is possible to have multiple cradles connected to the same PC—just plug them into available USB ports.*

## Two PCs for a Single CLIÉ

A Clié can keep two different PCs straight just as easily as one PC can keep a pair of Cliés straight. When you HotSync, the Clié updates the second PC with whatever data it previously got from the first PC, and vice versa. This is a great way to keep your office PC and home computer in sync, or even a PC and a Mac—the Clié can serve as a nonpartisan conduit for keeping all the data up to date.

Of course, the most efficient way to use a dual-PC system is to acquire a second HotSync cradle. You can buy an additional one for about $40, or you can get a HotSync cable instead, which is a little more streamlined for traveling.

# Upgrading from an Old CLIÉ to a New One

To those of you still living with a Clié S320, we salute you. But when you finally decide you're ready for a nicer screen, more memory, and a bunch of cool accessories that won't work with your old model, we'll be here for you. Specifically, we're here to help you make the move from an older Clié to a new one—an increasingly common task these days, now that the devices have been around for several years.

Unlike upgrading to a new PC (which requires an obnoxious amount of effort), upgrading to a new Clié is shockingly easy. Here's the process in a nutshell:

1. Do one last HotSync of your old Clié.

2. Turn off your PC, unplug the old HotSync cradle, then install the version of Palm Desktop that came with the new Clié. Don't worry—all your data will be preserved!

3. Plug in the new cradle, then HotSync your new handheld. When you do, a box appears listing your username from your old model. Click it, then choose OK. This will restore all your data.

NOTE *Whether or not all your third-party software is restored during the first HotSync depends in part on the age of your old Clié and which OS is installed on it. We recommended using Blue Nomad's BackupBuddy (see Chapter 13) prior to switching handhelds. On the other hand, if you don't have much third-party software installed, it's not a difficult task to manually reinstall it.*

# Obtaining Service and Repairs

Clié problems, while relatively infrequent, come in all shapes and sizes. Yours may be as simple as an alarm that won't go off or as dire as a device that won't turn on. Fortunately, technical support and repair services are available from Sony. Here's the info you need:

- **Tech Support**   (877) 760-7669
- **Web**   www.ita.sel.sony.com/support/clie/
- **E-Mail**   www.ita.sel.sony.com/support/clie/email.html

# Obtaining Non-Warranty or Accident-Related Repairs

Right up there with the awful sound of your car crunching into another is the sound of your Clié hitting the pavement. A cracked case, a broken screen, a dead unit—these are among the painful results. And unfortunately, if you drop, step on, sit on, or get caught in a rainstorm with your Clié, your warranty is pretty much out the window.

All is not lost, however. If your Clié is damaged, or develops a problem after the warranty has expired, you may still have options. For a fee (usually a rather steep $150), Sony will usually replace a broken or out-of-warranty unit with a refurbished one. It's not cheap, but it's probably cheaper than buying a brand new Clié. The bottom line is, if something terrible happens to your device, it's worth a phone call to Sony to see what options are available. You may be able to pay for repairs or buy a refurbished one for less than the cost of a new unit.

# Other Sources for Help

As we've noted many times already, you can find oodles of help on Sony's web site. In addition, there are several independent sites that offer tips, tricks, hints, and technical solutions. If you're looking for answers that aren't in this book or on the Sony site, try some of these.

| Site | Description |
|------|-------------|
| www.pdabuzz.com | This site has a message board area in which you can post questions and read answers to common ones. It also contains handheld-related product news and reviews—and just happens to be manned by the authors of this book. |
| www.cliesource.com | An all-Clié web site with extensive message forums categorized by model. |
| alt.comp.sys.palmtops.pilot comp.sys.palmtops.pilot | These newsgroups are available to anyone with a newsreader like Outlook Express. They are threaded message boards that contain questions and answers about Palm OS-based handhelds like the Clié. You can post your own questions, respond to what's already there, or just read the existing posts. |

## Where to Find It

| Web Site | Address | What's There |
|---|---|---|
| PalmLife | www.palmlife.com | Screen Clean |
| Fellowes | www.fellowes.com | WriteRight |

# Index

## INTERNATIONAL CONTACT INFORMATION

**AUSTRALIA**
McGraw-Hill Book Company Australia Pty. Ltd.
TEL +61-2-9417-9899
FAX +61-2-9417-5687
http://www.mcgraw-hill.com.au
books-it_sydney@mcgraw-hill.com

**CANADA**
McGraw-Hill Ryerson Ltd.
TEL +905-430-5000
FAX +905-430-5020
http://www.mcgrawhill.ca

**GREECE, MIDDLE EAST,**
**NORTHERN AFRICA**
McGraw-Hill Hellas
TEL +30-1-656-0990-3-4
FAX +30-1-654-5525

**MEXICO (Also serving Latin America)**
McGraw-Hill Interamericana Editores S.A. de C.V.
TEL +525-117-1583
FAX +525-117-1589
http://www.mcgraw-hill.com.mx
fernando_castellanos@mcgraw-hill.com

**SINGAPORE (Serving Asia)**
McGraw-Hill Book Company
TEL +65-863-1580
FAX +65-862-3354
http://www.mcgraw-hill.com.sg
mghasia@mcgraw-hill.com

**SOUTH AFRICA**
McGraw-Hill South Africa
TEL +27-11-622-7512
FAX +27-11-622-9045
robyn_swanepoel@mcgraw-hill.com

**UNITED KINGDOM & EUROPE**
**(Excluding Southern Europe)**
McGraw-Hill Education Europe
TEL +44-1-628-502500
FAX +44-1-628-770224
http://www.mcgraw-hill.co.uk
computing_neurope@mcgraw-hill.com

**ALL OTHER INQUIRIES Contact:**
Osborne/McGraw-Hill
TEL +1-510-549-6600
FAX +1-510-883-7600
http://www.osborne.com
omg_international@mcgraw-hill.com

# New Offerings from Osborne's
# How to Do Everything Series

**How to Do Everything with Your Digital Camera**
ISBN: 0-07-212772-4

**How to Do Everything with Photoshop Elements**
ISBN: 0-07-219184-8

**How to Do Everything with Photoshop 7**
ISBN: 0-07-219554-1

**How to Do Everything with Digital Video**
ISBN: 0-07-219463-4

**How to Do Everything with Your Scanner**
ISBN: 0-07-219106-6

**How to Do Everything with Your Palm™ Handheld, 2nd Edition**
ISBN: 0-07-219100-7

**HTDE with Your Pocket PC 2nd Edition**
ISBN: 07-219414-6

**How to Do Everything with iMovie**
ISBN: 0-07-22226-7

**How to Do Everything with Your iMac, 3rd Edition**
ISBN: 0-07-213172-1

**How to Do Everything with Your iPAQ**
ISBN: 0-07-222333-2

# OSBORNE
www.osborne.com

orders: McGraw-Hill Customer Service 1-800-722-4726 fax 1-614-755-5645  For more information: Karolyn_Anderson@mcgraw-hill.com 1-617-472-3555  www.books@mcgraw-hill.com/library/html